Clowns

Clowns: In Conversation with Modern Masters is a groundbreaking collection of conversations with 20 of the greatest clowns on earth. In discussion with clown aficionados Ezra LeBank and David Bridel, these legends of comedy reveal the origins, inspirations, techniques, and philosophies that underpin their remarkable odysseys. Featuring incomparable artists, including Slava Polunin, Bill Irwin, David Shiner, Oleg Popov, Dimitri, Nola Rae, and many more, *Clowns* is a unique and definitive study on the art of clowning.

In *Clowns*, these 20 master artists speak candidly about their first encounters with clowning and circus, the crucial decisions that carved out the foundations of their style, and the role of teachers and mentors who shaped their development. Follow the twists and turns that changed the direction of their art and careers, explore the role of failure and originality in their lives and performances, and examine the development and evolution of the signature routines that became each clown's trademark. The discussions culminate in meditations on the role of clowning in the modern world, as these great practitioners share their perspectives on the mysterious, elusive art of the clown.

Ezra LeBank is the Head of Movement for the Department of Theatre Arts at California State University, Long Beach. He has published articles in the *Journal for Laban Movement Studies* and *Total Theatre Magazine*. He performs and teaches across North America and Europe.

David Bridel is the Artistic Director of The Clown School in Los Angeles and the Director of the MFA in Acting in the School of Dramatic Arts at the University of Southern California. His plays *I Gelosi* and *Sublimity* are published by Original Works Press.

Clowns

In Conversation with Modern Masters

Ezra LeBank and David Bridel

Routledge
Taylor & Francis Group

LONDON AND NEW YORK

First published 2015
by Routledge
2 Park Square, Milton Park, Abingdon, Oxon OX14 4RN

and by Routledge
711 Third Avenue, New York, NY 10017

Routledge is an imprint of the Taylor & Francis Group, an informa business

© 2015 Ezra LeBank and David Bridel

British Library Cataloguing-in-Publication Data
A catalogue record for this book is available from the British Library

Library of Congress Cataloging in Publication Data
Bridel, David.
Clowns : in conversation with modern masters / David Bridel &
Ezra LeBank. -- First Edition.
pages cm
1. Clowns--Interviews. I. LeBank, Ezra. II. Title.
GV1811.A1B75 2015
791.3'3--dc23
2014037149

ISBN: 978-1-138-77992-1 (hbk)
ISBN: 978-1-138-77993-8 (pbk)
ISBN: 978-1-315-71975-7 (ebk)

Typeset in Baskerville
by Taylor & Francis Books

MIX
Paper from
responsible sources
FSC
www.fsc.org FSC® C013604

Printed and bound by CPI Group (UK) Ltd, Croydon, CR0 4YY

Contents

Preface

We are clowns.

Clowning has always been a mysterious art to us. Every time it seems there is a method to it – how to make a bit work, get a laugh, generate a revelation, invite an audience into a particular way of seeing – as soon as we think we've stumbled upon the answer to something, the proverbial rug is pulled out from under us, and we find ourselves lying on our backsides, scratching our heads. Sure, there are several timeworn structures that have good odds of finding the funny, but, in our experience, the notion that there are rules to clowning strikes us as … unlikely.

We are also clown teachers.

Leading our students into the unruly world of the clown, we have long grappled with this paradox: How can one teach a form that resists method? What in this ephemeral, illogical, and topsy-turvy discipline of clowning can be captured, formulated, and passed on to those who have the desire to learn it? There are many companion texts that have helped us absorb and articulate the practice of clowning, rich and rewarding books including manuals of commedia dell'arte *lazzi*; clown and physical comedy exercise compendiums; histories of mime, clown, comedy, the stage, vaudeville, and the circus; explorations of character archetypes; and treatises on humor theory. And yet we have continued to feel the absence of a certain essential voice, some guiding document that could support and develop our own studio practice and provoke new creativity in the classroom, on the street, on the stage, and in the ring.

We pondered. If we were to add to the literature on clowning, to contribute something that could be of value to ourselves, our fellow professionals and clown aficionados, and especially for our students, what would it include? We reflected on the clowns we love, those who have deepened or advanced the form, reached wide audiences, achieved extraordinary levels of excellence and influence. What distinguishes the most impactful of modern clowns? As we grappled with our questions, we came to a realization. The clowns who are masters are themselves. They make something wonderful out of who they truly, deeply, and simply are. They don't hide or conceal themselves in clown character, to appear as someone else, or someone good, or someone right. Yes, they borrow routines, shtick, and ideas from one another and their predecessors, and, true, they frequently belong to a long performance lineage and have learned, as apprentices, specific techniques that perpetuate a certain tradition. And yet whatever material they perform, whatever character they present, they enter into their clown persona as a way of being more generously themselves than they might be under usual circumstances. Every time we watch one of them, we don't view a form or a character or a concept. We see, simply, them. It follows that the book on clowning, the guide we are seeking for ourselves, should seek to capture, one clown at a time, what makes these individuals tick; what their stories consist of; and how they have translated the conventions of their artistic discipline into their powerful and singular voice. We realized that we didn't have the capacity to express these ideas effectively unless we went directly to the source.

Clowns: In Conversation with Modern Masters engages 20 modern masters of clowning in conversation about their origins, inspirations, techniques, and philosophy. The "Origins" section of the conversations shines a spotlight on each clown's youth, investigating the causal factors that led each of our subjects toward the world of clowning. We examine their first encounters with clowning, traces of clowning, circus, or related areas in their family history, and key moments that laid the groundwork for their eventual profession. In "Inspirations," we trace the onset of the clown's career, exploring the crucial decisions that carved out the foundations of their style and perspective. We discuss the role of teachers, mentors, and performers who shaped their development, as well as the twists and turns that landed them in unexpected situations where their careers changed direction. In "Techniques," we dig through the rich terrain of trips and slips, pratfalls and pies, characters and scenarios that shaped each clown's technical palate, taking into account both inherited techniques and original trademarks. We explore the content of their signature works, paying special attention to accidental moments, or failures, which led to significant discoveries. In "Philosophy" we discuss how each clown's work has evolved. Our clowns look back on long careers in order to compare past discoveries and triumphs with the current and future chapters of their careers, and of the field as a whole. We discuss their perspectives on clowning as an art form, and where they believe the future of clowning is headed.

By highlighting these four central areas in each clown's life and work, the conversations can be read either as a collection of differing thematic assessments, or as a master narrative that tells a clown's story from beginning until this moment. The exchanges – frank, forthright, and funny – delve into the history, family, culture, politics, aesthetics, and intentions of our subjects, reflecting their personalities, and teasing out the personal quirks and oddities that make our clowns hilarious, vulnerable, compelling, cruel, exciting, and uniquely human. Each chapter forms a portrait of a clown, and endeavors to capture the essence of their contribution to the art of comedy.

Clowning is minimally represented in critical literature and, as an art form, has almost no academic foundation. Clowns locate traditions of their craft that exist exclusively in custom and practice, and then adapt those traditions according to their own impulses. We wonder: to what extent does clowning – which is undeniably eccentric, illogical, and disobedient – facilitate the breaking of its own form, the redefining of its own principles, and the invention of original and unpredictable material? Does the absence of academic or text-based models offer license and freedom to its practitioners in their continued pursuit of the art? Or, alternatively, is clowning shackled by modes of thought and behavior that are more restricted than other artistic disciplines, owing to a lack of critical examination? Is there a preponderance of master–apprentice learning models, and, if so, does this limit the possibility of radicalism? Is clowning a revolutionary endeavor or a paradoxically conservative one? These are some of our additional questions as we journey into the field. By examining the connections and tensions between clowning's traditions and the idiosyncrasies of its practitioners, we aim to scrutinize both the essence of our clowns and the elusive nature of the discipline itself.

We are fully aware that the individuals included in this book form only the tip of the very large iceberg of clown practitioners performing around the world today. We acknowledge the limitations of our project in this regard, recognizing both a geographical emphasis and a gender bias in the choices of our featured clowns. We are also aware that our definition of clowning is not necessarily for the purist; we have been broad and inclusive, and incorporated those who have at various times performed in the circus, on the street, in theaters, on television, and in film. Nevertheless, there is much variety within our book. Placed next to one another, the interviews wrestle and provoke, reflections and experiences agreeing and disagreeing; speakers grapple with ideas and interpretations, sparking argument and insight. Taken together, they form a tapestry of foibles, quirks, and oddities, underwritten by serious intent. [Note: readers may consult the Appendix at the back of the book, arranged alphabetically, for brief elaborations on names, organizations, and other references that emerge in the interviews.]

In the classroom, we continue to wonder: How do we transmit the spirit of clowning to our students? How do we invite them to embrace and feel connected to a history, culture, and form that is so immediate and, in practice, untheoretical? How can we encourage our charges to ruthlessly and generously share their intimate, distinct selves with an audience? This one stumps us; we're not sure we'll ever figure it out. Nevertheless, our mission in this book is to peer deeply into the world of clowning, to uncover revelations about the intersection between form and content, convention and individuality. To begin our investigations, before the interviews commence, we will set out the contexts in which our 20 clowns have made their lives' work. From the origins of the clown in ritual ceremony to the masked obsessives of the commedia dell'arte; from the comic burlesque of British pantomime to the fantastical world of the circus; from the silent clowns of the silver screen to the renaissance of clowning following World War Two in Europe and the United States; from indigenous traditions to the razzle dazzle of Las Vegas – we will follow the development of clowning in order to establish the lineages, traditions, and expectations that have influenced the life and work of our subjects. Afterwards, the clowns will speak. We invite you to listen.

Acknowledgements

This book could not have been written without a great deal of logistical and practical assistance. The authors would like to thank the following for their invaluable contributions: Olya Petrakova and Amador Plascencia, who provided translation for several of the interviews; Kaitlyn Wayman-Dodd, Kyla Lowder, and Amanda Squitieri, for their meticulous transcriptions from the audio files; the American Conservatory Theatre of San Francisco, Jean-Daniel von Lerber, Philip Solomon, Dorothee Köß, Anna Bogodist, Mark Gindick, Bryan Brown, Jennifer Nock, Gabi Popov, and Charlie Varon for facilitating initial contact with many of the clowns in the book, and assisting in the collection of photos; and California State University Long Beach (College of the Arts) for offering financial support.

1   Origins

The clown has been with us for as long as we have been performing. Whether a part of sacred rituals first created in ancient societies and maintained in certain indigenous communities today, or a part of the far-reaching and multifaceted modern entertainment industry, the clown's function remains remarkably consistent: to turn established protocols (societal, political, cultural, logical, linguistic, or otherwise) on their heads, and to provoke a new understanding of, and appreciation for, the human condition through a celebration of foible and a mockery of power. By examining our lives from nonsensical and chaotic perspectives, clowns throughout time have given us a most vital permission, the license to laugh at ourselves and our beliefs. We can't do without them.

In the beginning ...

The original impulse to clown is connected to some of our earliest and most basic customs. Among the Pueblo tribes of New Mexico that sustain the cultural lineage of our prehistoric ancestors, including the Hopi and the Zuni, clowns have long ridiculed and contradicted the serious ceremonies associated with worship and harvest, marriage and death. Caked in white paint and tattered clothes, sporting mud-masks, or decorated in wildly contrasting colors, their appearance satirizes the formal requirements of their priestly counterparts while their behaviors disrupt the ordered procedures of ritual. They gleefully send up solemn rites and dances, engaging in patently ridiculous parodies of religious services, or indulging in grotesque mock-sexual activities; they overeat or consume excrement in the midst of the traditional occasion; they invert and garble speech and song, turning revered liturgy into obscene or impenetrable babble. And yet these chaotic and apparently destructive actions are not only permitted, but welcomed and celebrated. By contrasting and criticizing sacrament with the anarchic forces of discord and iconoclasm, clowns stretch the fabric of human tolerance, bringing resilience to societies and resisting our collective urges toward hierarchy, homogeneity, and perfection.[1] Though our spiritual aspirations may be laudable, they have been known to calcify into dogma; clowns remind us that we are equal parts devoutness and doltishness, as practiced in falling over, shitting, and humping as we are in prayer and purification.

In the 5th dynasty of ancient Egypt, around 2500 BC, this paradoxical relationship between the sacred and the profane was solved in one fell swoop; the
priest and the clown became the same person. Described by the Pharaoh as "a
divine spirit, to rejoice and delight the heart,"[2] the priest-clown's purpose, as
became the clown's role in countless courtly manifestations throughout history,
was to check the absolute authority of the ruler with the unspeakable truth of his
or her fallibility. Records from the kingdoms of India, Persia, China, and Europe
all attest to the power given the clown – or fool – to say what others dare not.
Whether ridiculing a king or ruler, or making them laugh at their own willfulness,
the clown maintained his function as counterweight to authority – and was permitted
to do so. "Jesters and dwarfs were the lowest of the Zhou dynasty entertainers, but
by jests and humorous indirect advice, even they could prod their government to
reform."[3] Aztec regent Montezuma II said of his jesters that "they frequently
pronounced some important truth,"[4] while in his *Praise of Folly*, Erasmus writes of
fools: "They're the only ones who speak frankly and tell the truth, and what is
more praiseworthy than truth?"

Medieval and Renaissance Europe

These examples suggest that as societies slowly shifted their foundations from the
spiritual to the political, the impact of clowns expanded to emphasize the critique
and ridicule of temporal power. The shifting relationship between the clowns,
buffoons, and comic players of medieval Europe with the Catholic Church further developed this theme. Prior to the middle of the fifteenth century AD, a
church-sanctioned Feast of Fools existed in a number of medieval French towns
and cities at the turn of the New Year, in which the activities of lay people and
lower order clergy – improvising parodic versions of sermons and making burl-
esques of any number of invocations – turned them into de facto clowns for one
day a year. In many of these carnivals, the elaborate and specific parody of
Christian lore, such as the townspeople of Beauvais' re-enactment of the flight
into Egypt on the back of a donkey, speak to the carefully constructed interplay
between popular festivity and spiritual teachings. But as the church became
increasingly concerned with its image as a seat of secular, as well as religious,
authority, it saw overt political implications in this kind of foolery, and those at
the top of the Catholic hierarchy grew uneasy. In 1444, the Theological Faculty
at the University of Paris sent a letter to all French bishops decrying the activities
of the masquerading miscreants, who,

> disguised as women, lions and mummers, performed their dances, sang inde-
> cent songs in the choir, ate their greasy food from a corner of the altar near
> the priest celebrating mass, got out their games of dice, and burned a stinking
> incense made of old shoe leather, and ran and hopped about all over the church.[5]

From this time on, albeit gradually, fools and clowns – no longer welcome in
their own spiritual houses – separated their activities from those of the church.

The tension between the jurisdiction of the church-as-state and the creative license of the now free-and-unsupervised clowns and players became a running culture-sore punctuated by painful incidents, including legal action and the banning of performances.[6]

The Renaissance heralded a phenomenal new energy in the arts. As the connection between performers (of all stripes) and religious or state ceremony eroded, a new identity emerged that shifted the clown's position in society irrevocably: that of the professional artist. In the case of the stage, it was the clowns and players of the commedia dell'arte – an itinerant street theater that grew into a highly polished indoor entertainment which conquered the courts of Europe – that made the crucial break with the past when they first formed themselves into a guild and instituted financial contracts with their patrons. No longer were these players integrally connected to the power centers of either church or court. They became free agents, answerable only to themselves, whose livelihood eventually became dependent solely on their public appeal. As a result, the commedia's "stock characters" – Arlecchino, Pantalone, Columbina, Pulcinella, Il Capitano, and others – began to exercise an unheralded artistic freedom in their efforts to thrill, delight, shock, and amaze with their foolery. Change didn't happen overnight; in many instances patrons held undue influence over their fates (as late as 1694 the Italian comedians were expelled from Paris for insulting the King's mistress, Madame de Maintenon). Meanwhile, the church continued to hound the players for their blasphemies and obscenities. But the tide of history had turned. By the time of the Enlightenment in the eighteenth century, free theaters and a new breed of patron – "the general audience" – had been thoroughly established.

Inevitably, and as a consequence of the economic necessities that professionalism dictated (competition, profit, market sustainability), the concept of popular entertainment was born. Audiences had to be attracted. And the clown – whose antics had always involved interacting with spectators in the service of laughter – was the star attraction. Some of the commedia dell'arte's best-known comedians – Tiberio Fiorello, Domenico Biancolelli, Evaristo Gherardi – developed comic behaviors, songs, and mimes that became the first of the clown's surefire hits, pieces of clown "business" or *lazzi* that had audiences rolling in the proverbial aisles. Of course, comic foolery had been the clown's stock-in-trade since time immemorial. But driven by the new twin incentives of profit and popularity, these routines reached new heights of sophistication. Acrobatic pratfalls, tumbling, bawdy tunes, tricks with props (clothing, food, ladders), wisecracks, elaborate set-pieces, imitations, mimicry, dance parodies, comic beatings and swordplay, situational gags – every possible dramatic avenue was explored for its clown potential, giving rise to endless permutations of *lazzi*, many of which we can recognize today in the nonsensical mischief of a Mr. Bean or a Nola Rae.[7] The content of these sketches, meanwhile, was no longer tied to a specific critique of ceremony or hierarchy. While commedia clowns remained rooted in a comedy of class tension (servants, such as Arlecchino or Brighella, were continually trying to escape the petty machinations of their masters, Pantalone or Dottore), the scope of their subject-matter expanded considerably, with the eccentricities of human nature – sexual obsessions, selfishness, fantasies – becoming increasingly recognizable targets for their wit. No longer was clowning devoted to exposing elevated rites or power-wielding regents; it became democratized, skewering the absurdities of regular folk, "people like us" who were now forming the majority of any given audience. (Perhaps the only precedent for this kind of comic character study in drama were the classical plays of the Romans – Plautus and Terence – and the Greeks – Aristophanes and Menander.) Along with their English counterparts Richard Tarleton and Will Kempe, the likes of Fiorello, Biancolelli, and Gherardi became justly famous for their skills, and – in the case of Biancolelli, or "Domenique" as he was widely known – rich beyond their wildest dreams; the much-beloved Domenique died with over 100,000 crowns to his name. The connection between art and commerce, laughter and revenue, had been forged.

Pantomime and the circus

As the commedia dell'arte began to suffer from aesthetic stagnation, a final effort by the authorities – by now, municipal governing bodies and town constabularies – to limit the activities of scurrilous comedians unprotected by official patronage, ironically paved the way for the next great clown adventure. Banned, in some cases, from speaking in the theater, the players presented silent comedies in fairgrounds (or "unofficial" popular venues such as the Théâtres de la Foire in Paris) instead – an evolution that only served to increase the clown's emphasis on physical comedy. Shorn of the trappings of state support, including lavish resources, clowning zeroed in on the basics: slapstick humor rooted in the unresolved love triangle of Arlecchino (now Harlequin), Columbina (or Columbine), and the newly minted character of Pierrot, the white-faced clown. (Other inventive responses to the speaking ban included the birth of comic operetta – after all, singing had not been outlawed – and the growth of popular puppetry, including a new manifestation of Pulcinella – Punch, as in Punch and Judy.) But the lasting consequences of the clown's "fairground phase" were felt in the birth of two distinctly new forms that took full advantage of the new priorities of physical and silent humor, long after the bans that had prompted them were lapsed. The first was pantomime, that gleefully iconoclastic romp that remains a lynchpin of the British comic calendar to this day. In its earliest incarnations, before it even earned the name by which it is known, pantomime was primarily an opportunity for great clowns such as John Rich or Joseph Grimaldi to ply their comedic trade in the theaters and music halls of Drury Lane or Covent Garden (or in the case of George Fox, on Broadway), while nominally following a narrative that, in truth, had little relevance to their tomfoolery. The legacy of these comic spectacles can still be felt in the all-singing all-dancing extravaganza of "Panto" that can be seen in Britain now, although the archetypes of Harlequin, Columbine, Pierrot, and his coarser replacement Clown (based on Grimaldi's portrayal of the "Joey") have long since disappeared. The second new theatrical form that emerged with incredible energy at the end of the eighteenth century, and incorporated the wandering clown as he searched for a new spiritual home in the aftermath of the demise of commedia dell'arte, was to grow from humble beginnings into one of the most spectacularly popular entertainments in history: the circus.

Initially a venue for trick-riding, whose circular performance area generated the centrifugal force that allowed riders to stand on their horses' backs, the circus began to incorporate comedy in order to offer some relief from the intensity and risk of the serious showmanship on display. Early circus clowns, such as John Ducrow,[8] were often brilliant horsemen capable of extraordinary equestrian feats such as straddling two steeds as they galloped full pace around the ring. But they came into their own, and won the hearts of their audiences, when they began inventing comic business that either mimicked and satirized the "straight" acts, or demonstrated a different approach to the horses, dressing them in an amusing manner, playing out domestic dramas with them, and making them, effectively, into scene partners. (The tradition of clowns partnering with animals continues today; Micha Usov feeding baguettes to his pigeons, for example.) The enormous success of these comic interludes soon anchored them to any and every new version of the circus, which underwent a period of explosive growth stimulated, in no small part, by its export to the Americas. No matter how sensational its acts, no circus was complete without clowns. In some cases, such as the extraordinary Dan Rice, the clown was the greatest sensation of all; Rice's own *One Horse Show* catapulted him to mega-stardom, until he was adjudged to be better known and more popular than Abraham Lincoln. (Perhaps unsurprisingly, he made a bid for a Presidential nomination of his own – in true clown style, he failed.) Through the medium of the circus, Rice, Frank Oakley (or Slivers), Felix Adler, Emmett Kelly, and a host of other clowns achieved similarly elevated status in the USA, beloved for their varying styles of humor; while in Europe, Anatoly Durov, Carl Bagesson, George Hall and Raphael Padilla (Footit and Chocolate), and the Fratellini brothers were merely some of the clowns who had their circus audiences in stitches during the heyday of the ring. A sudden flourish of brick-and-mortar vaudeville in the 1800s (known as music hall in Britain), variety shows that combined the earthy comedy of the circus with musical fantasia and other oddities, launched a whole new roster of stars such as Dan Leno and Little Tich. By now, the breadth of creative and comic possibility inherent in the art form was on full display: from the virulent satire of Durov, who skewered banks, the press, and even the Mayor of Odessa with the aid of his performing pig; to the whimsy of Kelley, whose morose attempts to steal popcorn from the public epitomized the poetry of suffering; to the flamboyant spectacle of Frank Brown (Flon Bon, King of the Clowns), whose stunts included leaping over 25 Argentinian policemen holding guns and bayonets; to the highbrow stylings of the Fratellinis, whose 40-minute routines at their Medrano circus, based on the strict hierarchy of White Clown, Auguste, and Contre-Auguste, resembled mini-modernist-playlets in their sophistication and depth. In the decades before and after the turn of the twentieth century, the ascent of these and many other famed clowns to the pinnacle of their respective popular cultures was complete. But a new frontier was about to open that would transform clowning yet again, this time catapulting the reputation of a certain clown into that of a worldwide phenomenon. In his remarkable journey one can trace the influence of so much that came before and so much that would follow.

The silver screen

Charles Spencer Chaplin earned his comedic stripes as part of Fred Karno's music hall troupe (or "army," as they were affectionately known), who perfected the art of the stage silent comedy filled to the brim with slapstick and sight gags (once again, dumbshow was a necessity – a response to censorship from municipal authorities). Tapping a comic strain that harkened all the way back to the commedia dell'arte, Karno's stories pitted the "little guy" against "the man," and delighted in the subversion of modern hierarchies; prisoners outwitted wardens, petty criminals or bums outran policemen, and the underdog wound up with the girl. Relishing a connection with their popular audiences, these comedies hinted at the implicit tensions in bourgeois society, seeking to resolve them through the unlikely victory of the working-class hero. When Chaplin, whose personal background included two stints in a workhouse, shifted his career focus to the fledgling film industry in the USA, he combined Karno's comic sensibility with his own powerful vision of the clown as a universal symbol of artfulness in the face of overwhelming poverty. Like a brilliant Arlecchino battling an endless stream of tyrannical masters, Chaplin's Tramp took on an entire system of cops, toffs, bosses, industrialists, and exploiters – and won. He was the ultimate trickster, an irrepressible fool and spirit of uncontainable mischief, who made a mockery of orderliness and etiquette and ridiculed the capitalist contract between the worker and the world. He also happened to possess an undisputed comic genius, a legendary insistence on perfection, and an almost superhuman affinity for every aspect of cinema – acting, directing, writing, editing, producing, and even composing his own music. Thanks to the influence and the permanence of film, he became and remains the clown of all clowns, an icon whose impact upon our understanding and experience of comedy is incalculable. Movies such as *The Kid*, *The Gold Rush*, *City Lights*, *Modern Times*, and *The Great Dictator* are thankfully always available to us, realizations of a complete artistic vision. Today, in far-flung corners of the globe, fledgling clowns continue to seek out the works of Chaplin, and his brilliant contemporary Buster Keaton, for inspiration. Several of the clowns in this book articulate the debt they feel toward these screen icons; one particularly indelible image captures the young Larry Pisoni, Bill Irwin, and Geoff Hoyle – with toddler Lorenzo Pisoni in tow – pouring themselves into their vehicle whenever a run of a Keaton film is announced, magnetized by the promise of inspiration from one of the masters.

Of course, Chaplin and Keaton were only two of the first in a glorious lineage of screen clowns. Ben Turpin, Laurel and Hardy, Harold Lloyd, W.C. Fields, Abbott and Costello, the Marx Brothers, Harry Langdon, The Three Stooges, Lucille Ball, Jacques Tati, Phil Silvers, Peter Sellers, Spike Milligan, *Monty Python's Flying Circus*, Morecambe and Wise, Bill Murray, Rowan Atkinson, Jennifer Saunders,

Mike Myers, Jim Carrey, Roberto Benigni, Catherine Tate, Sacha Baron Cohen, and countless others have explored the central premises of clowning in front of the camera: subverting expectations, behaving outrageously, debunking beliefs, and lampooning sacred cows. And their madness has reached millions thanks to film, television, and, more recently, the internet. But it could be argued that the overwhelming cultural dominance of the screen industry in the twentieth century was also, in no small part, responsible for a diminishing interest in stage spectacle, and a marginalization of the circus in general, and the ancient art of stage clowning in particular. With priceless comedy available at the local multiplex or beamed into the living room, what need was there to patronize the circus, the variety hall, or the vagabonds on the street corner? As screen comics became more and more popular, traditional stage clowns seemed out-of-touch or alien, and audiences abandoned them. By the time Chaplin died in 1977, precious few of his screen successors had ever experienced life as a clown in the circus or on the stage, and the music hall that had birthed Chaplin and so many of Hollywood's greatest early clowns was long dead. And yet today, at the time of writing, we are experiencing what could legitimately be described as a renaissance of the stage clown, a positive explosion of clown energy that can be felt from Broadway to Las Vegas, from the streets of St. Petersburg to the theater schools of the Western world. Who put clowning back on track, and dragged it from the outer edges of our comic consciousness, where it had dwindled, back into the cultural mainstream? For clues, we must examine the influence of the indefatigable theater pedagogue, Jacques Lecoq.

The new wave

Originally an athlete, and fascinated by the workings of the body, Lecoq's formative experience as a young theater artist occurred when he worked alongside Italian stage director Giorgio Strehler and mask-maker Amleto Sartori on a revival of Goldoni's classic play, *A Servant of Two Masters*, for the Piccolo Theater of Milan just after World War Two. By plunging into the "lost" art of the commedia dell'arte, the creators of this epic production (which lived on, in various renderings, for over 50 years) not only breathed new life into the comic masks[9] of the commedia, but also stoked their own desires to resuscitate the fundamental "territories" of popular theater, which had slipped into insignificance in the Hollywood era. Lecoq, whose greatest talent was in teaching, opened his own school in Paris for actors and theater artists, and devoted a significant part of his curriculum to these "territories": mime, the chorus, melodrama, commedia dell'arte – and clown. Over the course of almost five decades of exploration, Lecoq's dedication to these essential components of our theatrical heritage (never taught as history, always as living, breathing, changing forms) found articulation in the work of his graduates. The founders of Complicite (including Simon McBurney), Ariane Mnouchkine of Théâtre du Soleil, Steven Berkoff, and Julie Taymor have not only altered the face of modern theater; they have each brought a brand of populism to the stage that has revitalized the experiences of theater-goers worldwide. Hundreds, perhaps thousands, of Lecoq's students have found their way as teachers in drama schools, universities, and actor training programs where they continue the spirit of his work. When it comes to the particulars of clowning, Lecoq's legacy leads us directly to some of the clowns in this book: Avner Eisenberg and René Bazinet were both his students, while the irascible clown maestro Philippe Gaulier ("The Tormentor"), once Lecoq's student, then a part of his faculty, and now a lone teacher and one of the world's leading authorities on clown, passed on his unique brand of inspiration to Angela de Castro, Peter Shub, and Phil Burgers. (Sacha Baron Cohen, the award-winning comedian, has stated: "I owe my career and the discovery of my inner idiot to Philippe Gaulier.")

Lecoq is by no means single-handedly responsible for the rude health of clowning in the modern era. Others who worked with Strehler, notably Carlo Mazzone-Clemente, founder of the Dell'Arte School in Northern California, branched out on their own and pursued parallel interests. Additional French theater practitioners, including Jacques Copeau (a devotee of the Fratellini brothers whose daughter introduced Lecoq to theater in the first place) and Etienne Decroux (who taught Peter Shub and Geoff Hoyle) stimulated a recovery in the art of pantomime that reached its apotheosis in the work of Marcel Marceau, whose techniques offered a quite different pathway toward physical theater, comedy, and pathos – one that Dimitri and Nola Rae willingly followed. Meanwhile, in other parts of the world, clowning has prospered for differing reasons. The founders of Cirque du Soleil (surely the world's largest current employer of clowns) began their creative lives on the streets of Montreal with no formal training at all. Slava Polunin and Oleg Popov continue a rich legacy of Russian clowning whose star names include the Durov brothers, Karandash ("the Russian Charlie Chaplin"), Leonid Engibarov, and Yuri Belov, whose tenure as Director of Clowning at the Moscow School of Circus and Variety Arts intersects with Aziz Gual's clown journey. And Bill Irwin and David Shiner's creative lives grew out of their respective experiences on the streets and with circuses, and the "New Vaudeville" movement on two continents,[10] independent of the studio-based explorations taking place in Lecoq's school. Yet Lecoq's vision, so comprehensive and far-reaching, has undoubtedly energized contemporary clowning while keeping the discipline connected to its roots. "The clown has great importance as part of the search for what is laughable and ridiculous in man," Lecoq wrote. "Overturning a certain order it thus allows one to denounce the recognized order." Such basic truths point to the motives behind clowning, motives that Lecoq was philosophically inclined to explore. By exposing and celebrating our deepest flaws, the clown serves to correct our collective tendencies toward hubris and perfectionism, representing instead our innate fallibility and capacity for chaos.

Tracing some of the historical lines that connect clowns through the ages helps to illuminate the importance of lineage and succession, apprenticeship and mastery, to the discipline. Clown dynasties are common; the Gherardis of the commedia dell'arte, the Ducrows of the early circus, Frank Brown and father, the Durov brothers, the Fratellini brothers and Victor's daughter Annie Fratellini, the Marx

Brothers, Larry (father) and Lorenzo (son) Pisoni, several hundred years of Circus Nock, the Konyot clan, and the Larible family are just a few examples of the familial connections among clowns, the ties that bind one generation to the next. Patrons at the early incarnations of Slava Polunin's *Snowshow* may recall his little son's appearance for the curtain call, dressed identically to Slava. Initiation, whether at the hands of a family member or a master teacher who is directly connected to the "tree" of clowning, remains the primary entryway into the discipline. Trade skills are passed from one to the next through proximity, repetition, and endless rehearsal, frequently begun at a young age. Craft is hard-won through the guidance of an exacting superior. The nature of this kind of apprenticeship is chronicled faithfully in Lorenzo Pisoni's *Humor Abuse* (2009), in which the author-performer recalls, and re-enacts, many of the routines that he learned directly from his father Larry, ranging from simple trips and slaps to elaborate sequences of falling down stairs. But if clowning is a form that is perpetuated through a "passing of the torch," how can space emerge for artistic license and creative independence? Can a young clown set out in a different direction from that of his or her teacher? The capacity to express countless distinct perspectives is one of the signature elements of an art form. "We should put the emphasis on the rediscovery of our own inner clown," wrote Lecoq. How do clowns pay homage and do justice to their lineage while remaining true to themselves and their own idiosyncratic vision – their own inner clown? The conversations that follow attempt, humbly, to address these and other questions, in order to grasp the relationship of modern clowning to its past, its present – and its future.

Notes

1 No wonder, perhaps, that the clown's role as a "leveler" has become formalized in certain indigenous communities; many African clowns, such as the Woloso of Djenne or the Bambuti pygmy-clowns of the Congo, fulfill the function of peacemakers, puncturing political tensions through the use of destabilizing gestures such as lampooning injured parties, or appearing nude during hostile situations.

2 *Fools Are Everywhere: The Court Jester Around The World*, by Beatrice Otto, Chicago, IL; London: University of Chicago Press (2001).

3 Ibid.

4 Ibid.

5 Quoted in *The Delight Makers* by Ronald McCoy, a Nook Book, edited by The World and I Online (2012).

6 In Russia, the skomorokhs, traveling clown-minstrels of the medieval and post-medieval era, who wore masks and presented folk dramas, met a similar fate in the sixteenth century – outlawed by the Orthodox Church for being servants of the devil.

7 Mel Gordon's *Lazzi: The Comic Routines of the Commedia Dell'arte* (New York: Performing Arts Journal Publications [1983]) unearths over 200 years of stage business, much originally recorded in the clown's notebooks.

8 John Ducrow: "Prime Grinner and Joculator General to the Ring, whose Circumgyrations and Facetiae extraordinary will occupy the intervals between the acts" (Quoted in *A Calvacade of Clowns*, by Laurence Senelick, Santa Barbara, CA: Bellerophon Books [1992]).

9 The word refers to both the physical article – the leather masks of the commedia, which Sartori so lovingly recreated – and the archetypal characters themselves: Pantalone, Arlecchino, Dottore, Brighella, etc.

10 "Among the elements of New Vaudeville is that it is nonviolent and nonracist, and it is a reaction to the kinds of theatre we don't like" (Avner "The Eccentric" Eisenberg, quoted in *From The Greek Mimes To Marcel Marceau And Beyond*, by Annette Lust, Lanham, MD; London: Scarecrow Press [2003]).

2   Nola Rae

Figure 1 Nola Rae. Photo by Ella Simunek

Nola Rae (born in Sydney, Australia, 1950), after training at the Royal Ballet School in London, turned to mime, studying with Marcel Marceau. Rae blended clown, mime, and puppetry in full-length solo shows including *Elizabeth's Last Stand* (1990) and *Exit Napoleon Pursued By Rabbits* (2005). Rae founded the Friends Roadshow with Jango Edwards, The London International Mime Festival with Joseph Seelig, received the Charlie Rivel Award for Clowning, and was inducted into the Clown Hall of Fame. In 2008, Rae was awarded a Most Excellent Order of the British Empire by the Queen.

We talked with Nola in her home outside of London. (DB/EL)

Origins

EL: When did you first discover clowns or circus?

Nola: I never thought I was going to be a clown. I was a rather serious child. There was nothing to indicate that I would ever become a clown. I was born in

Australia, in Sydney, and when my father first looked at me, he said, "That girl should dance." I had long fingers, and he thought that I should dance because of my hands, but if he'd seen my feet, he might've changed his mind. So he dragged me across Sydney and plonked me in front of *Swan Lake*, and of course I was hooked. At the age of four. I started dancing quite seriously from eight. He did take me to see the circus. There was one in Sydney called the Ashton Circus. It was very run-down. I can remember looking up and thinking there were stars in the roof of the tent – but there were so many holes in the canvas, it was actually daylight.

I must say that my father was a connoisseur of humor. He used to take us to see silent films; he took us to see Jacques Tati and Pierre Etaix, so I got my first comic – not philosophy, but my first dose of comedy at the cinema. Then the family immigrated to London in 1963. My father wanted me to dance properly and to be educated at the same time, and we couldn't do that in Australia back then. So we came to London. I was quite morose, a serious dancer, and I don't think, until I got into the Royal Ballet School at the age of 16, that anybody ever thought that I might have comic possibilities. One of my teachers said that I could be an actress. But I wasn't interested in that because I didn't want to speak. I've got this feminine voice, and it makes masculine playing impossible. As a dancer I could play everything without speaking. So I didn't listen. I got a job as a dancer in Sweden as a corps de ballet dancer at Malmo Stadsteater, only to find out that being a corps de ballet dancer in that place in those days was like joining the army. You had to rise through the ranks in order to get anything decent to do. It could be ten years, and I wasn't prepared to stay around in Malmo that long. And then one of my friends took me aside and said, "Look, you're never – I can't see you as a dancer, but you'd make a very good clown." Sometimes a few words from somebody, even a casual acquaintance, sometimes they sink in. I said, "Okay, then I'll go for it."

Inspirations

Nola: I happened to meet Marcel Marceau. My father had taken me to see him once in London when I was about 16. I'll never forget that first show. It was a full house. I think it was the Apollo Theatre in London, and we were sitting up in the gods in the cheap seats. Everybody was leaning forward and you could have heard a pin drop. It was fantastic. After the show ended my father and I couldn't speak to one another, we were in silence for at least … we got on the train to go home, and it took us about 30 minutes to say anything. That was a big experience. But at the time I never thought I could do anything like that. So years later, there I was in Sweden trying to be a dancer, when my friend suggested I should think about clowning, and lo and behold Marceau came to do a one-night show in Malmo. Of course, I went to see it. And I knew he was opening a school, so I met him, and I said, "Can I come to your school?" And he said, "Yes." So I did.

DB: Did that cause any ructions with your father?

Nola: Well, when I said, "I'm going to give up dancing," he was quite shocked. He'd always seen me as a dancer, you know. But it took him about a week to get over it, and then he got over it. And he was pleased, you know. He met Marceau, and he was very proud. My mum, too.

I was in the first intake of the school, 1969–70. Marceau taught technique. He wasn't particularly good at teaching technique because he couldn't stick to one thing. He would do this, and "Now we'll do that," and "Come over here and we'll do this." We even tried doing facefalls, you know, which I wasn't very good at because I kept breaking the fall. I don't know why he thought he should teach that. His ex-wife Ella Jaroszewics was a mime in the Polish style, and she was a technical teacher. We did mask work. We did fencing because it makes you very quick in reaction. We did acrobatics, which I wasn't good at either. And we did improvisation. Now here's where Marceau really came into his own, because he had a never-ending fund of improvised stories. (You know, I wish I had written them down because I'd be doing them now.) That's where I learned a lot. I got used to improvising, which is a big thing in clowning. I think you've got to be ready to improvise right on the spot, so that was helpful. Also he was performing at the same time in the same building in the evenings, so I got to see him about 30 times, and that was a huge education because so few teachers are also great performers, and I think, looking back again in hindsight, this was what really sunk in.

DB: Did Marcel Marceau talk about where he came from?

Nola: Marceau, yes, Marceau never shut up, actually. He was a man who talked and talked and talked in about six different languages, sometimes three different languages in one sentence. He had a poetic way of talking as well. He talked about his old days. He started out small, just like everybody seems to do, in little café-theaters in Paris. And he said it took him about ten years to get the audience to accept the silence. He was doing mime, and his audiences used to whistle because they felt uncomfortable with silence. He toured around in a tiny Volkswagen Beetle. Three or four people, I don't know how they did it. But his work became very popular, and he started to put on plays – mimo-dramas as he used to call them – which gradually became more and more elaborate, because they had to have scenery, they had to have lights, they had to have this and that, and music. In a way he didn't want all this. He liked simplicity in his work. So after ten years – he seems to be a man of ten-year periods – he stopped all that and toured as a soloist, and he was certainly one of the most famous Frenchmen of the last century. Everybody knew Marcel Marceau. So I couldn't really ask for a better start to this kind of work. After Marceau, I tried acting.

EL: Oh, really?

Nola: Yes. Even when I was studying with Marceau I didn't know exactly where I was going next. Then I was introduced to somebody who was traveling to France to form a company to do theater in English, dramatic theater, mainly visual theater, and I joined. But as an actress, I was hopeless, absolutely hopeless. Because this was speaking, you see. I had a few small roles. We played *Orestes*, and I was cast as Hermione, daughter of Electra. At one point I had to say, "Not more trouble, Electra. What has happened now?" And I couldn't say it properly because I didn't know how to form the words or how to emphasize them. I would say, "Not … *more* trouble, *Electra*." Oh, it was dreadful. The company just turned away and giggled when I was speaking. But I became very useful to them when I started doing mimes on the street. This is where all my street performances started. It was quite difficult because Marceau had done all the best subjects. I'd think, "Oh, I'll do a painter," but no, he'd done that already. "I'll do this one or that one," but no, he'd already done it. So I decided to do something I thought he'd never done, which was about a typist, although I'd never touched a typewriter at that point. But I thought of a typist because I was pretty sure he hadn't done it. It was about a typist whose boss showers her with work. She goes to sleep and dreams she murders him, and then when she wakes up, he's staring at her. That's a very simplified version of it. So that was first seen on the streets of Aix-en-Provence.

DB: So you began miming on the streets to make money for your company?

Nola: Yeah, we had absolutely no money. We were living off charity. We were living off vegetables that they left for us at the end of the market. I really learned how to starve. Can't say I imagined acting would be that way. So we'd do a little parade with my fellow actors on the street, and then they'd form a circle, and I'd be in the middle, and I'd do a mime. Then we'd pass the hat, and we'd move on. I was nearly arrested several times. I remember once doing "The Typist's Dream," in Aix-en-Provence, and I woke up to find a policeman standing over me, a gendarme. He was saying, "Go away. Go!" And the French audience was saying to the policeman, "No! You go! You're in the way! We can't see through you!" And they pushed him away, and somebody came while I was speaking to him and pressed something into my hand from the back, a ten-franc note, which in those days was quite a lot of money. So I had some really interesting experiences on the street. I think that if you can play on the street, a theater is luxury.

Techniques

DB: And that started your career as a mime?

Nola: It did. Soon enough I left the theater company and I started building my own sketches. I have a collection of them called *Upper Cuts*, although I don't do them very much anymore.

EL: What inspired you to create *Upper Cuts*?

Nola: Well, every idea is different. Revenge. Sympathy. I do sketches that are contrasting, and sometimes I have an idea because it's different to the last one, anything that takes my fancy, actually. I've done about 60-odd sketches – there are about ten that I like, that I could do now. One is the Jester, which comes from some great fools from history, and I really like doing this character because he's very simple, and he is terribly powerful. Nobody says no to him. (I say "him" because, really, most of my characters are "hims," strangely enough. They can be androgynous, but they always have a masculine side to them.) The Jester, he comes on, he's terribly tired, he has to sit on the stage and recover. He stares at the audience for a while, then notices that the time has passed, gets up, and finds a flea. The flea does a few tricks, jumps from one hand to the other, does some acrobatics, and then the Jester drops the flea. And of course he tries to catch it, goes into the audience, goes through the audience's hair and handbags and beards and whatever for a while, and eventually he finds this flea in someone's shoe. And I like this. I mean, this is a sketch that allows me to do anything in the audience, anything can happen. I also do The Detective. This was sort of my homage to Inspector Clouseau, although in the end I changed my costume to one more like Sherlock Holmes. The detective has a dog on a stick, and he drops all his own clues and finds them again. Eventually he gets people up on stage. Again, it's audience participation. So this is coming from being on the streets; improvising on the street gave me a taste for audience participation. So the detective gets three people up on stage and ties one of them up and asks him to escape. It's great fun to do because it's quite loose. I like to be loose, not to tie myself up with too much technique. I like my clown pieces to have a certain looseness.

DB: Do you have any clown heroes or heroines?

Nola: Oh, yes, Jango Edwards. He lives in Barcelona. American clown, Detroit. He came to England in 1972, and we formed a company together called Friends Roadshow. Jango and I are quite different to one another. He's big and American. I was, in those days, skinny and English-ish. And he was a magnet for people. Our first company was six people – we toured in Paris, Bordeaux, Amsterdam – and the next time we got together, we were 12 because Jango is a magnet. This is where I met Matthew Ridout, my partner. Jango is just such a wonderful clown, and he taught me a lot about clowning. We went out on the street just to work, just to gain experience, and I couldn't do anything because I was too busy watching him. He's a fabulous improviser. Nobody could be as stupid as Jango on stage and get away with it. Of all the clowns, Jango is the one who can get away with sheer stupidity. And after being 12 in the company, we turned into 25, including a five-piece rock band. After that, Jango wanted to become a rock clown and he did, he became a rock clown. Can you imagine that? But that wasn't what I wanted to be, so that's when we split, and I formed the London Mime Theatre with Matthew, my partner, and I've been doing that ever since 1976.

DB: How did your work develop after *Upper Cuts*?

Nola: In about 1990, I decided to change quite radically and for once play a woman. Someone had said to me, I don't know why, but a few years prior to that, while I was touring in Australia, we were having a cup of tea and this lady said, "I think you should do Queen Elizabeth. You've got no eyebrows." (I shave my eyebrows because of the makeup.) And I said, "Oh, don't be silly. All that stuff, all those costumes, I can't be dealing with that." But this idea rattled around in my mind for a couple of years, and I decided, in the end, I would do Elizabeth because I had also studied the Tudors in school. And that was a big step forward. This was the first piece I actually read up on, because if you're going to do somebody historical, it's best to actually read about them! And some things come out of their lives, which you actually can use as a clown. And things actually strike you; for instance, the loneliness of Elizabeth. She was a little old lady, and all her friends died off in the end, and she was alone, and she was courageous, and she had a hot temper. She loved music. She liked to dance. Do you know Simon

McBurney? He directed it, and he was very interesting. He said, "What you should do, you shouldn't just jump in and be Queen Elizabeth the First. It'd be much better if you played someone who could never be Queen Elizabeth the First." So I based it on my grandmother. The character is my grandmother, just like her, fighting as she did with electricity and things like that. The toaster. The toaster is one of those things. She blew herself across the kitchen several times by putting things down the toaster that gave her electric shocks. It's a wonder she was still alive. And so that's how that story happened, through Simon. I actually put some ideas in front of him during a first rehearsal. He looked very patiently, and then he said, "Very rich, but this is not going to work." It was only two weeks before the show, and I said, "But Simon, there's only two weeks to go." And he said, "Ahh, bags of time." And we did what he said, and it worked. We took those two weeks and the concept worked. And it stopped me from doing sketches.

DB: That was the beginning of a new chapter for you?

Nola: Yes, a new chapter. After that I worked with John Mowat on *Shakespeare: The Works*. That was extremely successful. We did short versions of the plays. For *Macbeth* we wondered why Shakespeare wrote it in the first place, and we decided he was inspired by his wife, Anne Hathaway, doing kitchen chores. I was Anne Hathaway, the female character, which was fun to play. Then I did *Hamlet* for two gloved hands, which is a puppet piece. Something I must mention is that puppetry is important to me, as well. Then we did *King Lear*, where we asked "Who is more foolish, the fool or the king?" And finally *Romeo and Juliet*, where I played Romeo and John played Juliet, and he played all the Capulets, and I played everybody else. He also played my horse. That was good, too.

DB: Can you trace your love of puppets? Did it come from Marcel Marceau's teaching?

Nola: Marceau said, "For a mime, probably also for a clown, the most important thing is your face. You have to have a good face. It doesn't have to be a beautiful face, but it has to be an expressive face. And you have to let your face do the thinking." The other thing he said was, "The next important thing for a mime is hands. Whereas it could be feet for dancers, for mimes it's hands." So I said, "Okay." And years later I said, "I'd like to do something with the hands now. I'm ready. What? Something impossible. How about Shakespeare? Sounds pretty impossible. And how about Hamlet? Because then I can get a good pun with the *Tragedy of Handlet*." So that was really my first puppetry piece, as I was changing gloves to be all the characters. In *Elizabeth's Last Stand*, there's a little bit of puppetry there, just a small piece of puppetry: moving objects. Objects becoming other things. The real puppetry one, though, is probably *Mozart*. I always wanted to do something about the life of Mozart because he's my favorite composer. I suppose I could've done Beethoven, but, you know, Mozart was my favorite. And I didn't want to crawl around being Mozart as a kid, so I decided puppets was how to do the job.

EL: Do you see boundaries between puppetry, clown, and mime?

Nola: Well, generally, mime is when you have nothing, you're on the stage, and you do everything, you make everything concrete by the technique of mime. For the story, you don't have props. That's pure mime. Then you get mime that also uses objects, so that's half and half. But you can mix them up. For instance, the Jester with the flea, there's no flea there, but it's clowning and mime mixed up as it were. With *Mozart* I mime because I'm seeing unseen characters, and I'm reacting to them. There's a court around me and I'm talking to people, but they're not there, and if you call that mime, that's mime. In my next show, which was *Exit Napoleon Pursued By Rabbits*, there's no mime at all. I knocked it out completely. Instead I had object manipulation and clowning. So I can mix things up. There don't have to be boundaries.

DB: Did you think that *Napoleon* was more daring? Was there something different in the way that you created that piece? Was it a development of your work?

Nola: Probably. Someone looked at me, having seen *Elizabeth*, and said, "You should play Rasputin." Because Elizabeth does get very bossy and strange. So that wandered around in my head for a while. And I read up about Rasputin (and it's worth reading about, Rasputin could make a great clown). But in the end that got me onto dictators in general. I began to study the great dictators, as it were, and, of course, Charlie Chaplin's film *The Great Dictator* showed that you can do this and get away with it. So that's how the idea developed. I read a lot about all sorts of dictators, and in the end, what fascinated me, was the route they all take. Always the same, they do the same thing, they make the same mistakes. And so the show became about the route of the dictator. Just like in *Elizabeth*, when a nobody turned into Elizabeth the First, in *Napoleon*, a nobody became a dictator and got worse and worse until the whole thing exploded in their face. So that was a step toward political clowning. It's fun to do, too; the audience sometimes are quite ashamed of themselves because I manipulate them, just as a dictator does, and they come out and say, "I didn't do that, did I?" So it shows you how easy it is to manipulate an audience, but I don't do it for that. I do it for the fun of it, and also it says something in the end, because if anybody stupid like a clown can become a dictator, then it's dangerous.

DB: Does much of your clowning have political overtones?

Nola: You are influenced, yes, by your surroundings and by people in power. Margaret Thatcher, in *Elizabeth's Last Stand*. There are bits of Margaret Thatcher in that one. President Bush, in *Napoleon*. And around the time of the Bosnian War I made a show with Sally Owen called *And The Ship Sailed On*. It was based on immigrants. I'm an immigrant from Australia, and she went to Nigeria when she was a child. Our director was Carlos Trafic. Trafic was a clown who had to escape Argentina and ended up in Holland. The story was we were pushed together, representing two different cultures. I played a very stiff-upper-lip Scottish woman, Protestant, and Sally played an Italian Catholic widow. And we had to share this bunk, this cabin, and it's all about sharing and not sharing, you know. And right at the end, we had a beautiful finish, because we leave the ship just before we murder each other. We dock, and the lights come down, and there's a suitcase left on the bottom bunk, and it opens very slowly. Matthew built a desert scene in the suitcase of probably Australia, but it could have been the United States. I come up in a puppet version, only about as big as my finger, and then Sally comes up. We look around at the scenery, and then we start fighting, because even in a new country, even in a new world, even with lots of space, we're still fighting.

EL: Is there a moment when you remember experiencing failure in a performance?

Nola: I think I was playing once in Cyprus in Nicosia on the north side, and we got to the performance by the skin of our teeth because we were delayed. We'd just come back from Iraq, I think. Beirut, says Matthew. This is Matthew. He's got his apron on. He's cooking.

Matthew: I'm trying to keep quiet in the background.

Nola: And the president of the Turkish part of Cyprus was coming to the show, so it was full of bodyguards. They sat there and didn't laugh once. It was awful. He didn't even turn up in the end. Instead, on his seat in the front row, was a great big bunch of flowers. So that wasn't very pleasant. Plus, you've got to learn whether the audience is going to understand what you're on about. Because if you go to Africa and you do "The Typist's Dream," and they've never seen a typewriter, you're lost. There's been a few. Nigeria was a bit difficult because they are strangely haughty. Someone said to me, "Why do you come here and show me your English shit? Why don't you do something African?" All right, well, they had their opinions. Once in Amsterdam, I was chased around the stage by someone's dog. Dogs hate clowns. I spent a lot of time on top of a chair. I approached the guy who had the dog after the show. I said, "How dare you bring your dog to the theater?" and he said, "My dog's got a perfect right to come to the theater." I couldn't think of anything to say to him after that, apart from punching him. So that kind of thing. Sometimes when you're working on the street, not that I do this much anymore, people walk through your illusion, and you've got drunks to contend with, and things like that. To do this kind of work, even with clowning and mime on the street, you have to have concentration. But total failures? There's almost always something you can pull out of a show. There are some shows of course which are far better than others, and the shows I'm satisfied with I can count on one hand probably in a year, or even in a lifetime. But there's always something good you can pull out of a show.

EL: Can things going badly lead to opportunities or discoveries?

Nola: I think so, yes. Another thing about clowning – and Matthew keeps saying this – if it doesn't work, if no one's reacting particularly well, get on with it. Don't try and win them over by doing more. Do less, in fact. It always works better. You're more likely to win them over by doing less than by doing more. Sometimes you can put your head out on stage, and you sense, "Oh, this is going to be good," or alternatively, "I'm going to have to work here." You know in the first couple of seconds, and so it's up to you then. The pleasure, if there is any pleasure in showbiz, is actually winning them over, getting a laugh somehow, leaving without being murdered.

EL: You've done a lot of directing recently. How has that contributed to changes in your clowning?

Nola: The first thing I directed was *The House of Bernarda Alba*, and if you know that one, it's a very dark, tragic, murderous piece. Perfect for clowns. I was asked to do this by a group of lady clowns, and at first I thought, "Oh, god, lady clowns, I don't know," so then I workshopped them and I liked them, and we cast it, and it went really well. There's no point making a comedy into a clown piece because a comedy's a comedy, but a tragedy into a comedy, that's doable.

DB: They spoke? Was there text?

Nola: Only the maid, La Poncia, was able to speak. She had to introduce all the characters so that everyone knew who they were. I did the same thing with *The Wild Duck* with the waiter character, who, again, had to put the story before the audience. It's like a mime. I mean, this is why Marceau has title cards held up with the subjects on them because if you don't do that, the audience gets lost. The same goes for clown plays generally. They have to know; they have to be introduced to the characters. After that, the clowning takes over. In the end of *The Wild Duck*, Hedwig, the little girl, has to shoot the wild duck to show that she loves her father. (Her father's so-called friend has persuaded her to do it.) But I got fed up with all this, so I had her shoot everybody else. And throughout the play, there was a duck trying to get on stage, a half-man half-duck. He had flippers and a tailcoat. But he was always being thrown off by the actors or the clowns. The critics said, "Oh, it was like Tarantino," and, "Why on earth did you kill everybody in the end?" and I said, "Because I'm fed up with them," but they never asked, "Why did this duck try to get on stage?", which is quite strange. But you see, a clown can do anything. You can have ducks wandering on stage. You can shoot them. You can change the story around. I think there should be more clown plays. Clown plays take a really sad and tragic subject and turn it around. It remains tragic though. In the end of *Bernarda Alba*, the youngest daughter does hang herself. It's a really beautiful end because the audience doesn't expect it. So you can still keep elements of tragedy. I think that good clowning should have elements of depth and sadness in it at times. If it's "Ha, ha, ha," all the time, it's very tiring.

DB: Can you give us a preview of your new show?

Nola: It's going to be a new clown. Totally different from the one I've done so far. Who is going to be very naïve and very slow, which suits my age. First thing is him just coming on and doing something, and he has a lot of trouble, he loses his arms in his coat … This new show is going to be as simple as possible, hopefully, with only a chair, a clown costume, and a few props. And a toy bear as my partner.

DB: Does that feel to you like a return to something that you did with a show like *Upper Cuts*, which seemed very pure?

Nola: I'm going to use my mime technique, but generally it's going to be much more clownlike, with a red nose again. I've only had three red noses. The first one was *Mozart*. That was the first time I put the red nose on. But this one is quite interesting. I'm finding it quite difficult, in fact. I thought it would be simple, something an old girl could do, but actually to be slow is very difficult. Not to twitch around and not to flail about, which is what I usually do, it's quite a discipline. Plus all the things I've got to practice. Like the piano, and the manipulation of this puppet of mine, a teddy bear that must be at least 50 years old. It has done another show, in the very early days, before I was even a soloist, in Rotterdam. And now it's back. And it's all ready to go. With new eyes on it, and a new nose. It could all change, but that's the idea.

Philosophy

DB: Do you ever think about the question: What is clowning for?

Nola: I think life would be much grayer if there weren't clowns or comedians. A clown and a mime and a comedian hold up a mirror to the audience as it were, and the audience will see their ridiculous selves mirrored by the clown. Plus I like to laugh. There's nothing better than an audience laughing, with you rather than at you. It's a huge pleasure to have an audience understand you and go along with you. It's a power thing as well, I think. The clown is very powerful. Don't dismiss the clown as actually somebody who has no power. The clown has a huge amount of power. So that's another pleasure of doing it, another challenge also. Another thing I must say about the art, particularly of mime, and, yes, clowning too, is that they're so fragile. It's really easy to be bad at mime. Lots of people don't like mime because they've seen it done badly. You see bad acting, you hear bad singing, and you go back, hoping that something will be better. But not with mime. So it's a very delicate thing. But if you can actually crack that, it's great.

EL: Do you think the clown always possesses great power or authority? Are there times when a clown is powerless or impotent?

Nola: It's hard to say. I think what defines me is the fact that I'm Australian, and I have a certain sense of humor, which is generally a quite dark sense of humor, and Australians are quite stoic. I think that's a good thing to be in life sometimes. You know, I don't crumble too easily. I plow on, as it were, and I tend to persevere. I'm very stubborn. I won't give up ideas easily. I will say that being a woman clown can be difficult at times because lots of people think that women can't be funny, and I think that's stupid. Women have always been funny. It's just that they don't put themselves in front of audiences as much as men do, but that's changing now. The women are coming up very quickly, and we've got some amazingly funny women clowns, too, which is great to see. And the other thing, being a dancer, and this I think is really important from my point of view, is that I don't feel inferior. As a dancer, in my day at least, everybody came to see the ballerina. The men were always at the back, lifting us around, so we were the stars. So it didn't occur to me to feel inferior, even when I stopped dancing. It was embedded in me from an early age that I was as important as anybody else. That's also an attitude that I think is important; sometimes when I teach, I get lots of people who feel inferior right from the beginning and put themselves at the back – especially ladies. So I never had that, which is lucky for me, though I'm personally quite shy. I suppose I'm a shy exhibitionist.

EL: Do you think clowning is moving in a particular direction? Do you see any new developments?

Nola: I think there will be more and more female clowns, and hopefully more female clowns broadening their subject-matter, not just being women, as it were – well, it's good to be women – but broadening it away from women's things and going deeper and more surreal and more fantastic. This is what I'd like to see in clown. I'd like to see it from men, too.

DB: More surrealism and fantasy?

Nola: I've seen a lot of shows that have surrealism in them, and if it's done well, it's really interesting. Of course if it's not done well, it's just confusing. You have to know when and where to use it. You see, the thing about silent clowning and mime is that you can't lie. Everything you do is truthful. And the art is to be truthful without being confusing. So that's what we're trying for. We're trying always to think if the audience is going to understand.

EL: Do you feel like you're part of a community of clowns across the world?

Nola: I do feel I'm part of a world. Of course we're all different, hopefully. We don't want to be clones of each other. That's why I stepped away from Marceau as soon as I could because I didn't want to be a little Marceau. I found different material, different ways of doing things. But I do, I've got lots of clown friends. I love meeting clowns. I love being in clown festivals because clowns are generally really friendly people. They're really nice, so I enjoy meeting them, being with them. We get on very well. Yes, with most clowns I get on very well.

3   Aziz Gual

Figure 2 Aziz Gual. Photo by Eugenio Morales Montoya

Aziz (born in Mexico City, 1969) has performed in Ringling Bros and Barnum & Bailey's *The Greatest Show on Earth* in Mexico, the United States, and Canada, and collaborated in the creation of Cirque du Soleil's World Circus project, also in Mexico. He is founder and director of the street theater company Summit Clown, with whom he has created a dozen shows. He has toured in many countries, including the United States, Turkey, Italy, France, Croatia, Argentina, Brazil, and Costa Rica, and performed in countless festivals in Mexico, with his own shows *Huraclown* and *Laughing at Laughter*.

We talked to Aziz in his home in Cuernavaca, Mexico. He was in a relaxed frame of mind, and every now and again he would play his mouth organ, act out one of the bits he was describing, or demonstrate something from his collection of homemade props and costumes. (DB/EL)

Origins

In front of the apartment where my family lived, there was a lot of land, a big field, and the circus came and pitched its tent there every year. My brothers and I were frequently alone in our house. Our parents were always gone or not available. So, starting when I was just three years old, when the circus came to town, my brothers would grab me and take me outside and across the field to the tent, and we would sneak under the canvas. I can still remember the smell of the elephants. Gradually I formed an idea. I thought that if I became familiar with the clowns, it would open the doors for me in my neighborhood, and people would give me affection. They'd say, "I'll have that little kid come over, because he's funny." Also, when I was a child, in our bathroom there was a portrait of Emmett Kelly on the wall. One of my grandmothers had painted it. So every time that I would use the toilet, I would stare at the portrait. And it had an effect on me. I began to imagine.

Something happened when I was 11 years old. The circus was in town again, and I went with friends of our family, and I sat next to their daughter. I was excited – I had a big crush on her. She was a bit older than me. I would try to talk to her … It was a little ridiculous. Anyway, we sat in the front row. At one point the clowns asked for a volunteer to join them in the ring. Every kid in the audience raised their hand except me. I didn't want to be embarrassed in front of the girl. So of course the clowns decided to choose the person who did *not* raise their hand. They took me into the ring and put me on a camel, a two-hump camel, and they began to walk the camel around the circle as fast as they could. They attached me to a security rope, so it was safe, but I was still nervous, and people were laughing. Suddenly the clowns hoisted me up by the rope until I was hanging in mid-air. The camel left the ring, and now it was just me, dangling there, circling round and round. Everyone thought it was hilarious. Then came the grand finale, and the clowns pulled down my pants. Of course I wasn't wearing underwear that day – all my underwear was dirty and I had decided I would do without it. By now the whole audience was bursting with laughter, watching little me swinging on a rope without any pants on. To the clowns it was a great triumph. But for me, it was an invasive experience. I felt profoundly vulnerable and intimidated. Naturally, the daughter of our friends never spoke to me again, probably because I was just a kid without any pubic hair. I felt deceived. I didn't think that clowns could be that mean. I thought somehow they would be more careful. That day, I learned that the clown I imagined did not exist. So I said to myself, "I will become that clown. The one in my mind. The one like Emmett Kelly, from when I sit on the toilet."

And that is what I have tried to become. Empathic. I have always strived for empathy. To understand the people. It doesn't matter whether they are old or kids. We are humans. We are all vulnerable. The principal element beneath the clown is empathy. This is very important, because if you don't understand what people feel, or why people cry, you can't be a clown.

I was always an eccentric child in my father's eyes. My father is a very serious person, a lawyer with a serious vision. He does have a very humanistic side as well, but in the beginning he wasn't very happy about my decision to become a clown. He would tell me not to do Cantinflas. He said, "Behave yourself as a serious person, we are serious people." Looking back, I think my most difficult homework was to accept that I could never be the serious person that he wanted. You see, in Mexico there are a lot of complications. In the United States I can stand up and talk to the public, and the public is always helping me to reach my goal. "You can do it!" they say. They always have that impulse. In Mexico it's completely different; it's the opposite. Nobody stands up because they are scared of looking ridiculous, scared of being criticized. So to be a clown in Mexico I had to break through this. I had to break the ice of a frozen society.

Inspirations

There wasn't really a professional path to follow to become a clown in Mexico. I began by studying theater and pantomime. Marcel Marceau would come to our country sometimes, and I was able to study with him and participate in his workshops. I was young – only about 14 years old – and I would also observe workshops that he would give to teachers. But I knew that pantomime wasn't exactly what I wanted to do. I was interested in breaking the fourth wall. I wanted to connect with people. Eventually I learned that I needed to travel, to discover other ways to see the world. I was looking for a universal language, a language that was not literal.

I knew I wanted to be humorous, but I didn't know what it was called. The first person that told me I was a clown was in Russia, the artist Anatoli Lokachtchouk. From him I learned the very rigorous methods and structures of the comic numbers of traditional Russia. Some of these numbers were not only comedic, but profoundly philosophical as well. For example, here is one of their routines.

[*He begins to act this out.*]

There are two clowns in a wasteland. The first clown is a dumbass. He's on stage, a shivering wreck, hungry and cold, when he spots an apple and a piece of potato on the floor. He doesn't see anyone around, so he decides to eat the apple and the piece of potato. He fails to notice that there's a second clown, a big guy, right behind him. Just as he goes to grab the food, he hears the voice of the big guy say, "No!" He thinks it's God. He's terrified. He pleads with God for forgiveness, and he stays hungry and cold. But after a while, he can't resist that apple and that piece of potato. Of course, when he goes again to grab them, the big guy says, "No!" again, and the dumbass is terrified once more, and pleads with God again for forgiveness. This happens again and again, and the dumbass becomes more and more anguished, which entertains the big guy. Finally the dumbass, half-crazy, rebels. When the big guy says "No!" the dumbass suddenly yells out: "Yes!" and he snatches up the apple and potato, and he eats them. The big guy is shocked, and the dumbass, well, he gains some confidence. His body posture starts to shift, toward an authoritative stance; meanwhile, the big guy begins to take on the original body posture of the dumbass, becoming cold and scared. Eventually the clown that was originally the dumbass, who has become a boss, strides off the stage saying, "Yes! Yes! Yes!" Now, like in the beginning of the story, there's a clown all alone, in misery – a shivering wreck. It's the big guy, reduced to nothing. He finds some scraps of food somewhere else on the stage. He begins to start touching the scraps, and whispering "No," to himself, but with a strange kind of pleasure … This number has a lot to do with the difficult Russian lifestyle, and it has a peculiar message or lesson buried inside it. Plus it also contains a kind of nostalgia that is typically Russian too. Lokachtchouk was a maestro of this material. Also Yuri Belov, a great teacher, and director of famous clowns such as Karandash, and Leonid Engibarov, Oleg Popov, and Makovsky.

So in Russia, the clown has a strong poetic sense. You learn from the inside out. It is a fragile place, and a vulnerable place. On the other hand, in the United States, I learned that the humor is more corporeal. You must be very physical, and your clown personality, well, a lot of it has to do with physical comedy and visual comedy. It's an external approach. It's very interesting to see the perspective of American comedy. It's a very particular way and a special way to be humorous. My experience at Ringling Bros was fascinating. I believe that the clowning of the United States is more connected to the "here and now." In Belgium, there were a lot of English, French, and Central European people. They work very hard in a group, and each person is in charge of bettering themselves, but they also don't have as much fun as an American.

In the end, thanks to my travels, I found my universal language. It's a combination of influences. Like all of us, I had to find out the things that worked and the things that I identified with the most. I've found inspiration in both the Russian and the American ways. For me as a Mexican, I feel comfortable in a dialogue with both worlds, the internal and the external. But whatever the training, whatever the method, I never wanted to become enclosed in the technicalities of it. I feel that you have to be free to live in the moment, the moment that can't repeat itself. To live in the moment – that's the most extraordinary thing. That's when you produce the most gems, when you're living. You have to be able to relieve yourself of what you've already practiced or rehearsed and just go with what's in the moment. That's the authentic difference between clowning and theater. The clown isn't an actor or character. The clown is a person representing all of us in one way or another, representing our imperfections and who we are, with the grand desire of creating a universal "us."

Techniques

The most important thing as a clown is a real intimacy between yourself and the people. That has to do with the truth, and the energy and emotions of the heart. When you don't have the fourth wall, you can really see the people. You can see their faces, their eyes. If you're a true clown, there's something of you that wants to get as close as possible, to establish contact. Of course it's possible to establish physical contact only as far as the public energy will permit you. Maybe someone will allow you to touch their hair or touch their head. When it happens, it's very charming, and that person is sharing with you everything that the other people in the audience are feeling. It's one of the most beautiful things in this language, to eliminate those informal frontiers of the stage and the audience, and then all the frontiers that follow – race, background, language – you can eliminate those too. You remember the flowers and the old man in my show? When I did that number ten or so years ago in Mexico, a certain girl came back to another performance, dressed in red the way that the story was told, so that when I got to that moment when the old man was left all by himself, she came up onto the stage to be with him so that he wouldn't be alone. Then I had to do other things because this was new. I had to create other options. I had to find a different finale. That's something of the game of clowning. At the end it converts itself into reality. A real connection of the spirit.

I also believe every failure has a spiritual substance. You need to fortify yourself with failure; you can't give up. If you've earned the confidence of the spectators – if you've demonstrated to them that you are not abnormal, you are in fact one of them – then they see themselves in the mirror of your clown, and they accept that they are imperfect, and that failures will happen. When I was 21 years old, I had a very crazy accident on a motorcycle, so I was only able to paint. I still have a self-portrait from that time; I painted it on cardboard! I believe that the life of the clown can be very similar to recovering that liberty of being able to play with whatever you have, like a kid, and permitting yourself to use your imagination freely without being scared of someone saying: "You're a musician or not a musician, a painter or not a painter, a dancer or not a dancer, a singer or not a singer … " For example, I have these socks.

[*He demonstrates the following homemade props and costumes.*]

When I put on these socks, my knees play. Also, I have these masks. I have a lot of things because I'm always exploring. I put on all the masks – one, two, three, four – and now I don't see anything. The audience, who see the masks, need to tell me where they're at, like a piñata. All of these things are just things, ideas, that I have in my house. I'm also a painter. I'm always trying; I'm always doing different things. You see? The clown sets out to do what he or she feels and what he or she wants to do. And there's where you expose yourself to failure. But failure is relative. It depends on how you let it affect you.

Philosophy

For me, it's very brief and simple. Clowning is the language of the heart. The most valuable thing to cultivate in the clowning process is your inner voice, the way that you think you should do it and what makes you unique. Above all, always continue exploring yourself and take risks.

Do you know Leo Bassi? He's a transgressor clown. He doesn't only care about jokes. He's interested in hitting the people's conscience very hard, to awaken the people from lethargy, and so he doesn't shy away from things that could be considered violent. But after seeing one of Leo Bassi's skits, the people follow him.

He could come out naked, and people would be ready to go to war for him. He awakens that in people. Have you seen the movie *The Last Circus*? In this story, when a circus is doing their number, the military comes and takes the clowns, just like that. This happened in Bassi's family. He comes from that history, so he has another energy because of that. Yes, each one of us as a clown has to know what we would like to awaken in others.

I'm interested in awakening people's self-esteem and self-worth because in a lot of countries in this day and age it doesn't matter what people think about the government, it doesn't matter whether or not we decide to help or save the planet, there are always larger powers that are deciding what's going to happen to us, and they're always telling us that we don't matter, and that's why the people get into a state of desperation. Society needs to laugh because the global crisis is continuing to grow more complicated. I believe that people get sick a lot because of sadness, that society has invented something where it feels like you're only validated by having something, that if you have this, possess this, possess that, then you're happy. But there isn't enough for everybody. Therefore, clowning is very important for society because it reminds us of the importance of what each person can be. It cultivates the most simple and valuable things in life. The things that don't cost anything. Laughter.

When a country doesn't laugh, the country is in crisis. Because laughter will take over any pretensions, even the sacred ones.

I have mixed feelings about the internet. I believe that yes, in certain ways, it allows everyone to have access to this beautiful knowledge of humanity, although not everyone has the maturity to understand this, and so, a lot of times, things get frivolous. For example, a lot of people look at the internet just to copy things because this seems to be easier. Take a look at Charlie Rivel on YouTube. Charlie is the most important clown in Spain. He does this very simple number. He is 80 years old, a wise man, and he can create a piece of genius very easily. He comes in with his guitar and a chair. He's very old. He wants to get on the chair, but because he's so old, it looks like a giant mountain. He tries different ways until he's able to, little by little, get to the top of the mountain. Finally, he's up there, he looks – and he forgot his guitar. He gets down, and he takes another 30 minutes to get back on, and so a girl comes in and says, "Charlie, let me help you." And so she helps him, gives him her hand, and he's able to get up a lot easier. And then he sits down to start playing the guitar. So it's something very easy, but for him to do something like that, he had to be a clown his entire life. And because of YouTube, any young guy can copy the same thing without understanding the profoundness and significance of the entire life of an artist. While everything's good to learn in various ways – through history, from people – learning implicates a responsibility. If you're going to copy, recreate, do it in your own way. After all, almost everything is done already, right? Not much is new.

Look, I have another thing to show you. Give me one second.

[He comes back with a pair of trousers. He has painted a face on the crotch and another on the ass.]

I painted this. So I have a laugh, a smile, in my genitals, and then whenever I'm embarrassed, I turn around.

I guess that nowadays, I do the same thing that I used to do back when I was a little kid. I search for people to love me. Yes, that's what I used to do as a kid, and I turned it into my profession.

4   Larry Pisoni and Lorenzo Pisoni

Figure 3 Larry and Lorenzo Pisoni. Photo by Terry Lorant

Larry Pisoni (born in New York, 1950) founded the Pickle Family Circus in San Francisco in 1974. The circus, which operated as a collective and raised money for the local communities in which it performed, helped to kickstart a new movement in American circus, focusing on a back-to-basics approach that promoted clowning and human skills, and eradicated animal acts and outlandish spectacle. Pisoni's clown partners were Geoff Hoyle and Bill Irwin. The circus continues in the form of the New Pickle Circus, although Larry is retired.

Lorenzo Pisoni (born in San Francisco, 1976), Larry's son, grew up in the Pickle Family Circus and began performing with the company as a boy in 1978. He eventually moved on to work with Cirque du Soleil and many other circuses around the world. Lorenzo has a thriving career as an actor in film and theater. His solo performance *Humor Abuse* chronicles his young life in the Pickle Family Circus.

We caught Larry and Lorenzo in good-humored conversation as the latter was preparing a new show in Las Vegas. (DB/EL)

Origins

Larry: My first memory of a clown? My grandfather took me to the Clyde Beatty Cole Brothers show, on Long Island, and a little person clown put a hat on top of my head. I was four years old and I wasn't exactly happy about it. That was my first experience.

Lorenzo: My first memory. I think probably my father put a clown hat on top of my head.

[Laughter.]

Lorenzo: To be honest about it, I don't know what my first memory is. It's like, what's your first memory of gravity? I have a hard time remembering the clowns. Mostly I remember the people. When I think of Bill Irwin, I don't see his makeup – I see Bill's face. Even Slava's *Snowshow*. I would go and see that, and I would think "Oh well, that's just Slava … "

Larry: My grandfather was a comic. My grandmother was a dancer. And that's how they met. My grandfather did an ethnic routine. He was an Italian right off the boat.

Lorenzo: And he had his own show, right?

Larry: Yes, the Pepper Pot Review.

Lorenzo: Al "Wop" Pisoni.

Larry: Seriously. I have a poster. He was born in the States, however. My great-grandfather came over. He was a stonecutter. He came over before the turn-of-the-century, and worked on a New York Parkway, or Turnpike, whatever it is.

Lorenzo: The Taconic right? Didn't he work on the Taconic?

Larry: Maybe. He was a stonecutter, so he cut stones. But my grandfather didn't want any part of that, so he went into – you know in vaudeville there used to be ethnic shows. Irish shows, German shows, Jewish shows, and so forth, and there was an Italian show, and he started off in that. And then he crossed over to mainstream. He worked in New York, Connecticut, Jersey, pretty much in that area.

Inspirations

Larry: I had really hoped that I was going to end up as a painter. But I met Hovey Burgess in New York in 1967. I got sucked into it. I was in Hovey's company by 1968, somewhere in there, and was introduced to the commedia, and that was the start. When that company fell apart, I moved to San Francisco with the idea of starting my circus, but using theater people as opposed to circus people. So I taught at various theater companies in San Francisco; I was teaching at five at one time, and one of them was the San Francisco Mime Troupe. And I taught with them for a while, and then I decided that I wanted to be a member of that company, and I put my idea on hold for a while. So I did radical theater for three years I think, and then decided it was time to put my show together.

Lorenzo: Now mind you, Larry, you started doing this at 19. So that's kind of intense.

Larry: So what's the problem?

Lorenzo: No problem. As for me, I can certainly remember being very excited when you decided to make a clown act with me in it, not a passing entrance and exit, but really to make a narrative that I was heavily involved in. I remember being excited by that. But I still really don't think that I'm a clown, and it probably wasn't until 2007 when I decided, "Oh yeah, I enjoy this, I like what I can do to help other people be funny." So maybe it was that late, because otherwise it was just what I did. What I knew. The show I'm doing right now, in Vegas, is clowning. Structurally it is clowning. Now I'm the straight man, there are four other comedians. There is an Arlecchino. There is a Capitano. They come from those same archetypes, except we are wearing Tom Ford suits. And I'm holding a glass that looks like it's whiskey, in my own little homage to Dean Martin. So it's Vegas style, but yes, it's just straight-up clowning.

Larry: There's no getting away from the commedia when it comes to doing this kind of stuff. It is the root of it.

Lorenzo: And it works. It's just so easy to know, okay, if I'm doing X you have to do Y, and it doesn't matter how drunk the audience is, it will elicit a response.

Larry: It has to do with what drives your character, you know; it could be money, it could be food, it could be sex. There's status too, but it's not just status. You always want to know what it is that you want, what you are looking for. And then what happens along the way, that's the stuff that makes it funny. When I built the Pickle Circus on the West Coast, with this idea that it would be theater people as opposed to circus people in it, I guess that was born of a commedia model, in some ways. I was looking for something that was a little more accessible to an audience than just somebody standing there juggling seven balls by themselves. I wanted there to be a connection, something that creates empathetic moments. So yes, juggle the seven balls, but *be* somebody doing it, or have something happen to you that causes you to do that. Use the circus skills to advance some sort of relationship. Sometimes we were successful, and sometimes not, with that as an aesthetic. It was, you know I was very very fortunate to have met Bill Irwin. Bill Irwin had gone from Oberlin directly to Clown College, then turned down a contract with Ringling, and came to San Francisco. His then fiancée was working with a dance company in San Francisco, so that's what the connection was; so Bill came and auditioned, having just finished Clown College, and I said "Yeah, you're the guy." Especially because he'd worked with Herb Blau and done all of this theater. And then Geoff was part of Inter-Action in

London and had worked with Decroux and he had chops. So as far as clowning was concerned, it was not the traditional American approach; it was not the Ringling approach to clowning. We all shared commedia. We had all studied commedia. That's what we used for clowning. Also, Bill was a dancer, and Geoff had a background in English music hall, so he understood that genre. We were very lucky, we were extraordinarily lucky in terms of building our material. And we had great clown heroes. All three of us really admired Buster Keaton. Big time. But we also loved clowns like Grock, who we were impressed with, and Dimitri from Switzerland, and the Czech Polivka. There was a whole movement in Europe just before us, of theater clowns. And we were interested in that. So it was interesting that we had all of these similar influences.

Lorenzo: I'm a generation later, so my influences and mentors are ... Larry Pisoni, Bill Irwin, and Geoff Hoyle! I mean, for certain the three of you guys. And what's weird, I think, about that, or impressive – you know Bill left the circus in 1980? –

Larry: Yeah, we did the one outdoor season and then he decided he wanted to go.

Lorenzo: Yes, and yet sometimes when I do something on stage people say "Oh that's a Bill." Or "That's a Geoff." Or "That's a Larry." And then there are other times when I will do something that I think is like Geoff, and then one of them will come and see me and say "Oh, actually that's Dimitri," or "Actually that's Grock." And certainly I've seen David Shiner so much that there are certain things I do that are like him. But then of course my first memory of seeing a movie is Buster Keaton. You guys would, you know, jump in a car at the first sign of a Keaton film playing, because there was no VHS, so you would all go, and if there wasn't a babysitter you would just throw me in the car. So now I have all the DVDs of all the Keaton films because I feel like I have to have them. I mean I never watch them. But I have to have them.

Larry: You should watch them!

Lorenzo: I know, I know, I should watch them.

Larry: Promise me.

Lorenzo: I will watch them.

Larry: Yeah, yeah, yeah, you say ...

Lorenzo: So by proxy, I have some of the same mentors as these guys, and then I also have them as mentors too. And I do just have to say really quickly, it was amazing, when I was doing *Humor Abuse*, which was really the first time I had ever really decided to do something that was clown (-ish, it was still like an actor doing clown so it was a little sketchy), Hovey Burgess came and saw the show, and he said that's really great, but it's not clown. It's not a clown show. But it's really great. And I knew what he meant, and I agreed, of course everyone else thought it was a clown show, and then when Geoff and Larry and Bill came to see it, they couldn't help but give me notes.

Larry: I didn't give you notes because you wouldn't take them from me.

Lorenzo: No that's not true, you could just give them to Erica! But it was great, because then I would try to use them. And they were right. They were right. So that was really fun.

Larry: Although I don't think you should be exclusively forged by your teacher or your mentor. The point is that it should get better and better. With each generation. If it doesn't then it just becomes a museum piece. But, having said that, you know, there's a reason why painting students go to the Louvre and set up an easel and paint the masters and try to duplicate the brushstrokes. And there's a reason why sculptors, if you're learning to be a sculptor, you do feet for three years, and then maybe you get to do a hip. You know, I think that that's really important, but then you take all the stuff you've been learning for years and you make it your own. And you have your own approach to humor, or your own approach to making a gift for an audience, which comes from you. Otherwise you end up with a museum piece. And who wants to see that? I don't want to see that. I don't want to see someone do Dimitri's routine, or see someone else do Shiner's or Irwin's stuff. I *do* want to see someone else do something inspired by those people. That I'm interested in. Do something else. Make it your own.

Lorenzo: Just to add, I think that as an audience people probably ... They might not know it consciously, but when they see someone doing someone else's material, it may be funny, sure, you can paint by numbers, you might get Shiner's movie routine, but it's not going to be the same as when he does it, because he has those years and years of doing it on the street. I've heard you say Larry, sometimes you say to your students "Find something that you like and copy it, and we'll start there." But then, where the artistry comes in is making something that is about *you* as the performer. Otherwise there's nothing ... As animals I think we can perceive that it's not connected.

Larry: Well, we are mimics. We're all mimics. But there are variations all the way along. You know, I used to do this three-quarter front somersault onto a balloon. I've never seen anybody do it onto a balloon before, but I certainly had seen film of Ben Turpin doing it, or Keaton doing it. But my addition was adding the balloon. I did a variation of it when I worked with Yo-Yo Ma in Japan; I took a bouquet that I was supposed to give to someone on stage, and I did the three-quarter and stuck the bouquet under my butt and pulled the bouquet out as a variation, and handed it to whoever. So, it's just, you know, you make it your own. You make it your own.

Techniques

Larry: I always try and come up with an ending first. And then, work on how to get to that end. And if in the course of working to the ending I find some things that I like better, then that's fine. But all too often, I have seen people work on great stuff, and it doesn't have an ending. And I think that's a serious dilemma. If you have an ending already, if you have a move or a gag that you want to end with, then it's so much easier to go backwards, and just see how you get there. That has served me well for quite a few years, and that's how Bill and Geoff and I worked. We had a final image that we wanted. Play the song and get off the stage. I put it rather delicately, play the song and get the fuck off stage was what we really said.

Lorenzo: Yes I was going to say, you're leaving out the expletive. I mean, it's interesting to hear you say that, Larry, only because right now there's a few moments of the show here in Vegas, a few times, our task is to cover the scene change, you know.

Larry: Oh really?

Lorenzo: Yeah, it's really a novel idea.

Larry: How progressive.

Lorenzo: Yeah it's really cutting-edge here in Vegas. But, it's funny, when the demand is to move a piece of scenery, if all you have to do is cover an automations change, then the problem becomes that. And then to build over that gets tricky quickly. Because you have to move this one prop from here to there, and that becomes your task, so how do you make it problematic? And then how do you make the solutions? And we skipped that whole "come up with the last image" thing because the last image was just getting the prop to the other part of the stage and it wasn't our choice. So then in performance, we're trying this one night, trying this another night, trying something completely different, and, slowly, we're working it out. But of course people have bought tickets to the early shows that haven't gone so well, so it feels a little tricky.

Larry: Well my other philosophy when it comes to doing comedy is keep it real.

Lorenzo: Yes. Yes.

Larry: If what you have to do is move a piece of scenery, move a piece of scenery! Move it a lot.

Lorenzo: Yeah, yeah! We've found that's the way. Don't try to mask it.

Larry: Don't try to mask it.

Lorenzo: Just say, "Oh well, now I have to move this over here … "

Larry: Yeah, or over here …

Lorenzo: "Or it's going to be in the way."

Larry: Or over here …

Lorenzo: See, but I have to say "Just move it over there." And then the other people say, "No, over here."

Larry: Well there you go. Exactly. Finita.

Lorenzo: You find the problem and then try to solve it in a number of ways, some of which presumably will fail. That is like a C scale, you know what I mean? A scale with no flats or sharps. If you need to create a piece, that is the most straightforward way to do it. And then if you want to start playing something that is slightly more interesting, then it can go off, you know. Keaton wants to get the girl. How many things does he have to do to get the girl? And then, lo and behold, to get the girl in the end he solves all those problems, in one fell swoop, and then boom, he's got the girl. It's that thing. It's formulaic, but I think the artistry comes in when you start coming up with really interesting solutions to solve very basic problems. And then perhaps you start concealing the formula.

Larry: You have to create your own reality, and keep it real within that. So if the reality of it is that your foot is stuck in the middle of the stage, when we all know it's not really stuck, then you have to create the reality of your foot being stuck, and make it appear to be real for the audience, and for yourself. My personal feeling about humor is, I don't find silliness in and of itself very funny. But if you put that silliness in context with a straight person, you know, an authority figure … For example, you've got the whole Marx Brothers situation where Harpo was ostensibly silly, and Groucho and Chico are living in a surreal world themselves, so how do you create the dynamic? You have a Margaret Dumont. You have someone who is creating the obstacle, and then you can work all your crazy comic stuff. And I think they knew that. They knew that they needed someone that they could play off of. I like fantasy. I think you can do a lot with fantasy, but you have to create it in such a way that it relates to something, so you can invite your audience in, you know, have them participate in it. Otherwise the audience is excluded, and you don't get anywhere with that.

Lorenzo: Yes … In my show right now, I try to be the authority figure and the other guys can play off me. Mind you, I still have to have fun, because otherwise it's just me saying "No, no, no" all the time, and that's not exciting for anyone.

Larry: Dean Martin is a good example of that.

Lorenzo: Yes, he would seemingly break and find everyone funny … So I am creating the obstacle. And of course they allow me to create the obstacle, they push and push and push, and they treat me like a king, so that the structure is maintained. Because I think the other thing about fantasy, or having this world in which the everyday rules of people's lives don't apply, is that the logic has to be sound. So that if a person's foot is attached to the stage, and we all know that it's not, you can't have something completely silly and bizarre happen that has nothing to do with the fact that you're stuck. Because then you just destroyed the illusion. I suppose I'm saying the same thing that you did, Larry.

Larry: Well, you said it better than I did.

Lorenzo: Yeah, right … !

Larry: What about failure?

Lorenzo: Failure? What's that? Everything I've done has been 100 percent successful. *[Laughter.]* I mean I think that there is a buoyancy that one feels on stage when things work out well, and then when something doesn't, the ground comes out from under you really hard. Fast. It's that feeling of just bottoming out in a car, where the undercarriage hits that pavement really hard and you hope the transmission is still in the car. That's kind of what it feels like. To me anyway. And then, it's a struggle not to have a tell, that it didn't work. And to get back to where you are meant to go, I think that's where experience and skill really kick in. Because it's very easy to just sit in the failure. Although I think failure is also much more important than the successes, because of the humility that it builds, and also the information that you're given – that's a true gift.

Larry: Mmm … It depends on what you're doing, but when I sit in an audience, I really want the person who is performing to be successful. I don't want to participate in their recognition of not being able to do something that they had intended to do, or participate in a gag that didn't necessarily work properly. This brings up the notion of working with props that don't work. And my feeling about that is, if you're working with a prop, if there's a chance that it's not going to work, then don't work with that prop ... The value of rehearsal is that if it works 87 times out of 100, I'm willing to live with that quotient of risk. But it's got to work those 87 times. Otherwise I don't want to work with the prop. Bill and Geoff and I work with props all the time, and we always make sure that our props function. Always. Also, I see a lot of students who, when it comes time to give a presentation, they say, "Oh well, I'll drop the flower and then I'll pick it up." Only they drop the flower and the head of the flower falls off the stem. Something as simple as that. And then they panic. They break character, and they say "Sorry! That wasn't supposed to happen!" Play it real, if the head falls off the stem, then do something with that. But don't tell me, don't tell the audience that it wasn't supposed to happen. The value of rehearsal is that you find those things. "Oh! It falls off! I can do something with this, I can bounce it on my nose, then pick it up and put it back on, then bounce it on my nose again, take it apart again, and put the bloom on my nose and just let it sit there ... " You just discovered a little gag. You know, but do that in rehearsal; don't do that in a presentation. I don't want to see that.

Lorenzo: You know, as a performer, part of your job description is to take care of your audience.

Larry: Absolutely.

Lorenzo: And you can take care of them in a way that makes them feel uncomfortable, if you like, but you have to be ... I mean, you're hosting them. So be a good host. If something's gone wrong, we don't want to see that it's gone wrong. We don't want to worry about a performer. When a good performer is working with a problem and it is seemingly a struggle, we know somewhere inside that they are in control, and therefore we can relax and say to ourselves, "Oh this is great, the bloom just fell off the stem, oh this is amazing, it's just wonderful." I agree with Larry. Unless we are there to see a workshop of something, and we know it's not finished. I saw Robin Williams do a workshop with a new set years ago, and he would get halfway down a joke that wasn't working at all, and he would stop mid-sentence and say "I'm never doing that again," and move on to the next thing, and it was really kind of great. But we all knew that's why we were there. Because this was new material, and he'd never done it in front of an audience. And therefore, it was fun. But other than that I don't think there's any value in sitting in your failure, unless you're totally in control and made it fail on purpose. Anyway, I think success is scarier. When you have a huge success you still have to do the next show. And then, the tendency for me is that I somehow want to recreate the time I had before, and if I try to recreate it, it's slippery, right? Because, you know, there's that old story: So-and-so was asking for a cup of tea, asking for a cup of tea, asking for a cup of tea, and it kept getting laughs, kept getting laughs, and then all of a sudden he stopped getting laughs, and he went backstage and he said "Why aren't they laughing?" and someone said "Why don't you just ask for the cup of tea?" And as soon as he started asking for the tea, he started getting laughs again. It's that thing – you can't want the results. I don't know.

Larry: You do know. That's good. Good example. I'm proud of you.

Lorenzo: Thanks, Dad.

Larry: Are you proud of me?

Lorenzo: Of course I am.

Larry: Okay.

Lorenzo: Good!

Larry: We all go through this, too: "Let's do everything we know how to do, and let's do it a lot!" to "Let's just do one thing. Let's not carry four trunks anymore, and, you know, a whole bunch of stuff. Let's just do the one little thing. And make that work." I think the simpler it is, the better. But you have to go through that stage where it's necessary that you do all that stuff, so that eventually you can say, "All I'm going to do is just look at you." And that will work. "Look at you with a commitment that I am happy just to look at you." And we can tell a story that way. I've seen a whole bunch of my contemporaries go through that as well. Doing everything they know how to do, then just paring it down to something as simple as possible.

Lorenzo: Yeah, I mean, Bill doesn't even travel with those trunks anymore. He has that little one that's like two feet wide.

Larry: Well, he's getting old, he can't carry them anymore.

Lorenzo: Geoff doesn't even use props anymore.

Larry: I think that's great. In *Humor Abuse*, you do my old sandbag routine. Lots of sandbags. But eventually I pared it down to a version of that which involves just one bag, and one balloon, and that's all I need. And it seems to hold. Though I always liked doing all of the bags, but it's too much trouble carrying it all around, setting it all up.

Lorenzo: Let alone hanging them.

Larry: Well I never had to do that, I always had someone else do that.

Lorenzo: Yeah, that somebody else was me.

Larry: Well, you know, that's why they say you have kids, that's the reason you have kids.

Lorenzo: That's right. That's right. You know, I've never heard you talk about that, but certainly *Humor Abuse* was that. "Let's do everything I possibly can ... "

Larry: Let's do all of *his* stuff too.

Lorenzo: "Yeah, and let's do everyone else's material as well!" I do think that there is that paring away over time. You get better at polishing the stone, to get just what you want. Simplicity becomes so much more attractive than complicated stuff. And I also think that as people get older, they know themselves better, and there is less insecurity, less fear. You don't need the smoke and mirrors as much. It seems to me as you get older, you have more experience, and what are they going to do, not laugh? Well, I've been through that. That's not all that bad. And if you can find a situation and provoke a response with *nothing* – that's the skill. And then you know, oh wow, it's just so gratifying because it's not about the stuff, it's just about you and the audience sharing a moment, an experience.

Philosophy

Larry: You know, for the last 15 years I've been trying to write down for myself … Why do we do this? What is the purpose? I think for me, I just want to have … I always say to my students, it's not about being funny, it's about creating empathetic moments. That's my philosophy of comedy. Let them recognize Uncle Harry in the thing I just did, or Aunt Joan, you know? If someone is standing at one end of a tightrope and needs to get to the other end, that's a great metaphor for facing a challenge. And I sort of think it's the same way with clowns. Our challenge is to create a moment that is identifiable, and find the humor in it. That, more than anything else, is a clown's charge. To help everybody feel better.

    Lorenzo: It also seems to me that, especially in this day and age, here in Vegas anyway, audiences are watching the show but they're thinking about their iPhones. And I think the clown's job is to remind people of their humanity. To me, as I get a little older, it's not so much about getting attention, or feeling that the laugh's the most important part of it … I get great pleasure when people just take down their smartphones and watch what we're doing. To me, that seems like a good reason to do this kind of thing. For people to actually stop multitasking, and be right where they are, and see themselves, and recognize their own behavior. Don't get me wrong, I love gadgetry. I'm sitting here and I have my iPad and I have my iPhone, and I can't wait to get some new toys … But I think it's important when a group of people sit down in a room and they have an experience at exactly the same time.

    Larry: Right. After all, clowning has been around since we became sentient. I think that humor, you know, since the first time the guy in front of you let go of the sapling and it hit you in the face, and you went back to the fire and they talked about "Oh well, you know, look who got hit in the face!" (you know, it wasn't like the guy in front of you did it on purpose, but you were the brunt of the joke) … That kind of stuff has been around forever. And I think that it's good for us. It's good for us to acknowledge the humorous parts of life, and it's not necessarily ha-ha-all-fall-down funny, but it's part of admitting to the fact that we are, I don't want to say flawed, because that's a little too simple – that we all have challenges. And what's best is to approach or engage in those challenges in the healthiest way. Don't blame somebody else for your challenge, accept the challenge, figure out how to address the challenge, invite people to help you deal with the challenge, and so forth. So how that relates to clown, practically, is the props, the hats, the shoes, your clown ladder, these are all opportunities for metaphor. You know. So … I think that we are just sharing a human experience. We are attempting to work it all out. Together. Collectively.

    I use the word "courage" a lot. You have to have courage. When you walk on stage, when you walk in the circus ring, when you walk onto the set, you have to be ready to fail. You have to be ready for it not to work. You have to be ready to expose yourself to people you don't know, and there's courage involved in that.

    Lorenzo: With clowning you have to be much more vulnerable and naked than when you're acting. Because so often clowning comes from the performer, so therefore you have a lot more at stake, you are presenting a lot more of *yourself* intrinsically. When you're an actor, you can say, "Well Shakespeare wrote that line, I have nothing to do with it," or whatever.

Larry: Or "The director told me to do it this way," or "The costume designer said: 'Here, put this on … '"

Lorenzo: Right. Also I feel as though it's harder to go from being an actor to being a clown. It's a lot easier to go from being a clown to being an actor, I think.

Larry: I think it's interesting at this point to say that the traditional way for people to come to clowning was that they were acrobats, they were jugglers, they were rope-walkers, they were bareback riders, they were musicians, they had another discipline that supported their work as a clown. So even though a piece of material within a clown act might not work, you still had a little trick to do. You had a little skill that you could show. "I'll twirl my hat one more time because I missed that cue," or something along those lines, something actually physical that you could do. And in my day, coming into acting, the whole thing was, "Tear the person down and then let's build them up to someone who can do anything." I think if an actor goes through that kind of training, it's reasonable to expect that if you say, "Okay, be funny, do something funny," anyone who is just an actor is going to have a hard time. I didn't mean to say *just* an actor.

Lorenzo: Yeah, hey, hey.

Larry: But I think an actor who has a background in improvisation, or can sing a song, or can do a little dance, or something like that, you bring them into clown and they'll have no problem. But if their background is simply learning lines, breaking down the scene, working on a monologue, and so on and so forth, and then they're told "Okay, do something funny!" That's a hard one. I think that's a hard one. What are you doing, Lorenzo? What's the smirk?

Lorenzo: Nothing.

Larry: So who was catching all those glasses in that last play that I saw you in? Who was that?

Lorenzo: Hey, you know, I was just doing what the playwright wrote …

Larry: She may have written it, but you choreographed it. She said, "Okay, do this routine!" But *she* never did it.

Lorenzo: Right, right. I think a lot of contemporary clowns, because there is less premium put on skills as we know them – juggling, acrobatics, music – the skill then just becomes this whole idea of being able to make people laugh. I think that really limits what's possible. Because the really successful clowns can go from the sublime to the ridiculous. But you need the sublime in order for the ridiculous to mean something. So …

Larry: I also think it's not about *making* people laugh.

Lorenzo: Here we go.

Larry: It's about *inspiring* laughter. I don't believe you can *make* anybody laugh. I think if you're good enough to keep doing this, if you've reached a level where you feel like you've accomplished something and you're accomplishing something, then you will find that you still have to create. And the act of creation is a revolutionary act. Sure, there are people who are conservative in their approach.

"This is what it is, and it isn't that." But my feeling about clowning is that it is inclusive, it is *all*. And I know good clowning when I see it, and it's almost always something that inspires me, and there lies the revolutionary part of it. And with each generation, those of us who have been doing it for a while keep being surprised by people who are coming up in the work and making it their own, and inspiring those of us who have been doing it for a while to want to stay in it. I'm retired, unfortunately, because I can't work anymore, I can't move the way I used to. I can see a time when I might get on the boards again to do something, but not in the circus, I just can't. I can't get out of the way of the horses. But you've found a way to incorporate all of the stuff that you learned into your acting, and that's exciting for me. I had the great pleasure of meeting Cieslak back in the '60s, when Grotowski was doing a workshop in New York. And as soon as he found out that I was an acrobat, he just grabbed a hold of me, he said: "This is what we going to do … " in his broken English. So I look at you and I say to myself, "Oh he's got all the stuff, he can use it in his quote–unquote legitimate acting." Like what you're doing in Vegas!

Lorenzo: Yes, yes! Oh God.

Larry: But just as a sidebar, I saw you in a production with Sam Waterston, and Sam is quite a presence on stage, and you held your own with him. I think it was because of the circus that you were able to do that.

Lorenzo: It was also because I knew the light plot, and I would just stand in the right place.

Larry: Ha!

Lorenzo: Which I learned in the circus. I agree that some people are conservative and they have a narrow view, and I think there are some people who don't want to make people uncomfortable, and in that way they are conservative, very middle-of-the-road. But for me, I feel that historically the clown is the one that speaks truth to power. And that act is revolutionary. So if you're truly clowning, then that's what you're doing. Whether you know it or not, that is what you're doing.

Larry: I recently read that there are no clowns anymore. I wonder what publicist at Ringling wrote that? Actually I'm encouraged. I don't know firsthand, but through the internet I read about all the stuff that is happening in New York. I read about the stuff that's happening in San Francisco and Montreal and overseas, in Spain, and France, and so on and so forth. I think there is a bright future for the work, and it gets better and better. I also think I stopped using clown as a noun and started using it as a verb a long time ago, so you will see clowning in the context of a lot of other genres. You'll see good clowning in other kinds of performance venues, and I'm really encouraged by that. So, I think we're doing okay. I also think that actors are better prepared to address clown than they know. They just have to, well, young actors all have to get out of their own way. If I can say that. Lorenzo, you're not young anymore, I don't feel that it's a problem for you …

Lorenzo: It's true, I know. Yeah, it seems to me, this whole idea that clowns are dying out, I don't get that. I don't understand how that would ever be possible. Because we're all human, and we need clowns, and we have always had clowns, and why would it stop? One of the beautiful things about clowning is that it's always the same, and it always has been the same, and always will be the same. There is a constant, I think, that the clown fulfills in people's lives. The form it takes may change, but the purpose, I believe, will remain. Or not. I don't know.

5   Micha Usov

Figure 4 Micha Usov. Photo by Yann C. Arnaud

Micha Usov (born in Kharkiv, Ukraine, 1967) recently completed five years performing in Cirque Du Soleil's *Totem*. A graduate of the Circus Arts College in
Moscow, Usov is also one of the founders of the award-winning clown theater
Mikos. With Mikos he has won gold and silver medal awards at a number of major
festivals, such as the Festival Mondial du Cirque de Demain (Paris, France) and
the International Clown Festival (Ostend, Belgium). He is currently developing a
new solo clown show, *Inside*.

   We talked to Micha in Cirque's café for artists outside Cirque du Soleil's *Totem*.
(DB/EL)

Origins

I was born and raised in the Ukraine. The first time I went to the circus I was
about six. It was a circus of, how do you say it and be politically correct, small

people? It scared me very much. They were the same height as me, but they were adults, and I couldn't understand how that was possible.

Aged about 16, something happened. I had to choose my path in life, and I'd already started to go to technical school when this old guy approached me and said, "I think you could be really good on top." I got scared. "What? On top of you?" I said, "No, no, no, I don't want to be on top." He said, "You didn't understand me. You could be a really good top acrobat in a duo. Because," he said, "I'm from a circus school. What's your mother's name? Please give me the phone number of your mother." Every Sunday he would call my mother. "When will your son come to our studio? When he comes – I really want him to come – please make sure he brings the special shoes." He meant dance shoes. He was calm, and persistent, so after about a month, my mother said, "Go, check it out. But if something is wrong I'm gonna call the police." So I went. I opened the door to the studio, and I never left. I entered into the circus world.

But when we started to rehearse, they looked at me and said, "You're no acrobat. You're a clown!" Because when we were doing the acrobatic work, I kept failing, and it was funny. I was really kind of crooked and weird and naturally funny, I guess. I didn't mind; it worked for me. I hated the town where I lived; it was like living in a subway, you know, when it's so full and you have to fight to get a place on the train. And I hated Soviet aesthetics as well. Pushik hats! Pushik hats were made of a particular animal, and if you had that particular hat, then you were really cool. But our family didn't have enough money to be cool. So I always kind of dreamed of my own train, not to be a part of mass transit … Probably that drove me into the clown world.

My mother was kind of okay with it, but my grandfather, he didn't like it at all. He told me, "Look, you can go and get a real job in a factory. Go work with a machine. And then at night, after five o'clock, then you can go catch flies. That's fine." He thought that clowns caught flies. He was very pragmatic.

Inspirations

We had a dissenter appear in Russian clowning. Leonid Engibarov. He became one of our most highly regarded clowns in the '60s and '70s. He was very successful. The whole circus would always end with his routines. People would give him standing ovations and flowers. He was very simple. He had this real sincerity. For instance, he could balance on one arm, and he would say, "When I balance on one hand I feel like I hold the whole world in my palm." That's it. So simple. This type of clowning was something that people really needed at that time in Russia. Engibarov went inside. He didn't need laughter – that was the audience's business. He simply lived out his inner state. That was very much his approach to clown. An inner journey.

Aged 16 I started to actually earn income as a clown. I had two routines, two numbers. I was quite successful, and I was invited by a professional team to work in Kazakhstan. And then what happened was kind of interesting, because when I was 18 in Russia, I was drafted. And when I finally came back from the army, for some reason people stopped laughing at me. I would be doing the same thing, but nobody was laughing. For a moment I thought, it's probably time to change profession. Then all of a sudden, this enlightening thought struck me that no, this is a profession that I have to actually study in order to always generate something new, independent of any conditions or circumstances. I can be funny. So I applied to a professional clown school in Moscow. It was the best school for clown in the Soviet Union. Very good masters were teaching there; it had a great theater program as well.

In school we were expected to bring ten sketches a day. Every day, ten sketches of different people. Observations. In silence, with text, it didn't matter. We would study a person, we'd study a situation, and we'd reproduce it in class. We could develop the situation for ourselves, or stick to observation. So this was where one of my numbers was born. I was in the zoo, and I watched a woman feeding a donkey, but at that moment I couldn't understand, who was the donkey? She brought a carrot, and she was telling the donkey, "Eat. Eat." But the donkey just had his big ears and wasn't paying any attention. "Eat, come here. Come here, you silly, you came to me yesterday, and you're not coming today. You asshole." And then she started to scream at the donkey. So that was the number, except in my case, I used pigeons. I would have a loaf of French bread. I wouldn't break it into pieces. I would just be feeding the pigeons the whole thing. It was actually a really good number, I think.

After two years of studying, I was performing, and one of my teachers came up to me to say, "This moment, this is your organic state. You've discovered your organic state. This is how it is." When he told me that, it was so important. It was like a light was shining on me. I felt, finally, recognized for who I was. I understood that it's not important what I do; what's important is the state I am in. The next time I entered the stage, I couldn't even reach the end of my routine because people were laughing so hard, as if I was plugged into something.

Techniques

This state offers a different approach to clowning. When you're not seeking success of any kind. For instance, you have a number in five minutes, and you just want to share that, and that's it. You're not really expecting anything in return. You're not listening to the applause or the laughter; you're not seeking that. You just give. No strings attached. Nothing to do with achieving success. Success is very – today you have success; tomorrow you have no success. Something changes: a full moon, a dog comes to the station, a child begins to cry, and suddenly you can't do it anymore, you're not successful. But when you share, and only share … None of that matters. If somebody comes to your house as a guest, and you offer them a cookie, it's their responsibility either to eat the cookie or not to eat the cookie. It shouldn't hurt you either way. So I don't rely on any particular reaction from the audience. I am neutral. If they take it, I'm happy. If they don't take it, I'm not not happy. It's kind of like the sun. You don't ask the sun if it's happy shining or not. It's just shining. For some people, they really absorb the knowledge, and for some people, it's like a passing shadow, and they don't want it, and that's fine. That's correct, too.

I've developed my own system. It consists of three aspects: timing, character, and state/self. Timing is like a skeleton for the routine. Character is like the muscles. Self is the spirit. Without good timing, within 15–20 seconds clowns generally get boring, even if the character is really good. Without character, the clown can still survive, the routine can still go on, but the people will not see the nuances, the different sides of the character. Without self, it's just a technical clown. Now this could be very intellectual, but in my opinion, if you have self/state, but you don't have the other two, you still have a home, because in that state, your personality is not infringing, getting in the way of the self. And you don't need success. I'm developing a new show now, and I explain to all my collaborators, including the technicians, not to expect anything from the public. Only, with the help of the technique we have (of timing, character, and self), we build the show. We put our focus on structure: where to take a pause, what the texture will be of everything, what the decoration will be on stage, and so on. We're not working from a standpoint of reaching for success. Instead we are working as a service.

It's really nice. It's really all about limitations and boundaries, how these are only constructs of our mind. "Oh, you cannot do that!" But who said you cannot do that? Why? Nobody knows. For me, I have to imagine that I am the first man on earth. I imagine I'm Adam. Do I know what's good, what's bad? If somebody points to a palm tree and says, "This is a tree," well, we all know that it's a palm tree, but does Adam know that it's a palm tree? No, he doesn't know anything. So this exploration really opens up a world without any patterns. This is the art form I'm striving for.

To imagine and research and create my routines I have two different approaches. The first one: go to the art. Look at Rembrandt, find his inspiration: how he creates character, what is his image of the person, how do the eyes work, how does the color work? For me, it's all dependent on what I'm working on. If I'm building a routine that takes place in a restaurant, and there's a table, then I look for all the artwork that has tables. I do that with everything, and I find myself getting really filled up, and then my brain just churns out ideas. That's one approach. The other approach is to go to the people. "Look, look! I have this idea. I'm gonna try to do this. What do you think? Do you think this will be interesting?" You have to ask everybody. You even have to ask your mom. And this is interesting: when it comes to clowning, everybody understands what you are talking about, and everybody will give you their advice! Those that are selling ice-cream will tell you how to do better! Until recently I actually critiqued that kind of thing, but now I'm seeking out those ice-cream sellers so that they'll give me their advice, because in that conversation something happens – I find the answer by talking to people that are not directly engaged with what I'm doing. I learned that from Robert Lepage.

Failure is the best thing ever. It's the spot, the point, where we actually can go above ourselves. It doesn't mean that there's no exit; it means that there is a way out. That's where you can do your best work. All of my points of failure were really my points of success. In failure, you can find new gags and new understanding of your acts. You invest a lot more consideration into how to transcend your failure, and when you invest so much, something really extraordinary comes of that.

Philosophy

I really believe that the basic needs, values of all people are all the same. Everybody wants to be happy. Basically. For me, clowning is sharing happiness, because as a clown you're not seeking anything. You already have it. Just gift.

For me, there are clowns and there are not-clowns. Very few clowns, and that's always been the case. There are very few clowns in the world. A great Russian clown Yuri Nikulin said, "There are less clowns than cosmonauts."

Many people engage in the clown world, but many of them are far away from the profession. And that's probably why in America when you say you're a clown people really don't know what you mean because they don't know that many real clowns. To scream, to show the underwear, that's not real clown for me. The true clown is a poet. A philosopher. It's always been that way. If you take the stack of cards, there's a joker there. The clown is really a wise man.

At the end of my masterclasses, I quote Stanislavsky's last words: "Lighter; happier; more joyful."

6   Slava Polunin

Figure 5 Slava Polunin. Photo by Vladimir Mishukov

Slava Polunin (born in Novosil, Russia, 1950) created *Snowshow* – a stage spectacle that has been performed to acclaim in venues across the globe. The show won the Drama Desk Award for Unique Theatrical Experience and was nominated for the Tony Award for Best Special Theatrical Event. Polunin's theater Licedei created several highly successful shows: *Dreamers, Eccentrics in the Attic, From the Life of Insects, Asisyai-revue,* and *Catastrophe.* The members celebrated the twentieth anniversary of the theater with its funeral. They believed Konstantin Stanislavsky, who stated that any theater dies after it has existed for 20 years. In 1989, Polunin organized *The Caravan of Peace,* in which street artists and clowns from around the world were on the road for half a year giving street performances in many European cities. Later, he started the Academy of Fools, the center devoted to the resurrection of the carnival culture in Russia. Polunin has earned many prestigious awards including The Harold Angel (Scotland), The Golden Nose (Spain), Triumph Lifetime Achievement (Russia), and the Laurence Olivier Award for Best Entertainment (UK).

We talked to Slava in his Paris home. He had just returned from St. Petersburg, where he had "inspired" a recent circus. (DB/EL)

Origins

When I was about 12 years old I saw Charlie Chaplin's *The Kid*. It affected me so much that on New Year's Eve I put on a hat and big shoes, I took a big walking stick, and I walked up and down the corridors like Charlie Chaplin. After seeing Chaplin I realized that I wanted to dedicate myself to comedy, especially physical comedy.

I was born and raised in Novosil, which means "new village," a small city, maybe 5,000 people, between the Black Sea and Moscow. My father was the head of the collective farm, and he always made people laugh. But none of my family were performers, until me. I sang in the choir, danced, drew, and I watched television avidly. That's where I found Chaplin, and Marcel Marceau. As soon as I saw Marceau, I told everyone I could get my hands on, "Sit down. I'm gonna perform for you right now." And I imitated him. Before long I began to compose my own scenes and show them to others.

Everything was pouring out of me. So much was coming out of my imagination. I seized every opportunity to create something, and whenever there was a celebration of any kind, I concocted something new for it. Even the 8th of March, International Women's Day! I'd make a scene out of stealing apples, or something ... I was overflowing with ideas.

When I graduated from high school, I went to St. Petersburg. My mother requested, "You have to be an engineer." So I went to the Engineering Institute. But at night, in the evenings, I could do what I really loved to do, which is comedy. Years later, my mother came to visit me, and I took her to a performance that night. It was a musical show, and I was playing the main part. I was dancing, moving, the stage was filled with lots of bright lights and beautiful girls ... Mom watched the show and said, "You know, maybe you can make a living at this."

Inspirations

I went to the circus school, and I audited some classes. I looked at it and said, "That's not me." It was around '67. At that time clowning and circus in Russia were stagnating a little. They were ... stuck. Nothing was moving. There were just hundreds of clowns on a conveyor belt. The three great clowns – Popov, Nikulin, and Karandash – weren't working much at that time. That's when I realized that in the circus I would not find the things that I wished to see in a contemporary clown.

There was one incredible clown in the circus. His name was Engibarov. I really wanted to go in his direction. He never had the "ending" in his routine. He didn't have a period, a button. Instead he would end with dot dot dot, like Chaplin, who would just walk away, into another place. All of Engibarov's clowning was very strange. It felt as if he was writing poems. Actually – he *was* writing poems. But he was the only one.

In St. Petersburg I found a studio with a plaque on it that read "Pantomime Studio," but there was nobody there, no teachers, no students. So I said to the manger, "Would you mind if I use this space, since you already have the name on it? I could fill the void … " Over the next 25 years I brought together and worked with ten people who are renowned clowns today. The name of the theater was Licedei.

At first we studied Eccentric Pantomime. In Russia at that time, pantomime was resembling a hippie phenomenon. It was something very mystical and not very clear. There was no directive attached to it, so you could do whatever you wanted, however you wanted. For me that was essential, to not be burdened by any directives.

There were no instructors and no students. We would sometimes stand for hours in front of the mirror or trying to come up with funny scenes. We wanted to make each other laugh. Our ethos was all about laughter and fantasy. Fantasizing. I found amazing partners among the group, with great chemistry, wonderful levels of energy, senses of humor, so we would spend hours going back and forth, fantasizing, concocting, playing.

Our main teachers were comic films. We watched the work of masters every day. We knew all their gags. We learned their methods. We even created a whole system of gags, like a science of gags. One of the aims was to figure out how to make the audience fall to the floor from laughter within five minutes. The answer was to do 25 gags in those five minutes.

We also learned a system of movement that would help us achieve maximum results. We actually learned a lot from Disney. We studied animation to learn about effective movement, Tom and Jerry. The formula that we found is that the body must make the minimum movement between the maximum number of poses. We created a vocabulary of these poses, and we would go from one pose to the next pose to the next pose as fast as possible. So the audience wouldn't even have a chance to finish laughing at the first gag before the second gag began, and so on, and on. We called it Expressive Idiocy. There was a verbal version of it too. It was brilliant.

But something changed me. I was at a competition in Russia. My colleagues and I won an award for our performance. We were in the Mime category. I was walking with my friend Sasha when we were approached by a critic who had watched our show. The critic told me that I was not really a mime, I was a clown. The word he associated with it was "grotesque." He said that my essence was grotesque, that I would be a part of the clown world naturally, that I could organically belong to a circus or any other environment, because the grotesque is not limited or contained in one genre – it has no boundaries.

This word, "grotesque," has something to do with exaggeration. But exaggeration does not seem to be strange in the grotesque. It actually feels very organic, unlike a dramatic theatre where limitations are precluded by a psychological environment. The most important quality of a circus clown is the ability to be in that grotesque state. When successful, it seems very natural and normal.

When the critic pointed me in that direction, I found myself in the library for many years. I would go there in the morning at 9 a.m., and they would be pushing me out of the door when it was time to close. I studied everything I could in terms of theater, circus, stage. In particular I became attracted to the Silver Age. This was the time when poetry became the main spiritual leader in the arts in Russia. The Silver Age gave birth to the avant-garde in the 1920s. So everything that's in my head, really what identifies me, is the hippie time of the '60s and '70s, and the Silver Age, the age of the poets. After I sat at the library for several years, I asked Marcel Marceau for some advice; I said, "What was the most important thing for Chaplin?" And he said it was personality, character. (At that time Marceau was often in Russia, and I was always carrying his suitcase, helping him with anything … Whatever he needed, just to be close to him and absorb everything.) So then I started to really get engaged in studying characters. First I studied the literary world, and I analyzed all the characters – Don Quixote, Ivan the Idiot – and what I really tried to understand was, what are the qualities of their character that attract people to them throughout the ages? And then I started to look at the qualities of different characters in life. I looked at children. I looked at crazy people. I looked at everyone and everything that resonated with me, everything that I gravitated toward. Finally, after all that research, I realized that I was ready. So I ventured to the kitchen, and I started to paint my face.

My character was born. I went to the bathroom to see what kind of nose I could make for myself, and I saw the cap for the shampoo – that became my nose. Then I went to the closet to figure out what my costume would be, and I saw my wife had recently acquired this new yellow jumpsuit. I always affiliated myself with yellow because it's the color of something really sunny, but also it's the color of a crazy person, a lunatic. So there was my costume. And I went the next morning to the studio, and I picked up these two inflatable telephones that were lying in the corner. (I'm a collector. I collect everything because you never know when you're going to need it. I had a lot of junk in there. I've always loved this quote from Eisenstein, who said, "In every object there already lies an idea. What's necessary is just to uncover it.") I saw in the telephones the idea of loneliness. And then all of a sudden, everything fell into place. I came up with a story of a lonely man who talks to himself on two phones and lives in a world of illusions.

So I called the television show *Goluboy Ogonyok* – I was already well known for my pantomime – I called them and said, "Look, I have a great number for the New Year's Eve show." (It's really like the Oscars in Russia – it's the show, which everybody watches, the whole country sits down on New Year's Eve to watch this show.) They said, "Okay, come over and show us what you have," and I thought, "Okay, now I get to share what I'm doing with all my friends." And it was really wonderful because everybody loved it. It's something that really resonated with the country at the time. It was those slow and dull years of the Brezhnev era, when everything seemed to freeze, as if the whole country was standing in shallow water … Nothing was happening, people were wrapped in cobwebs … And they sat in front of their televisions and suddenly they saw this character who was screaming at the top of his lungs, hoping and trying to break out of the torpor. And the public responded with such fantastic energy. I became a member of everybody's family. I was accepted in every house. It was amazing – people wouldn't take my money when I was riding a taxi; they wouldn't take my money when I went to the restaurant. The personality that I created had somehow tapped into the psychology of that time. I said to myself, "Well, you know, I should really be doing theater with this character." And that's how I started.

Techniques

I had been studying old comedy forms, and I chose the route of the commedia dell'arte. I decided to build a troupe that consisted of different characters. I wanted to make sure that each person, each actor, would not only have an individual character, but would also appeal to a different social layer of the public. We created poetic characters, romantic characters, foolish characters, punk characters – a wide range of types. Naturally they clashed with one another, and there were many collisions; but at the same time they lived as a family, and despite their differences, in the end they found joy and harmony. This particular and unique chemistry between the players became very attractive to the public. It was hard at that time to be sincere in the theater, but because of the connection we created between ourselves, and between the troupe and the audience, we managed it. We were in pursuit of this state of open, joyful, sincere celebration, which was very rare at the time. It was difficult to find that state! But we did it. And the most important thing is that we were a group, seven to ten of us, experiencing that together. Perhaps it had the same effect in Russia as The Beatles did for Britain. There was a kind of co-living between the characters on stage and the members of the audience. Each person in the audience would find a character who was closest to them, and it opened up a wider associative plane. I called this poetic clowning. I was moving in this direction for nine years. And this opened up the doors for many artists to create in a similar fashion. Many companies were formed to experiment in that way.

We created tons of material. We did several new productions a year. But every two, three years, I would change the direction and the theme of the material, because my interests were changing as well. We also played to very different sizes of audience, from small-room theaters (70–100 people), to large theaters of 1,500 people, to stadiums of 5,000–10,000 people. Plus we experimented with film. The reason I mention these numbers and different media is because aesthetics demand a variety of responses. It's impossible to play the same piece in a cabaret theater that you would play in a 1,500-seat theater or on screen. It has to be a different production. When we went into a stadium, our genre became street theater, where we performed among the public and the public became part of the show. Then we would return to a small theater with knowledge that we gained from experimenting and playing in the stadium, having enriched our repertoire and gained many new approaches to our material. We did this continually, curving back on our material again and again, creating from different directions, varying everything. I was also making art installations – that was something that really interested me – and we brought those components into clown theater too.

The cobwebs and other effects that I have used in clown shows come from there, while the snowstorm I use comes from street theater.

I want to clarify something. If we talk about "the theater of clowning," the emphasis, for me, is on the word "clown." I'm cautious about the word "theater." In fact, clowns cannot abide by "normal" theatrical principles, not at all. Principles that guide actors are anti-intuitive to clowns. My troupe and I transformed these "normal" stage principles. We created our own system. Stanislavsky certainly didn't satisfy us. He said that there are three circles of attention, right? First, second, third. But the true clown works in the zero and in the fourth. For a clown, when all his attention goes inside, it goes in so deep that it becomes lost. That's the zero. Alternatively, the clown's attention is on the cosmos. Vast distances. That's the fourth. Sometimes I tell artists or actors, "I have to hit you on the head to get you out of this reality. You should either be lost inside or in the cosmos." Because you cannot be a smart clown. As soon as the public sees your mind in your eyes, you become an actor. The clown is a child, an idiot, all of these characters, anything else, but he's not *here*. He's somewhere else. So the first law of my school – I did establish the Academy of Fools – the first law of my school is that as soon as I notice that somebody is learning something, then I kick them out.

No rehearsal, no work. You have to live to the fullest and celebrate with your friends and your family. The clowns should never know when my prompts enter into their mind. I hide them as much as possible so that things just happen. They're sitting, drinking, eating, chatting, but what's already happening is that little pieces are starting to emerge, and I'm finding and collecting them and putting them into a little basket. (But we did establish a very clear, exact, precise system that gave us the results we were looking for.) I call it "Vsyaki Byaki" (Nonsense Show). It's doing things that mean absolutely nothing, that have nothing to do with art. Our own playfulness that has absolutely no meaning, no intention. One of the laws of Nonsense is that there must be treats. So we cook. We put a lot of attention on that, to cook something particularly tasty. There is a table that separates the stage and the audience. Also we have really good music that we play, so that we can dance. And it's very important that each of us only has one comp ticket for a friend to come, only one. Not comp as in there's no price, but you can only bring one person. It's very strict. If one of the members of the group does not like the guest that you brought, you cannot invite that guest again. So we only invite the best public. And gradually everybody shows a little something on stage. It doesn't matter what it is. You can just show your finger on the stage (not as an insult – I mean something tiny, insignificant …). But clowns are such envious people. If they see somebody having a success on stage, they have to top it. So then it becomes like a competition – they're one-upping each other, and they go till the small hours of the morning, and it doesn't stop. Every three, five minutes somebody puts on a new piece of music, people are dancing, somebody's making tea, somebody's eating, and during this time somebody's putting on their costume or preparing for their number. And then we have a whole system of prizes, and the system of prizes is very illogical. We give, for instance, a broken picture frame to somebody – that would be a prize for non-sense. So out of 20 bits that are presented in one night, three or four will receive these rewards for their ideas, including ideas that are absolute nonsense, where people don't really understand what the hell it is – we give these the highest prize, and it puts the audience into absolute stupor. And then at the end of the year we do a *Jubilee Nonsense Show*, and we go for about three days, nonstop.

At this point I start to analyze the material that we've created during the year. "Okay, so this year it seems like we're really attracted to dark clown," or, "this piece for instance is very lyrical and poetic." Then we assemble bits on this one theme, and we make a show out of those. So the show is really created out of our individuality, by each member of the group. It's really a self-realization of the individuals and that becomes part of the show. Spontaneity is above all. The most important part of our process is making sure that there's joy, there's freedom, and that there's anarchy. It's understood that at any point, the scene might be happening, but if the impulse is to run onto stage and scream and be part of that piece, then you can do it, because the spontaneity is very important. We do not put any importance on the culture of *something*. We want to break that, because the clown really has to listen to his intuition more than any reason or rationale.

Philosophy

I closed this type of theater in 1991, and I ventured into new explorations alone. I was interested in exploring clowning through exploring metaphysics, tragedy; to explore what it is to be a human being. In the last couple years I have moved into a different place completely. I'm no longer interested in theater. I'm only interested in how to make a human being happy, or what makes a human being happy. So I am interested in how to transfer the principles I have found in clowning into the principles of our daily lives. How can you capture and hold onto those incredible, illogical moments in your life? Because they bear happiness. I've created an organization that's called the Worldwide Academy of Fools. It doesn't matter what profession you have, you carve your life as a piece of art.

The carnival brought me to this search for happiness. You see, if you go back to pantomime, it exposes how a human being can be perfect. It's a perfect form. But unfortunately, what Marcel Marceau could do is impossible for us. He said, "Look at my mastery, reach for perfection." But he was on another level, and for you and I it's not that simple. The clown is not like this. He's not above you. He's a friend, and you can hug or embrace him. In fact, in the carnival there is neither artist nor public. We all live by the rules of the same game. And after carnival, the next stage is to choose a day, any day, when you're very creative and your life is filled with art. And after this, it becomes about how to subject your life to this creative state consistently, so that the whole of your life becomes indistinguishable from a piece of art, and the whole of your art becomes indistinguishable from your life.

7   Avner Eisenberg

Figure 6 Avner Eisenberg

Avner Eisenberg (born in Atlanta, Georgia, 1948), known as Avner the Eccentric, is a vaudeville performer, clown, mime, juggler, and sleight of hand magician. He famously played the title role in the 1985 film *The Jewel of the Nile*. Other significant appearances include his Broadway show *Avner the Eccentric* in 1984, an appearance in a Lincoln Center production of Shakespeare's *Comedy of Errors* in

1987, and the principal role Srulik the ventriloquist in the play *Ghetto* on Broadway in 1989. Eisenberg's solo show *Exceptions to Gravity* has toured extensively throughout the United States and abroad, including a sold-out three-month run at Theatre Fontaine in Paris, France.

Avner talked to us in his home in Maine. (DB/EL)

Origins

EL: What was your first introduction to clowns or circus?

Avner: Actually, I got interested in theater first. Must have been the end of my freshman year in college. I went into the theater, which happened to be the closest building to get out of a thunderstorm. I was a chemistry and biology major, and I got a part in a play. Then I started studying acting, theater. I remember the only D I ever got in college was in "Introduction to Acting."

EL: Congratulations. A feat indeed.

Avner: The only one. The rest were all As and Bs. Shortly after that, Johnny Simons, a director from Fort Worth, who'd moved to New Orleans, put together a commedia dell'arte version of Pinocchio. And my roommate, who had been the stage manager of that play that I got into, turned me onto the audition. I got a part, and that was my very first contact with any kind of physical theater.

Then my best friend from high school came to visit, during my sophomore year. We'd both been juggling since we were about 12 years old, and we saw our first street performers. There was a guy doing fire-eating and some little feral children doing tap-dancing on the street. So we decided to go out and juggle and pass the hat. We didn't have any juggling equipment. We juggled fruit, plus a pair of two-pound solid maple swinging clubs that I had collected somewhere.

DB: Did you make any money?

Avner: We made beer money, as I recall. Because I know we ended up at a bar called the Napoleon House with our little clique of fellow students, and we ended up doing a show in the bar.

After that people said to me, "You should take a movement course," and I asked for one at the university, and they said, "We don't have one. Take a ballet class." So I did. I looked like Ichabod Crane in tights. I was growing a beard for a production of Oedipus, also my sophomore year in college ... The white face and beard really looked awful. (Although there are lots of transvestite nuns who wear it very successfully.) I remember getting some books on clowning out of the library, thinking, "Well, that might be a direction to go," and I discovered a picture of Emmett Kelly, and I went, "Oh! He's got a beard!" So I developed kind of a hobo-clown-mime-juggler-eventually-magician-acrobat character. And then I saw Marcel Marceau perform in New Orleans, and I moved closer to mime.

DB: You didn't go into ballet ... ?

Avner: I did some comic roles in a couple of ballets. They wouldn't let me really dance, but I got to do some of the comic roles in *Nutcracker* and I forget what the other one was, *Sleeping Beauty*, I think ...

EL: So how did things evolve from there?

Avner: The theater department quit at Tulane. Big flap with the administration. They were one of the premier theater departments in the country at the time, and all of the big guns quit in this flap with the administration. So I went out to Atlanta and enrolled at Georgia State where I worked in the circus for a little bit. They were loading the circus in, and I just wandered in and got a job carrying things around for a couple weeks. Did a bit of street performing, did some birthday parties. My cousin reminded me just the other day of my very first public show. It was for a women's organization, and it was in a bank, and we had worked out this routine with paint and carefully put up a sheet. I think the sheet must have fallen down because the paint ended up all over the wall. I know we spent three days with toothbrushes and bottles of Ajax cleaning that wall. And I auditioned for the new Alliance Theater Company, which was just opening in Atlanta, and they did a piece that hadn't been done since the seventeenth century, called *King Arthur*, about the Saxon invasion, and they hired me to teach. This was a theater, ballet, and opera company, all co-mingled on stage. They hired me to teach the ballet, to do some basic acrobatics and juggling, and then they said, "Why don't you do the show? Put this leopard skin on and be a Saxon. And then put this bearskin on and be an Anglo." So I was the first Anglo-Saxon. Then I auditioned for the children's theater company and got a part in a couple of plays they were doing, and then moved over to a wonderful theater called the Academy Theater, which I actually got cast in because of some spectacular catches I'd made in a touch-football game between the two theater companies. I auditioned for the acting program at NYU School of the Arts and was accepted, but I still didn't think I was much of an actor … I ended up in something called Production Management, which sounded like a pretty good deal. I was very interested in technical theater. They put me in the design program, which was great fun and one of the hardest departments to get into. People had huge portfolios, designing lights, costumes, sets. I hadn't done any of that. But I sort of specialized in technical theater and prop construction. Still, I hated New York. Went out to California to teach Israeli folk-dance at a Hebrew-speaking summer camp in Ojai.

EL: Naturally.

Avner: Yes. Took a trip up to Seattle with some other counselors. I'd never been west of the Mississippi. Fell in love with Seattle. Flew back out two weeks later and got a bunch of jobs in Jewish education teaching folk-dance and beginning Hebrew, and went to the university where I took too many courses to graduate. But, while I was there, I remember in the springtime we had a big street fair, and a friend with a jewelry booth said, "Hey, why don't you come juggle in front of the booth?" And so I put little shows on and earned a whole bag of money and decided to go off to Paris. Went to the library. Couldn't find Marceau's address, but Lecoq had come to NYU when I was there, and I'd done the lights and tech stuff for him (they sort of stuck me with all the mime and movement things as the technician). And so I wrote to Lecoq, got into the school, and packed my satchel, and off I went.

Inspirations

DB: Can you talk about your mentors?

Avner: Jacques Lecoq. He's right at the top. I was very skeptical and rebellious. Remember, I was looking for a mime school. He wasn't teaching miming. Eventually, we did some of what we'd call illusion-pantomime in a portion of the course that he calls analysis of movement. And I think the way the school worked then (I'm not sure how it works now), you were accepted for a three-month audition period and then asked to leave or to stay, and about two-thirds of the students were asked to leave, and I was surely the one that was going to be asked to leave because I'd been pretty vocally critical. It must have been a month before the crunch when I really saw the depth of what he was teaching, the levels of nonverbal or what I like to call preverbal or subverbal communication, and then I started praying that I wouldn't be asked to leave. Luckily I was asked to stay for the rest of the year.

After I got back from Lecoq, I got very interested in commedia dell'arte, and you really couldn't study it anywhere. It was kind of a mysterious art form, and Carlo [Mazzone-Clementi] was starting the Dell'Arte School at that time. So I called Carlo. We talked and laughed on the phone for about 15 minutes. He said, "Okay, you come out. You work here." He's just like that. So I packed my satchel again. It was January. I left Minnesota in my van with a down jacket and a bottle of water beside me on the seat. The water froze before I got to Iowa; didn't unfreeze until I came down the mountains into Nevada. It was a cold trip. I spent the rest of that year in Dell'Arte, and then in the spring I had another residency in Louisville booked, and I couldn't stay. I said, "Well, I'll come back," but I didn't get back for ten years. Carlo, he was a wonderful one for sayings. My favorite one of his was: "The people who invented the alphabet were illiterate." Another: "It's not important what you know, it's what you don't know." And when I performed in the festival of American Mime, in '74, '76 – I'm not sure of the date – I did a one-man show. And it was the first time Carlo and Lecoq had been together in years and years. (Carlo actually introduced Fay and Jacques to each other. Bit of history.) And afterwards, to the audience, I said, "My two teachers are here, Jacques Lecoq, who taught me everything I know, and Carlo, who taught me the rest." Years later, I was in DC at a memorial after Lecoq's death, and I hadn't seen Carlo in a number of years. He was quite infirm; hobbling around on two canes. He looked like some kind of giant insect. Came hustling over to me and he looked me in the eye, and said, "What do you mean, I didn't teach you nothing!?"

DB: What was it about Lecoq himself and/or his teaching that spoke to you personally?

Avner: I think it's because of my science background, which I never really gave up. (I often think that this has been one long digression from some kind of scientific research.) Lecoq's approach was very scientific and, in a sense, evidence-based. He would say, "Look, this works, and you can see it, and you can try something else." He was very good at making lists and codifying things, and that really appealed to me. Plus, his standards were irreproachable. If something wasn't good, he said so. He didn't try to please anyone, except with his honesty, but he also – and he talked about this in one of his books, and thinking back I went, "Oh, of course" – he also said, "I never talk about how I would have done it." And I've noticed, a great majority of people who give criticism, they're really telling their students how they would have done it, what jokes they would have told. Lecoq said, "You talk about what works and what doesn't work." I believe there was a great kindness in that. And if you did something pedestrian in class, Lecoq would say, "Bah. My brother Albert could do that." And that's become a real catchphrase in my teaching. Now, last time I saw Fay, I mentioned that to her, and she said, "No, he doesn't have a brother Albert." So … I've changed it to, "My sister Carol could do that." Because I do have a sister Carol.

He organized it. It was a whole system as opposed to … Well, most of the movement teachers I come across, it's very anecdotal. Very much what their teachers taught them, without a true analysis of why things are how they are. But Lecoq's seemed to really be *sui generis*. It comes from beginning principles, starts from the breath. That's where my fascination with the breath comes from. Breath and rapport with the audience have become the things that I really concentrate on in clown training. He really introduced me to all this. Also, as someone famously once said, "It took Italians to invent commedia dell'arte. It took a Frenchman to explain it."

Techniques

DB: Did you know by the time you left Lecoq's school that clowning was the discipline for you?

Avner: Not at all. In fact, if we had an American high school yearbook and there was an award for Least Likely to Make a Living as a Clown, I would have gotten that award. I came back and started doing lecture-demonstrations on basically the entire Lecoq method, because it was quite secret – almost no one was talking about it. I went to things like the American Theater Conference and Southeastern Theater Conference, did some residencies in colleges and high schools, started to develop a bit of a show. I had learned rope-walking in Paris. I started doing Renaissance fairs where I did a 20-minute show, and I became known as the guy with the five-minute rope-walking act who will do anything to avoid doing it. So rather than demonstrating the skills, it was what became later the problem-solving aspect of clowning. Rope-walking is the solution. What was the problem? I don't want to do it. That's what the problem was. So I found lots of digressions, which eventually became the show that I would do. Digressions away from the focus, and since my training was theater rather than variety arts or vaudeville (although I have a lot of those skills) I think it differentiated me from the other skill-based performers at the time because it had a little story to it.

EL: You mentioned your concentration on breath. Can you talk a little bit about how you use that in your performance or teaching?

Avner: Absolutely. I'll give you my little rap. My clowning is very skill-based, not at all circus-clown-based, and I knew from the beginning, the trick was not to teach the skills, but to somehow figure out the principles at work. So that whole thing of the rope-walking act that I'm avoiding turned into, "The show starts in five minutes" – my favorite exercise. You come out with all your stuff, and you're just ready to do that first number, and then an announcement says, "Ladies and gentlemen, we're very sorry. We've got some technical problems. The show will begin in five minutes." So you're out there with all your juggling stuff, but you can't juggle because that's going to be the show that you do in five minutes. So what do you do now? How do you relate to the audience? Some people freak out and just go away. Fair enough, I suppose – they live only in their show, they haven't got a relationship with the audience.

So, for 25 years I've been teaching and watching people do numbers that really should be funny, and they're not. And I realized at a certain point that the basic emotion they were communicating to me was fear. And I would ask the group – and I'll ask you – "Do you ever feel a little bit of anxiety about performing?" Yes, everyone says "Yes." And I say, "What are you afraid of? What's your basic emotional state?" People always come up with some variation of "they hope it doesn't suck." They're terrified of being boring. They don't want the audience to get up and say, "I've seen this," and walk out. And so they grab the audience by the throat and say, "You get it, that's a joke!" But then I started asking my students, "What's your basic emotional state when you're going to watch a show?" The answer? "We hope it doesn't suck." (You probably have to watch student shows all the time, I assume. You're teachers. You must say your prayers. And you can't frown, you can't fall asleep, you can't leave. It's a terrible thing to be known. I hate going to theater because if I don't like it, I have to sit through it.) So there we have it. The audience and the performers, they're terrified of each other.

Now, you know what the freeze-fight-or-flight response is. It's our basic interface with the world. This goes back to my study of biology. Our neurology and sight are trained to notice differences and movements. If you're in the bathroom and a towel falls off the rack, you go, "Ah! Oh, just a towel." There's the freeze part – "Ah!" The fight-or-flight part is we see something in our peripheral vision moving, and we go into that freeze, and that pumps adrenaline. It gets our muscles ready. If it's prey, we might have to fight to get a meal. If it's a predator, we might have to run away. And all through the day, every time we see something, there's this little crisis that's then resolved. We can look at that in terms of breath. The freeze part is a gasping inhale, and as soon as we know we're safe, at a subconscious level we sigh, and we reset the clock. (Interestingly, this is one of the big arguments against television for children. Because what's television doing? Cuts, dissolves, pans, zooms. Every one of those makes your subconscious mind go "Ah!" And it never lets go. The latest on insomnia – I practice hypnotherapy and insomnia's a big topic for people – one of the latest suggestions is no electronic screens for two hours before you go to bed because it jacks your system up.) I'm gonna add another one. Freeze, flight, fight, or fidget. Which is the name of the title I give to my workshop – a physical approach to acting comedy. When you get jacked up and don't realize it, you start fidgeting. And we see people, they start walking like Frankenstein's monster, that stiff-legged, pelvis-stiff walk, that rocking back and forth, pacing around the stage in little circles, without being aware that they're doing that. That can be viewed in terms of breath. They're taking that breath in, they're breathing enough to live, but they're still holding it! They're trapped in the tension of held breath! So the first thing we find out in my class is that you need to finish things. And the problem that I find with so many clowns is when they finally actually finish something, and then take in a breath, it translates into a question to the audience: "Did you get it? Did you get it?" By God, it's like having a two-year-old in the house, going, "Mommy, Mommy, Mommy, look, look, look!"

So! It makes an amazing difference when people stop doing that and start breathing congruently. And that's the first bit, the beginning. To recognize when you're not breathing at the right time. It's really difficult to know, because the first thing that happens when you hold your breath is that you go numb. You shut down your perceptions.

DB: That's fascinating. Is there a particular bit in your work, in one of your acts, which you've built on scientific principles?

Avner: Okay, well, I'm going to do something. I have an exercise, which I'll do with you, David. I want you to pretend that I have a glass of water, and I'm going to hold it out to you, and I want you to take it.

DB: All right.

Avner: Can you see it? Yeah, so reach up and take it … Okay, good. That was very good. Now we're going to do it again. This time I want you to imagine that the glass is filled right to the top with concentrated sulfuric acid. Okay? Now, Ezra, I've got a question for you.

EL: Yes … ?

Avner: Just watch David with the sulfuric acid.

EL: I'm watching.

Avner: Now Ezra, are you holding your breath?

EL: Yes, completely.

Avner: Yes! You are. That's one of my Eccentric Principles: the work happens on stage, but it's the audience who experiences the emotion. So, David, you and I just made Ezra hold his breath. So now we're going to do it again, and you'll take the glass very carefully … And this time, David, the moment you know you're safe, in other words the moment you know you've got it under control, you've put the glass down, just let out a breath … Ahhh.

DB: It's finished.

Avner: And there goes Ezra. He just breathed out too. Okay? So you see, we also have to teach the audience how to breathe. Now, if they're already afraid, "Oh, my god, I gotta watch this thing," they're already in that state of mild freeze, right?

EL: Yeah.

Avner: When a performer walks on stage and sees the audience – "Ah!" It makes the audience do the same thing. Tension! So the very first thing that must happen is this: Inhale, Exhale. The message that you've sent the audience at a subconscious level, and this is something that has developed in the last eight years that I've been practicing hypnotherapy, is "I'm comfortable with you watching me," instead of the usual, "I hope you like this." All this is based on an old exercise, when the performer enters the stage, does not see the audience, then discovers them. I moved that discovery to this very first moment, and results are palpable. You feel the audience relax.

EL: So, may I make sure I understand that correctly? In the exercise as developed by Lecoq, the performer doesn't find the audience initially. It takes some time for that to happen. But you've made that into the first beat.

Avner: Yes, and it's a big principle. I started observing people going into rooms they haven't been in before, and they always take in a breath, and then let it out as soon as they understand the layout. You do it at home all the time. You go in a room, "Ahhh, great. I'm safe." It sends a very powerful message to the audience. You must remember, you breathe in for new things. You breathe out when you're in stasis, or comfort. And sometimes you hold your breath. Those are the only real options that we have, and that means that every gesture that we make is accompanied by one of those three states of breath as long as we're being congruent. When we're being incongruent, the audience, they catch it. They don't even know they're catching it, they just know something's off.

EL: Do you tend to analyze your own performances this way? And adjust them accordingly?

Avner: Yes.

EL: Can you give an example?

Avner: Well, the first thing is this: I might be crying on the outside, but I'm laughing on the inside. There's a basic optimism that I see in clowning, at least as I like to see it practiced. The clown finds everything interesting, the initial response is, "Interesting." And it's already funny to think about. You picture a guy who falls off a building. Well, first he is, "Ah!" *[inhale]*, but he catches the face of a clock. He catches the minute hand on the way down – "Ahhh … " *[exhale]*. And he says to himself: "Interesting." See, to say the word "interesting," you have to have breathed out, you have to have let go of that tension. And then our guy is free to think, "How am I gonna get out of this?" We really want the audience to follow our thought process. We don't want to be clever. Keith Johnstone talks about this, he says, "Clever's the last thing you wanna be. It's a subtle way of telling everyone else that you're smarter than they are." He says, "Give them what they want." And I've found that people laugh and clap for completion, not for cleverness. You give them clever, they go inside, not out. "Oh, wow, I never thought of that." But they're not with you anymore. They're in their world. So if you watch my rope-walking routine on YouTube, for example, you'll see it's one problem after another, and each solution (and this is becoming grad school level), becomes the statement of the next problem. There's a formula. You see the problem, the breath goes in: "Ah!" You accept the problem, the breath goes out: "Ahhh. Interesting!" And new breath: "I know what to do!" Breath is in, you're ready for effort. And now: the choice you make to solve the problem, if you do what anyone can do, it's not clowning. Remember? "Bah! My brother Albert could do that!" Grock sits down at the piano and can't reach the keyboard. "Interesting." Stands up, walks around the back of the piano, and pushes the piano to the bench. If he were to push the bench to the piano, we'd say, "Well, I can do that." And in fact, in Grock's routine, I don't know if you've seen it, he gets up, rolls up his sleeves, goes around the back of the piano. His partner looks at him, goes, "Hey!" Points to the stool, moves it in, and Grock goes, "Oh, my God! How did you think of that!?" So he gets two jokes out of it!

EL: Have you ever had a moment in performance when you felt like you were experiencing failure?

Avner: First of all, clowns are all about failure! If you don't fail, it's not going to work. You can't be afraid of failure. To give the short answer, I put my head down and do the material. I trust the material. I don't *ask* them to come with me. I *trust* them to come along, and I trust the construction of the material. You're getting all my good stories now. I was in a show with another comic act and a bunch of Russian acrobats, and there was a night when there were just no laughs. It was remarkable. It was almost as if the audience took a vote. And at dinner, this other guy said, "Avner, I feel terrible. It was a horrible show." I said, "No, it was a good show. It was fun. It was a challenge." And then he asked, "Well, what do you do when they don't laugh?" And then I had this real epiphany. I said, "Thank God! I've got enough problems out there without people laughing at me." If they laugh, it's a disruption. It's an interruption. You have to deal with it.

And that brings up another of my Eccentric Principles, what I call Validation Therapy. Validation Therapy is an idea that comes from Milton Erickson, the psychiatrist who invented the kind of hypnotherapy that I practice, in which you join the world of the patient rather than trying to pull them out into our world. For example: a guy thought he was Jesus Christ. The psychiatrist couldn't do anything with him. He was incarcerated in a mental institution. Erickson watched for a few months, went up to him one day and said, "I understand you're a carpenter." Got him to help him build a bookcase. One of Erickson's students had a more dramatic version. Different guy thought he was Jesus Christ. Student brought in two four-by-four pressure-treated eight-foot pieces of lumber, some big iron spikes, a sledgehammer, and a tape measure, said, "Hold your arms out. We need to take some measurements."

So using Validation Therapy I've found there is just one simple reaction to the question of laughter. If you're laughing at me … "I know. It's funny. I agree with you." And if you're *not* laughing at me, if you're telling me I stink, "I know. It stinks. I agree with you." I simply agree with you! When the audience doesn't laugh at a joke and I look at them and go, "I know, I didn't say it was funny," it lets them relax. They were gearing up for a fight with you, they were expecting you to expect them to laugh, but if you say, "I know. I didn't say it was funny," then everyone is congruent. And that makes us all happy. That has become the real key to all of this. "I know." Of course you don't really know, but they think you do. And it validates whatever they're feeling. And as soon as you do that, validate their feelings in therapeutic terms, you've created rapport, and that's what we crave.

So did I ever feel failure? You know, a comedian goes on stage to say something that they think is funny. A clown goes on stage, does something funny, and doesn't understand why people are laughing. I think that's a major logical division. And that's the great paradox of clowning. If you don't get laughs, you're not much of a clown. But if you try, you can't get them. Yeah, sometimes they're not laughing, and I just solve my problems, and often … This actually goes deeper into neuroscience. There's a wonderful book called *Laughter* by Robert Provine. And one of the important things that he points out is that laughter is a social activity. We seldom laugh out loud when we're alone. And sometimes we feel alone even if we're in a crowd. For example, an old couple came to see my show in Maine. They were sitting in the second row, didn't crack a smile, came up to me in the lobby after the show, and the woman came over, took me by the arm and said, "Young man, I want to thank you. That was the funniest show I have ever seen." And her husband said, "Yes, it was all I could do to keep from laughing." I realized something very important. Laughing is internal – you do it in your brain. When I used to do a two-act show, whenever there was a quiet audience, my stage manager would make some sarcastic remark like, "I've never seen dead people sit up like that!" And I would say, "Well, wait till the end. Let's see what happens." And sure enough, that would be the show that got a standing ovation. They saved up the energy. So as long as you don't identify an audience not laughing as a failure, how can you fail? You go out there, and you do your job. If they don't laugh, you get to go home early. And of course, we build in accidents that let them go, "Oh yeah, I've had days like that," which stimulate the empathetic rather than the sympathetic response. That's what we want the audience to say. "I've had days like that, and I didn't solve my problems as elegantly as you just did. Bravo."

EL: Are there times when you are really surprised at something unexpected?

Avner: Sure, all the time. My answer is, "Wow, that's even more interesting than I thought it was." I did a show for a friend. I don't usually do outdoor shows because wind is a real problem, but he runs a festival of Saturday nights in April in Gainesville, Florida, and I agreed to perform. It had been raining. There wasn't a critical mass. It was muddy. People were spread out in this public plaza. I just did the material. But the feedback was amazing. My friend told me, "Avner, you got them in the palm of your hand within the first three minutes, and you kept them there for the whole hour. I don't know how you did it." And he had gotten tons of feedback from people. So yes, when something unexpected happens, that's the time to let go of the tension that goes, "Wow, that didn't go the way I thought," and to just say, "Wow, that's interesting. Oh! I know what to do!" And if you stay on that train, there's gravy at the end of it. But often with a student or directing project, you'll build a number, a routine, and then you'll put it in front of an audience and watch it and just go, "Aww, that didn't work. Where are we not connecting? Where are we not letting them go, letting them make their own decision?" And it's fascinating. It's lovely. But it means always saying, "Well, that didn't work. Let's try something else."

Philosophy

DB: Avner, do you have a philosophy of clowning? Do you identify for yourself what clowning is for?

Avner: Yes and no. Let me talk around this subject and see if we come up with something. I went to my first clown convention at the World Clown Association, and I was asked to kind of give a keynote address. I don't think they really wanted to hear what I had to say – these were very much wigs, makeup, and big shoes clowns. I mean, it's as much a fashion show as a theatrical event, but it has its place. And I asked them – I was sitting with some members and the president of the organization at dinner – I said, "Well, how do you guys define clowning?" And there was this long silence, and they said, "Well, you know, it's complicated. There are so many different kinds." And they really codified. They've got their first Auguste, their second Auguste, their White clown, everything has a pigeonhole. But when I work with clowns, I say, "You know, forget about clowns. Be a character." So I remembered the Supreme Court on pornography, and I started my talk by saying, "You know, clowning is a lot like pornography. You can't define it, but you know it when you see it."

I think for most people, clown is a noun, but for me it's a verb. It's a series of attitudes and techniques that allow clowning to happen no matter who you are. The fact that you've dressed up like the American circus clown doesn't make you a clown. There was a wonderful article a few years ago on how to look like a tennis player, what to wear, how to spin your racket, blow on your fingers, straighten out the string, do everything but hit the ball, and I think a great number of clowns approach clowning from that point of view. But for me there's no such thing as *a clown*. There's only *to clown*. Everything the clown does is a problem to be solved, even in getting onto the stage. And an audience links up with you in recognizing the problem in an empathetic way, and they're delighted and relaxed when you solve your problem. So that's where I put clowning – it's problem-solving. I also started calling it Eccentric Performing, because I wanted it to be more inclusive. After all, there are straight-ahead storytellers, public speakers, occasional business people, a variety of arts people who aren't at all interested in doing comedy, and yet these principles work perfectly with them.

DB: Do you see the clown serving a particular role in today's world?

Avner: You can be a socially aware clown, pushing for whatever your agenda is. But clowning is not the agenda itself. Clowning is the attitude and the techniques that you use to attack your problem. You need to have the philosophy, the heart, the intellect to be attacking your subject with a particular kind of humor, which is based in problem-solving, and you must live with your problems, and not describe them.

EL: Are you aware of any new energies coming into the field of clown comedy?

Avner: Yes, I think so. It's very much vacuum-based. Where there's a vacuum, people tend to flow. When I was coming up, in the mid-1970s to early 1980s, every theater had a second space, and there was a lot of government money supporting theaters, and their mandate was to produce and present new work, so it really paid off to have a full-evening show. And even though it's been largely discredited, in that period I feel there was a group of us who put in our 10,000 hours toward full-evening shows, particularly the Flying Karamazov Brothers, Bill

Irwin, Penn and Teller, and myself. And within a two-year period all four of us landed on Broadway with full-evening shows using what had been vaudeville and variety arts, and Mel Gussow looked at these four shows and coined the term "New Vaudeville." In Germany there are a huge number of venues presenting variety acts; consequently, there are hundreds, I'm not exaggerating, of very professional and competent and exciting duo trapeze acts. "You want leather, we got it. You want feathers, you want virginal, we got it." They're everywhere. Why? Because there are at least 20 variety theaters that run year-round looking for that kind of work. Here in the US, Renaissance fairs became the place that a variety act could get work. Consequently there are a lot of people with 20-minute shows, but it's based on hat-passing and gathering a crowd, and they have a hard transition into the theater. So it really depends. There are a lot of festivals now. In France, in Spain, there are a lot of street festivals, and they hire street acts, but they don't have to pass the hat, so there are a lot of very clever, semi-theatrical street shows now. They're just wonderful, but they're not theater shows. So that's what I mean by vacuum-based.

EL: This is a two-part question. Do you sense an evolution in your philosophy, in your beliefs? And also, do you have a sense of being on the cusp of something that is beginning to change or evolve?

Avner: Evolution, yes, and it's still evolving. It was great when the first George Bush was President because I became a kinder, gentler clown. When I developed the idea of applying the golden rule to working with volunteers, that was a major, major step forward. I think I was as guilty as anyone of getting laughs at the expense of someone's incompetence on stage, and now I just gag. I can't watch performers humiliating people, making them do hoochy-coochy dances in front of the public. It drives me nuts. Or juggling clubs around them when there's this implication, this threat, that they might get hurt. I can't stand that. I've developed a whole philosophy and lots of techniques for what – I hope – creates a situation where the rest of the audience says, "Wow, that looked like fun. Maybe I can be next," and the person who's going on stage never has that dread of, "Oh, God, why am I doing this?" That's been the latest sort of research that I've been involved in. I love it. It's great fun, and it's great to see people change.

Cusp, you know it's hard to tell when you're in the middle of something. I think we have to wait and see how history treats this period. Randy Nelson of the Karamazovs said, "You know, we're dinosaurs, and the meteorite has already hit. We're extinct. We just don't know it." I get a fair amount of requests asking, "Can you get me a booking in Maine," and I say, "Sure, but how are you gonna get an audience?" They say, "Tell them that I'm a clown." I say, "Well, that'll keep 'em away. In droves." I had to take "clown" out of my publicity. I never let that word ... because it comes with so much baggage. Speaking of baggage, I was going through customs, coming back from Mexico, and the guy said, "What's in those bags?" I had these big rolling cases full of props. I said, "Those are clown props." Now I look more like a philosophy professor or a rabbi. So the officer said, "Are you a clown?" and I said, "Yes." And he said, "Seriously?" I said, "No, if you're serious it doesn't work."

8 René Bazinet

Figure 7 René Bazinet. Photo by Marcel Hubli / Copyright Roncalli

René Bazinet (born Germany, 1955), over the past 30 years, has performed in many of the most famous North American and European theaters. He starred in Circus Roncalli and Germany's Wintergarten, Teatro de la Fenice, and the prestigious Opéra de Paris. He has traveled the world performing for Cirque du Soleil as one of their most veteran clowns. Recently he directed clowns for the Cirque du Soleil production *Zarkana*. His two numbers, "Baseball" and

"Western," continue to be performed in *Saltimbanco* currently touring for Cirque du Soleil.

We met René in his Montreal loft. (DB/EL)

Origins

Every case is particular, isn't it? Every case is very particular, so everybody has their story, everybody has their past.

I was born in Germany. I was brought up there, and I was quite … It wasn't easy. I was quite a difficult youth, and a mother with a single child in 1955 was kind of weird for those people. I had what you would call today ADD. Very nervous, very frenetic, very erratic: just a case, basically. Perhaps I got that from my biological father, who was a musician, but I only have photos of him … I figure that somehow it's in the genes. Anyway, I couldn't do anything about it. I used to entertain my teachers. I used to entertain whoever I could. I was very sensitive, so I could feel when people were into violence, and I would stop it by making them laugh. You know, I was so sensitive I could feel it before it happened. So I became kind of a social worker at a very young age. I didn't realize it until much later. It was very natural for me to go into that field and make people laugh. You know, because they're violent. I'm in a violent world. I'm sorry, but I am. That's the way it is, isn't it?

When I was very, very young, when I was five, six years old, I was entertaining people. To survive. It's a survival technique. I had a Jewish mentor when I was a little older, and she described to me in detail the whole mechanism of what was going on in Germany. You know, the sense of humor is really a survival technique for very difficult situations. Take the Jewish people. There were some very beautiful, wonderful Jewish comics that the Germans just killed. So I grew up in a desolate place with a lot of money but no fun. It took me a while to understand that, but I was very young and adrift.

Being a teenager I was also very sensitive. Years later I notice, and still today, I'm talking about my sensitivity. I haven't killed it, I haven't killed my inner child. I kept it alive because that's all there was, this inner child. In those days, that's all I was, this kid. And a kid doesn't know much. He just reacts. I was very lost. I was very compulsive, the brain completely making up stories all day long. I was solitary in my youth, so my mother kicked me out, and I was in the streets. The streets were my territory. But I couldn't be in a gang. I knew what they were gonna do, and I was trying to make them laugh instead. I just wanted peace and harmony. Today, that's basically what everybody wants, but in those days it wasn't evident, because everyone was so violent.

I hung out with gangs. I used to steal. I taught them how to steal books. It was like the underground. My mother married a Canadian military police officer. Sergeant Major Bazinet. He asked me if it was okay for him to adopt me, and I said, "Well … " I was called René Fiener. My mom's name. And I said, "René Fiener. René Bazinet. That sounds great." I was 14 years old. And I go, "René Bazinet. That sounds great. Why not? Let's do this." And then they went to

Canada. I stayed in Germany in a boarding school for a year, and then they kind of tricked me into going to Canada. "Come for the summer vacations." I said okay. That was it. I was in Canada. I said, "I'm not going back to Germany?" I was very pissed about that. But it was a blessing in disguise, as they say.

I got lost in drugs, especially psychedelics. I loved psychedelics, but I took too many, to the point where I started thinking, "I gotta get outta here. I wanna get out of this. I don't really like this planet. I don't like the people here. I just wanna get out of this place." But I overdosed. I stared death in the face. I stopped breathing. That was the big turning point in my life. I had a conversation with voices. They seemed like angels, but they talked very, very quietly, and they said, "Just one little step, and you're with us." And then I changed my mind. I said, "Well, maybe I was wrong. Maybe my intentions were mistaken. Maybe there's something much bigger here that I wasn't aware of. Maybe there is something that's calling me." And so I asked to stay. I remember it was four o'clock in the morning in Ottawa, and the first ray of the sun, *swoosh*, struck my face, and I was breathing again, and I got the second chance.

Inspirations

When I got that second chance at the age of 18, I said, "Well, how can I say Thank You for the rest of my life?" And that's basically how I got into performing. One thing led to another. I went to theater school. I tried to be an actor, but everybody was laughing. And then I was physically so talented that people said, "My God, this guy's a mime." So I studied mime. There was a teacher there at John Torell College on the West Island, and he came from Lecoq. He created a one-man show with me at the school. I realized, "My God. I can entertain people without even speaking. Just through physical language I can communicate things to people that they understand, and I can talk to them, talk even faster than they can think, because their emotions are faster than their thoughts." And so I got into exploring this talent, and then the teacher sent me off with a letter of recommendation to Lecoq, and all of a sudden I was in Paris in September, 1978, and I started school at Lecoq, which was a great, wonderful gift because he's an amazing pedagogue. After all the LSD this guy just blew me away. "Shit, this guy has really got his stuff together." His neutral mask, becoming water, becoming air, becoming earth, becoming wind, becoming Coca-Cola, becoming glue, becoming acid, becoming *everything*, becoming the different kinds of light, morning light, daylight, moonlight, electric light, neon light, becoming colors, becoming everything that exists. How does it move? What an amazing gift for me, to be nourished at that age.

At the Lecoq School, I met Philippe Gaulier, who was a teacher there, and when I quit Lecoq, he quit, too. Gaulier appreciated me, and I appreciated Gaulier because he was – you know, Lecoq was the meta-meta-master, but Gaulier was human. He would go right into humanity. And I thought, "Wow, this guy's real." It was very natural for me to be able to open up and understand what he was teaching: as soon as you defend your personality, you're not really funny. You're just defending your whatchamacallit, the carbon copy of your life. You're not real anymore. As soon as you defend it, you know you're not real because you're defending it. After all, you don't defend the truth. If the sky is blue, you don't have to get nervous about defending the blue sky. But if you're defending it, well, you're not a clown yet because you're still hanging onto your personality and proving to everybody that it's a good one. So I learned with Gaulier that personality is not real. It's just not real. There's something new that's waiting for me, and if I have the courage to go and look for it, well, this is the place.

Gaulier had a contract in Germany in the Frankfurter Autoren Theater, and he took half of the class that was finishing Lecoq to do a show there. I played Arlecchino, because I'm the guy who knows how to do that. And people saw me there in Germany, me being back in Germany, my mother tongue and the whole bit. I fit like a hand in a glove. Some people saw me, Jacobo Romano and Jorge Zulueta. They had the group Accion Instrumental. And they took me on and gave me a job right away. Jacobo was living in Paris. So it all worked out because I was going back to Paris. I stayed with him for about a year, doing shows, one after the other. He believed in me. And I started to write text. He was into classical music, he was into Freud, really into psychoanalysis – his wife is a psychoanalyst – and this whole thing was very deep and it was very Argentinian, and music, and automatic writing, the discovery of the subconscious. It was a continuous schooling for a clown. Though I wasn't a clown then. He used me as a performer who knew how to write, how to play on the stage and become anything he wanted to, rather than being funny. We created five shows from scratch in five years while I was there. He really used me because I love creating. I have a very wild imagination. I created and created and created. "René, what would you do? Okay! Let's do that!" Because it worked. It was one of those things.

So after one year I said, "I can count my ribs." I was very upset, and I was out. I hooked up with Gaulier, who had left the Lecoq school, but was still in Paris and had opened up his own school with Monika Pagneux. Monika Pagneux was for me a goddess. She looked at me and told me everything I did last night, just by looking at my body. I thought, "Holy shit how does she know? She's a witch! Just by reading the body? God! I want to learn from her." So I took some workshops from her, but in the afternoons I was in the streets. And that's when I met David Shiner.

I was doing a pantomime. I had a white face. How can I say, I did sketches, I improvised sketches. I didn't imitate people, I did sketches: walking in place, finding something and eating it, and all of a sudden noticing it's chewing gum, then taking the chewing gum and blowing it up into a ball, a huge ball, going into the ball, not being able to get out of it, finding a pin in my pocket, bursting it, being stuck with it, taking it all off, then putting it in my mouth, and not being able to get rid of it, swallowing it, and having to go to the toilet because I needed to take a crap, and then doing the whole toilet scene … You know ten years later I sold this to Cirque du Soleil, the toilet scene: it started on the streets of Paris.

Hand to mouth, hand to mouth. Being in the streets is … being in the streets. My mentor Aneta Lastik said, "Hang around with the rats too long, and you get poisoned." Good old Jewish wisdom. "It's a bad environment, it's going to rub off on you René." Well, I turned out to be an alcoholic. A very low career, anything is possible, anyone can do anything at any moment, there's no organization, it's a free-for-all. The deepest thing that was evolving was that I got to appreciate my sensitivity because there was magic around. When you're very sensitive there is magic somewhere; there are things that happen in synchronicity, that you haven't noticed before, and you start to notice it, that's the highest state. I went into studying Lao Tzu, I went to Taoism, I read it every morning when I woke up and every night before I went to sleep. I went into esotericism. "I have to understand; I don't get this, I don't understand this, I am a tool of this, but I am not master of this, I am just a tool! I realize it's magic, and I realize it's very beautiful, but I don't know how to deal with it." I might as well have been put in a loony bin, because it's the same thing in a way. But then I met David and he was *really* into meditation. At first I wasn't interested, but he was into it, he said, "I want you to, you gotta meditate." So we became great friends, because of that similar sensitivity and the similar interests and a belief that life is not only about eating and fucking and shitting and then you have a heart attack and die. It's, no – there is something much greater going on. So I think that belief took hold of me at that time – even though I was almost bipolar, really up and really down – and it helped me to say, "Well, is there maybe a balance somewhere … ?"

Techniques

I always wrote my own stuff. I always repeated the sketches that I knew, that is, some pantomime sketches and two clown sketches, and the story I learned at Lecoq which is called "The Crow" which is like a mime, storyteller, making sound effects, ya know? Becoming the crow *[makes crow noise]*, doing the crow from far away, doing it close up, like a film technique. It was my signature piece for many years. I played that in Tokyo as I played it in Tel Aviv as I played it in Tunisia, and they all loved it. It was just the contact was very different in Japan than in Tunisia, because Japanese are very well behaved and Tunisians are very wild. I used to work in prisons in Germany, and they don't give a fuck about you. They smoke and look at you, they go, "Fuck you!" So I said to them: "Oh, okay. What are you doing? What are you trying to tell me, you? Yeah you! I know you can't touch me because the police are right there. The guards are right there. Now what in the hell is going on?" And they went: "Holy shit. Somebody's talking to me." "Yeah! Somebody's talking to you! It's me!" I stuck up my nose and said, "It's me! What's your problem? Why are you doing this to me?" And they said "Holy shit!" Yeah. But that comes from the street because I am not just a clown, I'm also a human. Don't you fuck with me.

Until '88 I stayed in Paris, then I joined David in Munich and we put a show together, and then we toured for about a year and a half in Germany. We'd go to all these little cities in Germany and do little one-night gigs. So that became a very great friendship there and a partnership, of course, because we made people laugh. Him solo, me solo, but some sketches together, and we had about 20 minutes, and people didn't want to leave. So it worked. But then the circus contacted David. And David didn't wanna leave. He said he didn't want to go to Canada and do this thing. But after a year and a half, we were, I was kind of tired, and I said, "David, come on, just go and show them what you're made of. Go and conquer your own country, and we'll meet up later and we'll do another show together." So that's what happened, he became a star, and sure enough, a year later, he'd talked about me so much to the circus, they had to contact me. I mean what are friends for? He sent them to visit me in Paris, and I basically sent them to hell actually. I was horrible – I was just so rude in those days. But I was a bit alcoholic, you know? And in the morning, you didn't talk to me in the morning in those days unless I'd had my two double espressos, then I could function. "What? What? You and your fucking circus, who, what the? Who is this guy?" I was very rude and arrogant in those days, and I didn't want to go. I had made money with galas and variety theaters – but the circus? "Fuck that! Who wants to join the fucking circus? Jesus Christ, it's ridiculous! What do you want from me? You've got David." And they said: "Yeah, but David … We're in Los Angeles right now with *Nouvelle Expérience* … " They weren't careful in those days because a lot of agents called him and all of a sudden David didn't want to do the tour anymore. Big times, right? Mmm. So they called me. "Come and visit and see the show on Santa Monica pier. Please? David is considering maybe not doing it anymore." "I ain't gonna replace David." "Well, come and see the show."

So I went there, and of course I fell in love with the show because *Nouvelle Expérience*, I tell you, I was sitting there, and I was almost in tears. I said, "My God, this is a magical box. The potential of this is enormous. And the show is beautiful! And the magic that they create and produce is amazing! But I will not jump in for David. Because David is David and René is René." You know? And I told them that and they got very flustered. I went back home and told them, "I won't do this, but if you ever do a new show, call me up." And they did. A year later, for *Saltimbanco*. Actually Guy Laliberté caught me in a very weak moment. I was in Stuttgart in this little variety theater, and I was playing for old ladies in the afternoon. And I don't know if you know old German ladies, it's horrendous. "The music's too loud … " There's all this complaining going on while you're playing. It was a very weak moment, and who did I see on the veranda of this theater? It was Guy walking toward me. He didn't win me over, but he sent Franco Dragone to talk to me. Franco came to visit me there in this little theater in Stuttgart, with all the drawings of the characters for *Saltimbanco*. And after ten minutes I said, "This guy is a visionary." And after what I'd seen they could do – and it was his show too, the *Nouvelle Expérience* – now I figured I was talking to the real man. I felt wide awake. My soul was elated because now I was talking to an artist! Not talking to a businessman! Talking to a visionary! And he pulled me in. He reeled me in, and he asked me, "What would it take for you to do the show?" I said, "I'll tell you exactly what it would take: let me play an aristocrat, a child, a horny satire, and Death." And he said, "Okay. We'll write it in." And they did. So I said, "Okay, I guess I'm going to join the fuckin' circus." It was too much of a beautiful invitation.

Four years I played in that show. All over the US, the big cities, then we did Tokyo, and then Europe. When I stopped *Saltimbanco* I was kind of burned out for a couple of years. Guy invited me to put up *Quidam* with him, to train the Russians. (Most of the performers in those days were Russian.) So I gave them training, how to play – I gave Lecoq training and mask and physical and Feldenkrais. I taught these people for three years and we became a very strong group. Debbie Brown was taking care of the choreography and we were such a great team. There were very powerful people doing the creation, and it was beautiful. And audiences were just blown away by that. But that was years ago. It was a whole different epoch, a whole different time.

After Cirque du Soleil I went back to Germany and did variety theaters. And there are a lot of them there. More and more. So in those days, the end of the '90s, beginning of the 2000s, I was mostly in Germany doing the variety theater as the *maître de cérémonie*, like I did in *Saltimbanco*. I was the guy smoking with the tails and sometimes a cane, the whole bit – like the German 1920s, with the top hat. I did that, plus "The Crow," plus the sketch I did in the circus, so I was doing three people's jobs, in a way, and having René Bazinet in a variety show is good business because he runs the show and does two numbers!

[Laughter.]

Sometimes I did some gigs with David. He'd call me. "Let's do our gig together somewhere for a month or two." And we did that too. So it wasn't a straight line; it never is a straight line. God writes some crooked lines! It's organic. It's a process. Then I started teaching at the Cirque du Soleil studios. I teach Feldenkrais, and then I do the neutral mask, which I love. That's part of my style and I insist on it. I know at the circus, when I go back there sometimes, there are certain people there *apparently* that don't like me, "Oh, René with his pedagogy," but I'm okay with that. Because I have to admit, if I am a director, I am a pedagogue at the same time. I can't separate the two. I can't expect people to know everything when they come to work. Sometimes I have to teach them how to do it.

Failing is my business. As a clown, this is what Gaulier gave me. Gaulier gave me the understanding, "Okay, it's nice that you still have your inner child, but in order to actually mix that into a profession, into a craft, you need to understand why people are laughing." People laugh when you are wrong. But you have to sell it. You have to pretend you don't know you're wrong. So you have to be a good actor. You have to be able to lie: "I don't know. I don't see the banana peel right there in front of me." I did that once on the street, I remember. There was a banana peel and there were two thousand people. And I picked up the banana peel, showed it to everybody, put it on the floor, and pretended it wasn't there. And everybody knew, "Oh but he's gonna fall on the banana peel!" Yeah, but when? When? And when I did fall – everybody laughed. It was a surprise. For the kid, the child always has this element of surprise. The animal has it as well. We don't have it anymore because we are in a box. We think we know everything. But clowns have it. They remind us of the phenomenon of being surprised by doing something weird or doing something *off* that is so personal to them. I think the more personal you are with your own shortcomings, the more universal you become. It's very strange, that. Tarkovsky was one of the first people who said it: "The more personal I become, the more universal I get." And I go, "Holy shit, that hits me. That hits me. That hits me." Because it's true. The more personal I am with my own mistakes, the more universal I become. Even though people don't know about my mistakes, but they are so *me* that everybody sees themselves in them.

It's a craft. It's a craft to pretend not to know all these things that are gonna happen in the next 15 minutes. To have them occur spontaneously. But the spontaneous comes because that night, that particular public, with you together, is a one-time happening. Because last night was a different time, and tomorrow is gonna be a different time, but tonight, in front of this public, for them, it's the first time. And if you know that, you can easily pretend it's the first time because you're also living in the same ocean there. So you "Boop!" and you "Ahh!" and everybody laughs. But you have to study it because it's a craft. To pretend. To sell it.

I'm performing less and less. Last few years I've done less and less on purpose because I'm tired. I just turned 59, and I can't do ten shows a week. It's not possible anymore. I can't sell myself, my body, play the prostitute for some rich … I can't do it anymore. So I'm focusing on teaching. Also, I have a son. After Cirque du Soleil, I got together with a dancer, Hélène Lemay, and we made a child because we wanted to, and bought a house outside of Montreal and did the whole thing, mowing the lawn and painting the fence and taking out the garbage and buying the milk for the baby … That's a one-way ticket, isn't it? You get the kid – it's a one-way ticket, you can't go back. My son is 18 now. That's also a reason I stay in Montreal. Because I've never seen my dad – my biological father – and I'm gonna break that cycle. It's very easy to run away and make money all over the planet, but you're alone in some motel. My son, I always told him, I said, "Whatever you do, please don't become a clown." Because the price is very high. To be a good clown, holy shit, the price is just, for me, I don't know. But it's personal. What I paid was a very high price, and I know that most of the greatest clowns they're all a bit, you know, in therapy, because it's too much. It's mad! They laugh at you your whole life! You show your imperfections, you show how crazy you are, you show how weird you are, you show how *wrong* you are, and they love it! They pay you for it! That's weird. It has side effects. That's why when Franco asked me, "What would it take?" I said "Those four characters!" Because I didn't say I just wanted to do the clown, I wanted to do a respectable aristocratic figure, a horny satire, and an old merlin, kind of sorcerer character. So I have a balance in my brain. I have a balance in my daily thoughts, in my daily feelings. It's not just the weirdo. I need that balance, otherwise I'd go cuckoo.

Philosophy

For me, a clown is somebody who has kept alive his or her inner child. Really alive. The inner child is the innocent one. The inner child is the one that suffered.

For the inner child, everything is new. I remember when I was very small it was all new. Everything was new, new, new. "Ah, look at that! Ah, look at this! Hah! Oh wow, I never noticed that about that! Holy shit. Wow, look at that!" Everything was interesting and new and innovative, because it was all a new moment, a new moment, a new moment – the child lives in that. Like the animal, lives in this newness all the time! It's all animals do! They don't reflect. They are there, happy, and all of a sudden they're being chased and they're dead, ok, it's over. What they're not going to do is, "Oh my God, I wonder if there's a tiger." No! They're just happy and then they die! There's just this chase, and hearts are beating and all of a sudden you're dead, okay. It's over and done with. But they're not walking around sad and complaining about their lives and blaming others for everything that goes wrong in their lives, the weather and the politics and everything is horrible, "Let's just get some guns and kill them all." Jesus! What an embarrassment this is, this humanity. God! I love animals. I really cherish them. But anyway, I'm going too far.

You see, the child goes from his guts, his or her guts, so it's the gut feeling, it's the joy, the pure joy of being new. And if I'm in an audience, if I'm in front of a good clown, I become the child myself. It's children watching a child. Because he reminds us that life-is-not-that-serious, hello! And it takes us out of the seriousness, out of losing a job or gaining a job or keeping my wife or not, and all of this fucked up bullshit you've been accumulating for thousands of years, it just takes us out and says, "Hey! *[Whistle.]* Cuckoo! Yeah you. How 'bout this? How 'bout that?" And everybody is like, "Oh my God. Oh, I love him. Oh, I wanna invite him for dinner." That's a clown. A kid who says, "I refuse to take it seriously. I refuse to take this seriously. I'm sorry! I'm in another world. I don't know where you guys are, but it doesn't seem very happy to me. Because you're all pretty heavy and weighed down, hitting people and getting violent over whether you're right or wrong … What the fuck are you guys doing? Discussing and then shooting! Why don't you just sit down and eat something, relax! Or just have fun!" And it's difficult because we're hypnotized, like in the film *The Matrix*. We're completely in it, we're completely in this trance. But if a clown's inner child tickles the inner child in the audience for a moment, or maybe minutes, we are being reminded of, "*[Gasp.]* Oh! Isn't that sweet? Oh look! Oh my God. Ah yes. I'm relieved. He's human. He's like my brother. He's like my sister. I wanna take him home." You know? Who do you wanna take home? Your child! The child, the little being that is innocent, that is walking around and going, "Hey, isn't life wonderful!" That's the clown! And he or she who can keep that kid alive, they usually went through a lot of pain already because most of the kids that I've met have been, you know, hit, marked if you wanna say. So we're walking on a high-wire in a way when you want to do this job. There's a difference between a grown-up and an adult. I think the planet is filled with grown-ups – that means children in grown up bodies – but there are very few adults, in fact. No. I'm still a kid. I'm working on growing up. I can't say that I'm an adult. And I'm 59.

We all were children. No matter what culture we came from. That's what saved my ass when I was in Tunisia, when I was in Japan … Even though people think very differently, they do remember their childhood. No matter how different they are, they were children once, and children are kind of easy. They're not so weighed down. So when you exhibit the pure child, all the world will go, "Hey! There he is!" That's what I see as the doorway into the new world. We need to accept that we have been weighed down for so long – we are caught, we are in a trance, we're in a very deep, deep hypnotic trance – the entire world.

Because we bought it, hook, line, and sinker – what we *should* be doing, and how we *should* live our lives, and how much money we *should* make, and all that crap. It weighs us down. Our value system has been impregnated, we've been indoctrinated for a long time … The power of the aristocracy, the king, God being like, the king, you know? What a weird idea. The altar being in the back. Well, the king had to have his back against the wall because that kept him safe, didn't it? What a strange God to be so insecure. It's weird. The whole story's so weird; it's so perverted. So to demystify this mythology of the materialism, that's the goal, so that this all … crumbles slowly. This whole mythology crumbles slowly, and the child will come out and the newness will come out of us and we'll recognize that we're just human. We don't represent anyone else. We're just us. You don't have to salute the judge's clothes just because of what he represents. It's not him anyway. People are in a trance, and unless you are out of the trance, you cannot do anything. You have to be interested in coming out of the trance, to see it from the outside and to understand everybody and why they are so hung up on what they are supposed to do and the mood they are in today and how horrible this whole life has become. The other day I walked into a store, and the guy was in really a bad mood. I stayed there for 20 minutes studying him. Because I wasn't in a bad mood, and I wasn't about to buy his bad mood either – it's very expensive. So I stayed in my mood, and I got him to smile after 20 minutes, just as an exercise.

I think this kind of consciousness, this kind of awareness, might be our saving grace in the future because we need to become aware that we are not these clothes we wear. We need to become aware that we're not what we're supposed to do. We're not that. We can use that, but we are not that. We are much bigger than that. We are grander than that. We are way beyond that. We are an awareness-function of infinite intelligence. We are just the awareness-function. It's a temporary experience, being on the planet and running around in the human body. Why is everyone making such a big deal about it? Why not just savor it and make something beautiful out of this experience and relearn how to become human, not with their rules but with new rules? "Holy shit, there is something looking after me. There is something running the show. It's not me. It's bigger than me. It's bigger than all of us put together." I mean it. You're really deep in the shits and you really want to jump out the window … There's a voice: "Ehhh, I wouldn't do that." It pulls a rabbit out of a hat: "Hey!" All of a sudden there's a check in the mail and a hole in your hat, wink, wink. "Check. Your. Mail." There's another entity. It's much bigger. I don't know how to explain it. I could never explain it. An infinite intelligence. And I think that one way of knowing that you have been chosen by this intelligence is that your life becomes a living hell. Because that means he really likes you. Because he wants you to *wake up*. That's how I see it.

9 Barry Lubin

Figure 8 Barry Lubin. Photo by Maike Schulz

Barry Lubin (born in Atlantic City, 1952), after spending five seasons traveling with the Ringling Brothers and Barnum & Bailey Circus, joined the Big Apple Circus, New York's famed one-ring circus, where he became the "Face of the Big Apple Circus" as his character Grandma, starring in the show for 25 years. Lubin is featured in the PBS mini-series "Circus," which chronicles a year on the road with the Big Apple Circus. He has been inducted into the International Clown

Hall of Fame, the Sarasota Ring of Fame, and received the Lou Jacobs Lifetime Achievement Award in 2007.

I sat down with Barry in his apartment in Stockholm, Sweden. (EL)

Origins

My recollection of my first circus? Getting splinters in my ass, seeing an outdoor show in Atlantic City, where I grew up, and not being very happy about the splinters in my ass. And then I didn't see another circus until after I auditioned for Ringling, back in 1974, and the dean of the Ringling Clown College, Bill Ballantine, offered me a ticket to come see the show because I couldn't afford it myself. On the other hand, in Atlantic City as a teenager I worked at the Steel Pier, an entertainment complex that had movies and various shows, and at the very end of the pier, about a half-mile out to sea, was something called the Water Circus. They had diving clowns, they had elephant acts, they had all kinds of circus-y things. But it's not something that I ever imagined for myself. In fact, when I was watching it on the day of my audition, to be honest – I don't know why – I found myself ... a little bored, frankly. I was sitting way up high in the old Boston Garden and thinking, "I don't know what I'm supposed to be looking at." But I also knew that it would be a lot of fun to be a part of it and to travel the United States, and to actually get paid to commune with all these people and animals. I was at a point in my life where I didn't know what I wanted to do. After dropping out of Emerson College in Boston, I was a bill collector, which was a terrible job, and anything looked better than that, especially the circus.

I was always attracted to show business. I didn't think it was going to be something I would do, but from an early age I was very interested in performance, especially silent performance. The clowns that performed at the Steel Pier Water Circus – the first half of the show they did these amazing dives; the second half they put on funny costumes and did clowning. It was really fun.

My father was a performer, in a way. I mean, he liked to make people laugh, and he gave speeches as part of his job and they were very funny. And I found out that my great-grandfather ran a legitimate theater in Philadelphia and he was also an amateur clown on the boardwalk in Atlantic City, so that's kind of cool. Plus there was a very famous guy at the beginning of American cinema named Siegmund Lubin, who, we think, might've been a distant relative.

My father was very interested in movies. For a couple of summers when I was a kid, he rented an old movie theater and showed silent movies for whoever would come. It was the beginning of my education. I would help him rewind the film in the projection booth, and, when I could, I'd stare through that little glass window onto the big screen and drink in the silent movie greats. Plus he also rented films for guests at all the hotels in Atlantic City, classics like *Some Like It Hot* with Jack Lemmon and Tony Curtis. I would just sit there and watch them, and dream. It just seemed like the coolest thing you could do was to be a movie star or in a situation comedy. So I was harboring those kinds of fantasies, of becoming a famous dancer, or ending up on Broadway. I think a lot of people feel that way.

Also, I remember looking at the papers while I was growing up in South Jersey, and wanting someday to be in the *New York Times*.

Throughout my last three years of high school I made experimental TV, basically comedies. Me and my cronies, we acted, we directed, we wrote, we did absolutely everything. We tried to emulate Ernie Kovacs – he was so innovative and so good at the quick, visual, television joke. We loved characters like Jonathan Winters, Red Skelton. Jerry Lewis was a big influence on my early creative career and still is, really, to this day. But when I got to college I had less access to the TV equipment, and I got discouraged. I was taking a year off to earn some money when Ringling came to town. And I became interested. I think at that time, which was the early '70s, a lot of people were looking for an alternate kind of thing – not to go down the chosen path, but to go in a more interesting direction. So as conservative as I was (and I still am), I found myself attracted to it.

When I got there for the audition, spring of '74, a gentleman named Jim Howell – one of their clowns at that time – was assigned to a couple of us auditionees, and we basically asked him as many questions as we could. He told us about the life, what clowning really is, and it was amazing. I was very lucky that I was inspired by this guy. Just recently I saw him and I told him how much that meant, and he started to cry that, ya know, that he had influenced me that much. That was pretty cool. So Ringling invited me to go to their college. Circus wasn't in my family's vocabulary. A Jewish mother wants her Jewish child to become a doctor, not a clown. So my family didn't encourage it. Not for a long time. Well into my career, my mother would seriously ask the question, "When are you gonna get a real job?"

Inspirations

I arrived at clown college and I was immediately intimidated. I mean, the first thing I remember is somebody doing a double backwards somersault off the high-dive at the pool. All I could do was juggle three balls, and not very well. And seeing people doing roundoff backflips on the grass and juggling what looked like 23 clubs, I said to myself, "I'm in the wrong place, I should turn around and go back to Boston, and finish my senior year at Emerson, cause this ain't it." It was touch and go at clown college for me because even simple things like doing makeup came very slowly for me, and I thought I would wash out just for that. I learned acrobatics in the end, but well after the audition for the producers of Ringling. (I figured out a backwards somersault on a trampoline, and I was really proud of it, but it was too late, I was just doing it for myself.) And juggling … Hovey Burgess was my juggling instructor, and he took an interest in me, thank God, and I really loved it, especially ball juggling, but skills were never gonna be my thing. I tried stilts – terrible. Wire-walking – terrible. I didn't understand that if you wanna get good at these things, it takes a lot of time.

But I made my way. I got into Ringling itself. I realized that what I had was a character, and that was something else. That's what differentiated me right from the beginning, knowing that creating a character was the most important thing I could do. To look like the other 27 clowns would mean that nobody would see me, but to look like somebody who walked in off the street – which is what Grandma looks like – that would create a whole different impression and it might get a lot of attention. Actually, it did. Immediately, on my very first show, I got an enormous amount of attention. No laughs, because I didn't know how to get laughs, but attention. (One of the great things I had learned in clown college was: if they're not watching you, you can't tell how you're doing.) I had lots of eyes on me. Most of the audience looked like Grandma, too. It was Venice, Florida – a hell of a lot of senior citizens – and it must have seemed as though one of their own had ended up on the hippodrome track and in the circus. So the producers of Ringling saw that there was something to this, even though I wasn't getting laughs, and they encouraged me to continue developing this character – which didn't have a name at this point, but looks exactly like Grandma does today. So I developed it. It became easy to tell who I was, in contrast to some of my fellow clowns who, as distinctive and wonderful and original as they were, looked like a typical Ringling clown. Now, there's a period called "Come in" which is the pre-show at Ringling (it's not called "Come in" anymore), and during that time I was allowed to go up into the seating area and improvise, and that's where I began to work on the character, to really find it. It was from the direct relationship with the audience. One on one, or small groups in the crowd. I needed to cut down the distance, because in Ringling you can be on the arena floor and you can play to thousands of people, but you can't see any of them. So I would go up into the audience before the show and kind of make my way, and try lots and lots of different things, and that's where the character of Grandma was really born.

I was lucky enough to have Lou Jacobs, who's a legend, as one of my instructors at clown college, and I continued to work with him at Ringling. He would say the most basic thing, which would be terribly annoying when you're looking for more information. People would say, "Lou, what's funny? How do you make people laugh?" And he would say, "If they laugh, it's funny, and if they don't, it's not." And everybody would say, "Come on, you gotta have more than that." And he'd say, "Ya know what? That's it. That's really it, ya know? Try your stuff out. If they like it, ya got a winner. If they don't like it, they told you. They're the only ones who are ever right." So that was something that I could never get out of my head, and when I pass along information to new clowns or people who are interested, I say that. Trial and error. Simplest thing in the world. It doesn't give you enough information if you're looking for a specific idea of what's gonna make people laugh, but it's enough to begin.

David Nicksay was the main clown teacher. And I didn't understand this when I was young – I do much more now – but he would say, "It's not an acting job. It's not like you're climbing into a character. It's that you're finding the character within you." And that can be one of the hardest things in the world. Because you have to take a look at yourself. Not always the most comfortable thing to do. He told us, "It's already there. That's the beauty of clowning. You just have to find it. You have to find the aspects of you that you can bring out in your character." He also talked about going up into the seats, mingling with the audience. He said,

"Go into the seats in an area where you will be performing in the main show later on. Once they know you, they're gonna remember you and they're gonna to pay attention to you, and, therefore, you're gonna know how your material is going over."

That was the main reason why I went into the seats in the first place. Before that, I just went into the ring and did this little routine, and it died every single show. Although people were looking at me, it wasn't working. So I would go up into the seats, I would climb up into the worst seats in the house, and I would get to know the audience up there. They were always very grateful. These were the end zone seats, as far up as possible. I would entertain them, and they were just so happy to have somebody connect with them, ya know? They thought they were gonna have a passive experience, and instead they got something more. So it was pleasing for me and pleasing for them. Plus, I was kind of conspiratorial with them. I would say – I'd get as many of them to hear this as possible – I would say, "I'm gonna be appearing in the show, and I'm gonna look over at you, and when you see me cheer like crazy! Go nuts! Yell, scream, go crazy!" So during the show, I would go out into the ring – and you're talking about an arena full of clowns, 28 of us, and sometimes a lot of other people as well – and I would look up and wave and all of a sudden this enormous eruption would happen from way over there. And the whole audience would look around to see who did what. Who just made somebody laugh? Did somebody's pants fall down? Did sparks come out of their ass? I mean, what was it? And I never revealed that it was me. I just went on my way, and nobody realized. I would do it two or three times during the show and then immediately act as if, "I didn't do anything." That was enormous fun for me.

I wanted to be improvisational, and my influence was the opposite of circus clowning – it was Lenny Bruce, who improvised an awful lot of his act every night. I admired that so much, I wanted to do that. Of course, what I hadn't figured out at the beginning was that he had a base upon which he could improvise. He had his prepared stuff that would get the laughs, and then he would spin off from there. I had nothing. I was going out there and purely improvising, show after show after show, half an hour a show, 13 shows a week – basically I was just racking up the hours. But there was no consistency. I could get a laugh here and there, but up in the seats I was only playing to three people. I was working in small circumstances. It was important – I was creating relationships with people, finding the basis for my character, learning what people liked and didn't like about the character, and that was vital. But I had no consistency.

And then something happened at the end of my first year. At the end of "Come in" there was something called "Blow-off," the very last thing in the pre-show when almost the entire audience was seated, when the best clown would go out and do the final warm-up of the audience to get them as excited as possible for the blackout that would lead to the opening production number. That was a great honor, and it was never somebody who couldn't handle it. It was always somebody who was really good. That year it was Dougie Ashton, an Australian clown. But he got sick one day, at the Nassau Coliseum in Long Island, and without asking I went out there when the house was completely full. The floor was empty, the audience was in, and I knew that because Dougie wasn't there, there was gonna be five minutes of time not covered by anybody else. I went out there, and I had every eye on me. I think it was 19,000 people. And I failed miserably. I got nothing. Absolutely nothing. It was such a colossal failure because I knew I had them, and if I gave them anything at all I was gonna get this rock-star reaction. But I got nothing. It killed me. It devastated me. It ripped my guts out. Took me weeks to get over it.

I realized that I had to figure out how to get those laughs on a consistent basis. It took me 18 months into my career before I had one gag, one laugh only that was consistent. It had a high batting average, and it was something to do with popcorn. I can't even remember exactly what it was, but I could pretty much count on it. Though it wasn't a hundred percent, it was up there. And from that, I started building. I went for the consistent laugh. I went for having a repertoire. Going from the person who thought that I should be improvising all the time to someone who needed to have a product that I could count on to deliver to an audience. It was certainly a different way of going about it. And I went through plenty of failure. Still do! But I started to realize that I needed things to count on, and that was a very big influence, that horrible experience. Since then I've had lots of tremendous failures, and I always encourage people to have them. They're invaluable. I've even failed in the worst place you can possibly fail at, which is the International Circus Festival of Monte Carlo, which in my business is like the Academy Awards of Circus. I died there, at the end of my third year in clowning. And it was a turning point. I could've said, "I can't handle it. This is terrible. I'm leaving. Enough." But instead I said, "Well, it can't get any worse than that." And I kept going.

Techniques

I had created this little old lady character named Grandma – which the audience named, by the way, I didn't, but it certainly was a good name – and she was noticeable and likeable. But how could I deliver with her? I realized that it was all about surprise. It was all about setting her up, with a very slow walk, and the appearance that this is truly an old lady, and then doing something completely out of character. And I've made my living doing exactly that. A great example: when I was with Ringling, I would slowly walk up the stairs during the pre-show – nothing more than that, walk slowly – and then at the very top of the stairs (this can be 80 rows in some of the bigger arenas) I would lay down, and I would slowly fall down the stairs. Slow, totally in control. People would leap out of their seats to save me. They would pick me up, and they would see my face, which was a clown face, and they would drop me. And I will tell you that a hundred percent of the time, they would drop me because they felt duped. Now, I wasn't going for duped. I was just – in my mind, this is just the stupidest thing in the entire world, and it's fun. And the crowd loved it.

Another thing I would do. In some arenas there were banisters on either side of the seating section, and sometimes, again, they'd be 80 rows high. I would slowly, slowly, slowly, walk through the top row of seats, then I would climb slowly up on the banister – and then I would go headfirst. Like a toboggan. Basically, I would shoot at very high speed 80 rows down, and I would brake by using my body, my arms, and my legs, and at the time I wore a winter coat, that was Grandma's costume. You could smell it burning. In one town, Tucson, Arizona, I went through three coats because I burned through the material. But talk about breaking expectations! You see the old lady walking. "Oh well that's nice. I don't know what's going on. It's an old lady." And then shooting at 50 miles an hour headfirst, plummeting down toward the ring … Incredible! Breaking expectations. I used to feel that these giant arenas were my playground.

I started doing lip-syncs because of Jerry Lewis. Now, to see Grandma be slow and plodding, and then break out into a rock and roll song – again, breaking expectations. I remember working with people early in my career who would say, "A little old lady would never do that." And I would say, "That's exactly right. Because I'm not an actor, I'm a clown." Besides, I would break any rule for that laugh. It didn't matter. The same people said to me, "This doesn't fit into the act. Yeah, it got a laugh, but it doesn't fit into the act," and I would say, "I could care less. It's getting a laugh, and I'm not gonna do away with something that's getting a laugh." Anything for a laugh. It's a great lesson. I don't mean bad taste. I mean: if it's getting a laugh, that's much more important than portraying what a little old lady would normally do. It goes back to David Nicksay, "You are finding what's within yourself."

My first real, true routines began when I got to Big Apple Circus. 1982. I put together these little bits that I had learned in Ringling, and suddenly it looked like a small act. I was working with incredibly talented people who inspired me. We worked really well together, especially in a trio – Michael Christensen, Jeff Gordon, and I became what was called "The Group" by Europeans. (I thought, "Well, that's kind of cool.") I also started working directly off the ringmaster as authority figure because – talking about David Nicksay's lesson "Find out who you are and use it" – I don't like authority. And in a one-ring circus it's possible to have good chemistry with the ringmaster. So I would play off this figure, Paul Binder at the time. I would interrupt him. I would screw up the proceedings. I never came through the curtains. It was always as if I were an audience member finding my way into the circus ring. (Come to think of it, I've always seen myself as more audience than circus. I've been in the business 40 years, and I still don't see myself as a circus person. I'm the audience member who's in awe of the circus. A friendly outsider, somebody who wants in.) It was a matter of working up a repertoire; sometimes within themes, sometimes the three clowns conspiring, and sometimes I was inspired and suddenly envisaged a new act that might work. One of the first things I invented there was Aretha Franklin's "Respect." It followed an incredibly stupid, low trapeze act. I think it might've been the lowest, fattest trapeze act in American circus history. And for no reason, at the end of that stupid act, the ringmaster said something that led to, "Yeah, I'm doing this because I want a little respect." "Oh, you want a little respect?" And ya know, the music would start and away we'd go, a lip-sync with Jeff Gordon and Michael

Christensen. It came out of left field and it worked. People liked it. But how does that go with a trapeze act? I'll never know. It doesn't make sense. But it *is* surprising. It's the unexpected.

Then I came up with this treadmill act for a friend, and I realized I might as well do something with it myself. I started going to the gym, and because my ex-wife was working there I got into a private section. It was very quiet. I thought, "Okay, I'm just gonna screw around on the treadmill and see what happens." I went in day after day and just experimented. "What happens when it's going slow? What happens when it's going fast? How can I fly off of this thing and be safe?" I was even busted by a trainer one day because I went off the back of the treadmill and slammed into a wall. I can slam into a wall without hurting myself. But this trainer came in and he was so upset, he tried to take my membership away! But that was the beginning of it. And then I was talking to the Big Apple Circus, and I had this idea of having it as part of a *Men in Black* parody. They liked the idea, got me a treadmill, and I carried on screwing around. Eventually I trotted it out in front of an audience. And a big part of what made it work is that it was out of character for a little old lady. Seeing a little old lady on a treadmill was fun for people. And then I combined music with it. I did "Chariots of Fire" as a slow-motion gag, which hadn't been done on a treadmill before. In fact, I don't think there had been a clown act on a treadmill prior to that ... I guess it was kind of unique in that respect. I did it for a full season with Big Apple, something like 300 shows. Then I left the show, but I took the act with me and it developed a new life. It wasn't under the same restrictions of time. I did it exactly the way I wanted to, having learned what worked and didn't work. Trial and error. I still do the act. It has changed enormously over the years, and my pet name for it is "five minutes of hell" because it kills me. It is so hard to do. Anne, my girlfriend, says, "Well why don't you pick a version that's not gonna kill you?"

What I've noticed in the latter part of my career is I've been doing simpler things, and getting much more out of the audience. It's not that I'm working less hard, but I realize that the smaller stuff, the simpler stuff – the holding still, for example, which I did right at the beginning of my career but didn't get laughs – now, it's paying off in a much bigger way. And I started doing this with a partner, Joel Jeske, and he and I both noticed it about each other. We were getting so much out of nothing. If you described it to somebody they'd say, "You're not doing anything. That's not an act," and I'd have to say, "Well, we just got 30 laughs," so what is an act and what isn't an act? The biggest laughs I get now are from a water act, which is basically two bottles of water where I spit water and then I teach somebody from the audience, a real audience member, how to spit water. And that's all it is. And it sounds like nothing, and it is next to nothing, yet it's some of the biggest laughs I've ever gotten in my career. Why is that? I don't know.

I left Big Apple in 1998 – one of the times that I took off not knowing if I would come back – and Paul Binder said, "Okay, let's consider licensing Grandma. You'll play the opening engagement and try-outs, and open at Lincoln Center, and then you'll hand it off to somebody else." The first person being Mark Gindick. So we made that deal, and Mark and I started to consult and collaborate. We became good friends. He watched the new show repeatedly, and we rehearsed when we could. But when the time came for Mark to take over, after all our preparation, it was a kind of disaster. It didn't work. There was a guy who wanted his money back and somebody else who wrote a letter that said Grandma must have been having a really bad day. I thought, "This is not gonna work. Now I'm gonna have to do the tour." Which is not what I wanted to do. So I started to work with Mark a little more seriously, and he did one more show that week. And it was not good, but it was not as bad. And then by the third and fourth show he was really starting to get it. The great thing for Mark was that he realized after a short time – and I trusted his instincts – he had to make it his own. He had to find the way to not be me. Somebody who talked to me about the licensing said, very smartly, "It's not gonna be Grandma. It's gonna be Grandma 1A. Don't expect it to be you – but expect it to work." And they were absolutely right. So Mark did it for a couple years. And I remember distinctly watching Mark, and when he had great success I was really proud and really jealous.

Mark would come up with some bits that I just couldn't do, and he would kill as Grandma; then I would try to emulate him and fail enormously. I didn't have the same chops as he did, whether it was dancing or acrobatics. But he had that kind of physicality, so he would do a bit and I would learn from it. I would find myself asking if I could borrow bits that he'd come up with. He always said, "Yes, of course! It'd be an honor, please!" Mark had a Britney Spears lip-sync from a different show called "How To Be A Man," which was funny as hell, and he put it into the circus show as Grandma, and he said it was rockstar kill. So I had to ask, "Mark, can I use it?" and he said, "Yes, of course!" So it was this interesting thing where I was informed continuously by the people who played Grandma, and I couldn't always do what they did. And Mark's mother's famous line … There was a period where I hadn't hired Mark to play Grandma for a little while, and she said, "Are you gonna hire Mark again to play Grandma? Because he does you better than you." And I went, "Fair enough."

Philosophy

Now this is kind of an interesting story for clowns. Bill Irwin is one of my heroes. I went to clown college with him, and I've watched his career. I admire him enormously; he is one of the great talents of all time. And he is the darling – at least he certainly was back then – of the New York press. They just would fall all over themselves for him. They would review bad shows that he was in and give him a spectacularly good review. He had features in the *New York Times* … And I wanted that! I wanted Bill Irwin's career, not realizing that only Bill Irwin can have Bill Irwin's career. I should've just wanted Barry Lubin's career, but I have the-grass-is-always-greener-on-the-other-side disease. So I developed an act that I thought would work for the New York press, which is the stupidest way to go about anything. I designed it in my head, not that it would usurp Bill Irwin in any way, but so that it would get me that kind of press, and they would have to start writing about my talent in those same terms that Bill was getting written about. And it was a colossal failure – I mean, it might've been the worst thing I ever did. A complete piece of crap! And it was miserable. But it's good to look back on something like that and realize how misguided I was, how far from my true purpose – which should have been, and always is, paying attention to the audience on that particular day. Not the *New York Times*. The audience; today's audience. They're the only ones.

Eight or ten years ago, I went from an artist who wanted to get, to an artist who gave. Let me explain. I was clowning for a purpose. I wanted to get money. I wanted to get love. I wanted to get adulation; I wanted the press; I wanted fame. I had an agenda. And at a certain point, it was around 9/11, it changed from that to, "I just wanna be. I just wanna give what I have." The gift is in giving. It's not in the receiving. It's really a 180-degree difference between giving to get and giving to give, and I think that's easily the most important thing. With that comes this realization that it's a very spiritual experience to be a circus clown, who looks like an idiot jumping around and doing headstands on a whoopee cushion. There is this circle of love thing that happens. There is this giving and receiving. The clown is somewhere in the middle of the circle, and the audience is looking at the clown and the clown is looking at the audience, and … The energy and the love that you give to an audience, they give back to you. And if you're successful at what you have to offer to them, they give it back to you tenfold. It's a circle: I give to you, you give to me, that inspires me, that gives me energy, that makes me know I'm doing something right, I give you the next thing. You are steering me in the right direction because you're always right. So I will be steered. I will be inspired. I will be given energy. And even if the audience has a low energy, you can produce it, to start the circle.

A person evolves, therefore their clown evolves. The world is evolving, therefore you have to evolve your own way so that you're in the moment, no matter where in time that moment is. I have friends who are lost because they're trying to recreate what happened way back in the '70s, when they felt they had the real connection. It's not the connection that the audience accepts anymore. So I think that to remain relevant, my job and any clown's job is to pay very close attention to what it is that the audience wants and what it is that you want to give. And I've always been very clear from the very start that all I want is laughs. That's all I want. I don't need to do more than that. If you take something from it that touches your heart, that's a great bonus, but that is not my intention. My intention is to make people laugh.

I think character comes in time. You can connect very quickly to who you are, but the character and the comfort and the ability to go out and stand naked in front of an audience, that takes time. As I have progressed in my career, I've seen a lot of people who are now in their fifties and sixties who have this enormous amount of time, who stayed with it. They may not be in the circus. They may be in theater or they're doing festivals, but they have evolved so far that there is a comfort to their stage presence that is immediately accessible to the audience. There's no setup involved. I just saw Michael Davis perform. I saw him at a juggling convention gala show in New York City a little over a month ago, and it was like a primer in show business. It wasn't what he was doing; it was that he was immensely present. He was just there. There was no pretense whatsoever. The material was good or it wasn't – well, it's phenomenally good material because he's been around for a long time. But it was just this immediate connection with the audience. That's the lesson. If you connect with the audience, they care. That's the maturity that I think comes with time. There are so many years of experience behind me now; there is a comfort from the audience. Now I see myself as just part of their life, which is different than it used to be.

There's another thing I'll mention, from my experiences in Hungary. When I played there, it became clear to me that people had to celebrate life, but at the same time they wouldn't give themselves permission to laugh because they were just so devastated. Perhaps the clown's role is to not only entertain you, but to let you know it's okay, no matter what. After all, in society we all have to laugh. I was asked in Budapest – this was in 2006 when I performed at a circus festival there – a journalist said, "So what did you think of the audience in Budapest?" This was after I'd been there for a week, and I said, "I think they're amazing. They're very generous. I had a great time with them." She said, "Well that's really interesting because they're such a depressed people." And it made me wonder: in the depressed parts of the world, is this where the clown is most successful? Is this where the clown should be? My daughter, who was a young teen at the time, she had a wonderful thing to say, she said, "Dad, everybody needs to laugh." You're a billionaire, you gotta laugh. You can't find enough to eat today, you gotta laugh. You gotta find the humor, the relief, the release, in something.

Comedy comes in many forms. I happen to love the clown because it's so unique, and I love the circus because everybody goes. Little kids and ancient people and families and people who are out on a date. And the clown, the way I approach it, has to find material that reaches all of those people at exactly the same moment. I can't clown for the little kid over here and then do something different for the senior citizen over there. I have to do something that works for everybody. And that, to me, is the great joy of clowning and the circus.

10 Jango Edwards

Figure 9 Jango Edwards. Photo by Ian Patrick

Jango Edwards (born in Detroit, 1950) has performed his unique clown shows all over the world. In the 1970s, he was part of the Friends Roadshow with Nola Rae, and a primary organizer of the International Festival of Fools in Amsterdam. Later he went solo, building up fan-bases in Holland, France, Germany, and Austria, where he made many TV appearances. In 2009, Jango created the Nouveau Clown Institute in Barcelona, which has attracted artists from 31 different countries for clown inspiration.

I met Jango at his apartment in Old Town, Barcelona. (EL)

Origins

The first time I saw a clown was the Shrine Circus. Emmett Kelly. Detroit. I was about seven years old. He was the Auguste, the tramp. He was poetic, he was sad, but he was not sad. He lived a life all in rags but his riches were in his heart. That and Bozo the Clown on TV. And then I got into Lucille Ball, loved her stuff, and then Red Skelton had a major effect on my life. Guy that had the most effect, died when I was 12 years old, was Ernie Kovacs. Those were the times when Kovacs, Skelton, they were clowns, you had clowns on TV.

I didn't have any interest in clown at that time. In school I was a student leader, captain of the football team, head of the newspaper. Those were the '60s, and I had my own business when I was 17. It was the time of the riots in Detroit. I had a lot of money, took a lot of drugs, had a lot of women, but I was not happy with my life. So I started going to school. I studied mostly religion and politics, esoteric studies. And eventually, because my work was seasonal, every year I would go to Europe with a certain amount of money in my pocket, no credit card, and rough it like a hippie. It was also the love generation. I was reading a book called *The Fourth Way*. And I was looking for something of value in my life, and I had 40 hits of acid. I was selling acid at the time. It was the '60s. I took the 40 hits of acid with me and I took the book and I traveled down to Morocco, and in 30 days I took the 40 hits of acid and I read the book. And on the thirtieth day when I took the last two hits of acid in the Atlas Mountains in Morocco, suddenly 40 sheep walked over me, and at that moment man, by chance, everything fell into place in my life, and I was 20. It had nothing to do with clown. But it had to do with two sentences in the book that changed my life. And the sentences were: "Know who you are," observe yourself, know who you are. The second was: "Help yourself by helping others." And that made sense to me, because I didn't know who I was, I was trying to find my center. *The Fourth Way* was a teaching about all the religions of the world, and combining them into one. You know, awareness is something the world has lost. You are born free, and in our family of clowns, we call ourselves soldiers, there's no leader, we're fighting for the freedom that we already have.

So I sold my business. I saw the movie, *I Clowns*, by Fellini. When I saw that movie I thought, here's a way that I can help people globally, it's a low form of humor, but very profound. There's something about it, we're not funny, I'm not funny, but we make people laugh, we help people reflect on themselves. All I wanted was to bring some peace to people, and that's what I do. The best clowns, you'll never see them because they're not on stage.

Inspirations

I applied to Ringling Bros, and I got down to the final 100, and they turned me down. I've got the letter from Bill Ballantine. Thank God he turned me down. So I came to Europe.

I actually started my work teaching. When I went to London in 1970, a guy named Ron Wilson invited me to go to his school, after I didn't get accepted by Ringling Brothers. I went to his class that day, he took me home for dinner and he tried to fuck me. I don't mind bisexual, man, woman, whatever, but I wasn't interested in this guy, so I left. Now I was in London, I didn't know anything. So

I worked on the streets, raising money from spinning around in circles. Ten or 15 minutes, and then I'd vomit. People were giving me money for being mechanical. The body controls the mind. I found this one continuing education course, a night class for clowns. The lady said to me, "What are you doing here?" I said, "I'm a clown from America." You know, I lied my way through all this shit, and she said, "Oh cool." I took the class, two hours a week for five weeks, and she said, "Jango, you know what, I have to go back to the circus, I have to leave the job, could you teach for the next six months?" I said, "Sure, why not?" And that's how I started. Once a week I taught for two hours. I spent all week learning something, went to the library, read mime books, I learned mime, learned gymnastics. They showed me on the English news, they showed me teaching. I started like that, teaching. I told everybody I was a clown.

I met Nola while she was sweeping. She was cleaning the theater for the guy who was gay. I met her there, and she came over to the Oval House, where I was doing this workshop, and she showed me mime, which I hate. I hate all that shit. It's only a vehicle. I only like the heart and the mind. I showed her how to be crazy. She was great technically. And then we became friends, and we decided to do a show, so we made a show, and called it the London Mime Company. While we were rehearsing we met the London Black Theatre Company, it was a carpenter and another guy and they were doing black theater, and we didn't have a long-enough show, so they were rehearsing and we were rehearsing and we said let's unite, and we did a thing we called Friends. London Black Theatre Company, London Mime Theatre Company, and then it became Friends, Friends Roadshow. We had a center in London, in Amsterdam, over 400 people inside the community over the years, we all worked for nothing, bread and cheese, cheese and eggs, all sleeping in a communal situation. Then when I had money, I started giving people 20 dollars a week. Mistake. End of the community. Eventually I left the group, and I told them all the truth that I never was a clown. I called them together, said I'm gonna start my own group, Jango and Friends, I never studied clown, I just lied to you for the last five years.

All this stuff, there's a myth about me, which I built, because clown is about myth. Because my name's not even Jango, my name's Stanley. I created Jango to get attention, to get work, I didn't even tell people in my own group, I played the character the whole time. All these people came to my class, I didn't know fuck-all. I was saying stuff then that I say now, but I didn't know what I was doing. But I knew clown had to be protected. It was an endangered species. Little did I know, three years later I'd meet Fellini and become good friends with him.

Let me tell you about Carlo [Colombaioni]. When I met Fellini, Fellini came to me in Rome, and he came backstage. I was doing a piece called "Jesus H. Christ and the Heavenly Choir," and I wore this big foam cross. We became friends. Fellini was friends with Carlo. So Carlo came and he taught, he showed me the Fellini film, and Carlo said, "Everything in it, I did." He showed me all that stuff, and I said, "Carlo, I'm gonna pay you to come every year and do a master class." And he came and taught, and I'd cry and laugh, and weep, the stories he told me were amazing. He became my teacher. Carlo only spoke

Italian, and I only spoke English, and I learned from him, because he had a big stick, so you had to, he'd whack you. He was teaching by feel, not by method or category. I was like his son.

Every day Carlo would hold court; he would tell us a story about clowning.

Carlo brought me to the level. He made me humble. Humility is key in our work. You didn't want to get up in front of him, he was a tough old guy; he'd beat you.

He said, "Jango, why don't we make a movie, you and me, about the death of two clowns?" So we laid in the stage, laying there dead, and then he looks over, and one by one the clowns come and give a eulogy, all bad, all start good and end bad. The guy edited it, two years later the film showed up in the mail. That was the day he died. Carlo never saw the film.

Ten days before he died, I called and said, "Carlo, how can I be a better clown than I am now?" I asked his wife. She told him in Italian. I heard him laugh, "Tell Jango, you will not get there from here." I put down the phone, I will not get there from here, what the fuck, he's a prick. It really fucked me up. He's my master, my sensei. My father used to tell me, "Stanley, if you don't go you won't get there." Just do the shit, just do the fucking shit, don't ask me about it, I try to tell people. Don't analyze. I just walk here and do something. I can make you laugh, doesn't matter where. A great clown never ever makes the public adjust to them.

Techniques

I saw this guy in Leicester Square. He had a matchbox. Finally he opened the matchbox; there was a feather in it; then he put the feather on the matchbox; finally he jumped up on the matchbox. Nothing. He did nothing, and he would pass the hat, and he was making money off it. I thought that's absolutely nothing, and I thought if I could do something, a little something, I could probably make money too. I learned a squat flip. You flip on a tripod and flip on your feet. I was young, didn't care about my body, now it's all fucked up, did 3,000 dives and missed sometimes. My body was going. Doc said I'd be paralyzed from the neck down, I figure I'd do box mimes.

Jango can't be sick. It's not possible. When the clown gets sick it's not possible, you destroy the myth.

I started, I took a cup of water, I said I'd jump in this cup of water. No one thought I could do it. I started in the street with my suitcase. I would do it, and people couldn't believe it. It's not so difficult, you just do the tripod. When you feel the plastic you flip up. I got the idea from that guy who jumped on that feather. I began to study people, that's what clown is about, helping people, and you only have to help one. Just one, the rest is a holiday, but to do that you have to help yourself first. Without that you have no right to reflect other people and tell them what they are, and what they look like. You don't have to change, but you have to know who you are, and you have to tell the truth. Me, I've been taking drugs for 40 years. I tell people that right away. I can tell people I'm a junkie, I was a junkie, I still am, I smoke grass, I take coke sometimes, but I can control it by being honest. I lied for a few years, but when you lie you hide yourself. You don't have to change anything, but you have to be honest, and this is very difficult for people. It's life changing. I don't do nothing but make people look at themselves.

I got myself smuggled into Russia. Joined this communist youth group. I go to this meeting in this house, and I meet these 17 clowns; they have nothing, nothing, I mean nothing. Slava, this yellow thing, that's what he had, that's all he had. And they were doing stuff to risk their life. They survived by being clowns. A lot of it was comedy on the government. Popov too, but Popov was more hidden, things like putting a rabbit in the washing machine, put it in black, comes out white, that kind of thing.

I met these guys every day. They gave everyone a backpack from the Moscow Festival. I gave them cassettes of music I had. I had John Towsen's book, and we met every day, we had fun. There were three parts to the festival – one was cultural, one was political, and one was environmental. I was in the cultural one. Something like the San Francisco Mime Troupe and the Pickle Family Circus, that was happening over there, but another kind of people. This wasn't happening in the States, that's why I came.

Every day one of the artists would perform in the State Theater. So on the ninth or tenth day I got to do a show. Two thousand people. Nothing political; don't take your clothes off.

I'd been playing in bars, living on a farm all fucking each other. We did the La Crosse Mime Festival. Avner, everyone was there. They took us, and then they saw what we were like and they banned us.

So I did this show on the ninth or tenth day. I did a show called "Garbage." I had a general's jacket and a phone booth; I hung up the jacket on the phone. I did my poetic stuff. I did a piece called "Weezer" – it's about pissing. I did a classical mime piece. And I did a Superman bit. Until the end, I did the diving glass of water; normally I did a G string, but they said don't do that, so I had a one-piece clown striped suit. But after it was over, I was excited. People liked the show, so I said "Ladies and gentlemen," I said, "people say we're enemies, but we're not enemies, no one's my enemy, we're people, just be human," and I said "I wanna thank Slava Polunin," and when I did that, that was a mistake, after the show was over my translator said, two journalists want to talk to you; they arrested Slava. I go upstairs, these two KGB guys, they say, "Tomorrow you go, we take you to the airport, we'll pack your things, go to the hotel." I see the clowns in the distance, looking at me, and I think, "Man I really fucked up." For me I was just being honest. I go back to the hotel. The next morning they escort me to the airport. This guy comes to me and says, "Two of the clowns want to talk to you, meet us in Gorky Park," a good distance away from us. They said, "Don't look at us." He said to me, they just want you to know, their life has now been lived in vain because their eyes have seen you. I thought, fuck. I wasn't even a clown, I didn't know nothing.

I gotta tell you another story.

There was a guy standing on the street, in garbage. Perfect suit, Armani, dressed to the T. He's standing there, what the fuck is that? I stop and I look ten minutes, 20 minutes. I'm thinking to go. Just at that moment one guy comes up gives him a coin in his hat, he goes up behind him, BOOM, he hits the guy on the back of the head. I started laughing. That's what he's gonna do? The guy said, "Hey did you see that he hit me on the head?" All you need is one. Guy who got hit in the head, he stood next to me watching. You got two people there, it changes. The mentality of humanity, you don't want to be the only victim. After a half hour there's 400 people there, giving other people money, just to see them get hit. This is clowning.

Other end of the spectrum, one day I had to play a halfway house for treating methadone patients. They come in: 2:00 they have a program; at 2:30 they get their methadone. I get $500 to play there. I arrive late, at 2:40. They already had their methadone. Seventy people, sitting in a room, and I gotta play for them. It was a challenge. How do I do this? What the fuck do I do here? The guy said, "Jango you gonna play?" I said, "Give me a moment, I have a lot of good information in me, I've done a lot of shit," so I took five minutes, went outside, I put on a nice suit, came back with a pad of paper, an ink pad, and a pen. What I'm gonna tell you, man, it doesn't sound like clown, but in our family, this is clown. I made the adjustment right there, and I was able to bring these people in, no matter what the cost, to win them, no matter what the humiliation was for me. It didn't matter what anybody thought afterward, it was history, but I had to go there then. I said, "Hey I'm Jango Edwards. I'm a famous clown, but you don't have to do anything, don't worry, you're in a good mood, I don't bite. But I'm not gonna do any shit for you, don't move, I gotta gift for each one of you, each one, don't move." I walk to the first guy, open the ink pad, unzip my pants, take out my cock, I roll it on the ink pad, stamp it on the paper, sign my name and date. There's 70 guys, after the first ten, they're all following me, paper in their hand, walking around in a circle, me making my ink dick prints; man I tell you I was embarrassed, but I won. They were all happy. They clapped. Never did something like that. That was one of those moments – I'm there, I'm a clown agent, I'm double-0 clown. From that point on, I have not lost ever, but sometimes it's a bitch. I have played some tough situations. I played a prison, took me an hour to get in, two hours to get out. When I went to play there, 90 percent of the inmates came. Afterward, two guys from the inmates' board gave me my diploma of graduation from the prison. I'm a gangster now. I go home, look these guys up – one guy killed nine people in his family, the other killed three women. I thought, man, this is clown. This is the stuff you live for. You don't live for success or money, you don't live to do Cirque du Soleil. I don't get that stuff. I'm comfortable and I love my life. And I'm gonna end the conversation there.

No, one more thing. A producer in Cannes, he came up to me, said he wants to produce my show. I say "Yeah, I got a show," "The Ballet of the Bathroom." I can do it seven times a day. It's a dance/movement thing in the bathroom. A few months later he calls me up, says we want to do your show.

We start like this, I say, "Fly me and my assistant down to Cannes, we'll find the right bathroom." We tour bathrooms, we find one – in the Majestic Hotel. I tell him, you pay our flights, we'll do the show just for the door. He says, "Okay, I'll do that." He says, "How much are the tickets?" I say, "$250 a ticket." He says, "Who's gonna buy a ticket for $250?" I say, "Hey, then I don't get paid." I figured I'd have a holiday. Three days, it sold out. Dig it man, $3,000 a show, sold out, seven shows, $21,000 in one day for taking a bath. I filmed it, sold the television rights for $18,000, released it on DVD. I made $52,000 in one day taking seven baths. So when people come and tell me you can't make any money at this job, I say then you're a fucking idiot, man. You can put garbage on yourself and make money.

In the end, when they arrested these people in Russia, I got sent home. Four weeks later I get a phone call from a guy who's from the Communist Party in Italy in a theater I played in. And then suddenly five months later I get a postcard, these 17 clowns dressed as birds sitting on a tree, going onto the lake, saying they're okay. And they invited me back to Moscow, and there's an entourage of people waiting for me when I get there. They take me to the theater, there's a wax figure of me in a museum, two shows touring called "Jango." I'm a social icon. I'm more famous in Russia than anywhere in the world.

Philosophy

The stage is the least important, that's the easy place. I've done it all – I played for the Queen, for the Rolling Stones. I can do anything. I have no limits. But the world is fucked up. It's not gonna change by the governments; it has to change by people. Things like Occupy Wall Street. It happened here first. Not anarchists – people. And this gives us some hope. It's all about fear, that governments separate us, passports, borders, religions, political parties, it's all to control.

We're trying to build our army of humanity. You're born a clown. You're born free. Clowns are freedom; clowns are outlaws. Not that we're against laws; we eliminate the laws we don't need. The only hope I have is that I do everything I can, and I help myself, and I help one person. I spend 20 hours a day awake. I don't like to sleep. I work till I pass out, I get up and I work.

My friends, we came up with comic formulas, 30 of them, one word, or sentences that are absolutely essential in doing a sketch, and when you know them you just put them down on a table, and say does this one apply, no, does this one apply, yes. Almost mathematical. And those 30 formulas, I teach them in a 50-hour class.

It takes 50 hours to tell them. It's what I do here; the Nouveau Clown Institute does that. I was diagnosed with cancer nine years ago. They gave me three years to live. I told myself I gotta get this school together. It's the highest level of education for clowns.

And the thing is, it's not about being the greatest clown, it's not about being famous, it's about communication. It's not about bringing attention to yourself; it's about bringing attention to the world of the clown. And that's why we create families. Every family is connected.

I can use the formulas. It's not because I'm doing something good, it's just because I know how simple it is.

Clown theory is my class. I teach absolutely nothing. All I do is open the door to things you forgot. We're so conditioned. We're so fucked up. I'm still too. We're not born competitive, jealous, worrying about money, all these things trap you.

I had this moment of inspiration by being mechanical, and started to watch people. I realized people don't know what they're doing; they don't even know how to walk. People can't slow down. They're mechanical.

Every clown in our family is great, we're all equals. Symbolically we're all walking on a mountain, different ways, no way is the wrong way, I'll see you at the top. We have two things in common, heart and mind; the rest of it we do it our own way. We share everything we know, what we've learned, with anybody who wants to learn.

Clown is the greatest act in the world. The definition of clown has been so prostituted, so fucked up, when I say clown, I mean I can do anything.

If I can do anything from clown, I'd like to show people what they forgot.

I wrote 146 shows for myself.

I spent 16 years learning to be a clown. Nobody showed me. I made a lot of mistakes.

I was doing 300 shows a year. I did 12 shows in one week. All different.

Suddenly I went, "I'm there. I'm a clown." I was 36. I started at 20. A clown can do anything, anytime, anywhere, for anyone. And that week I suddenly realized I did all that stuff. I played for everyone, for a methadone clinic, for the Rolling Stones, backstage. It's about change. The moment people talk about competing, real clown is not a competition with anybody, it's a warrior. From then on I looked for risk – risk is one of the formulas. When you stop risking, you're not part of the family.

I tell people, "Steal. Steal from everybody, because nothing's original." And this puts a bad taste in people's mouths. I say steal it, don't copy it, steal it. It's *how* you do it. I studied all the English, the Italian clowns, the Indians, it's all our background. People steal from me now. People need help to sustain our profession, to make it grow. I've been doing my show for 45 years all over the world where people don't speak English, and I speak English.

Now I direct women, because they're emotional people. We put women in this bad position, when in reality, and I've been with 400 women in my life, I treated them bad, and I went back and I apologized, and love is all there is to life. And I create love. Clown is love, clown is affection, clown is global hugging. Old hippie, I'm a hippie. I'm not a hippy, I was, still have long hair.

Best thing to do, touch a student, say, think about why God put your eyes in the front of your head. Think of where you're going, not where you been.

People take care of me, because I've done a lot. And you are what you've done. And you've only got one moment. Don't waste your life.

You coming in here isn't easy for me. Spread the word.

Here's an exercise: smile for one minute, then okay, stop. "Ohh my face hurts," one minute, one minute. You think you're happy? If your face hurts in one minute, what the fuck are you doing your whole life? And that's why we get sick. Every day smile for one minute. See what happens. You will discover a new life.

11 Peter Shub

Figure 10 Peter Shub. Photo by Tofaan Hashemi

Peter Shub (born in Philadelphia, 1957) studied with mime master Etienne Decroux and clown genius Philippe Gaulier in Paris, France. He has performed and toured with Circus Roncali, the Big Apple Circus, and Cirque du Soleil. He was awarded the Silver Clown at the 1993 Monte-Carlo International Circus Festival. Recently, he performed his solo clown show *Vestiaire Non Surveillé* at the Off Avignon Festival in Avignon, France.

I met Peter in his apartment during the run of his show in Avignon. (EL)

Origins

EL: What was your first experience of clowning or circus?

Peter: In New York, going with my parents to the Ringling Brothers Barnum & Bailey Circus. I didn't like it so much. There was too much going on. I think what I liked most were the toys you could buy that glowed in the dark, and popcorn and candy – I loved that. My parents were more enthusiastic about the show – the trapeze, and even the clowns. It was the furthest thought from any of our minds that I would one day end up being a clown. I think in their minds I was headed toward medical school or to become a lawyer like my brother. It was by accident that I ended up playing in the circus. I never had any dreams to run away with the circus. Actually I didn't like it that much. I preferred conventional theater.

EL: Did you have exposure to other kinds of performance as a child?

Peter: Yeah, my mom loved theater, so she would take me to children's theater. Every weekend I saw something, and she tried to encourage me to join a theater group, but I was too shy, and too introverted, so I never did that kind of thing. I was a swimmer, and a tennis player, and I played guitar. I didn't like group activities. Too introverted. I was beaten up a lot at school. I don't know what it was – maybe they didn't like the way I dressed, or perhaps it was because I was a Jew in a Polish neighborhood. So I was fast, and I was conditioned to run away. I ran track in school. I wanted to be a fireman when I was a kid. I was fascinated by it. I loved the fire engines. For me that was more exciting than the circus. But I knew that in the end I would probably just stand there in a fireman's outfit watching the house burn down. I'd be too scared. I was terrified of fire. "Why don't you guys go in there? I'll take care of the water."

EL: Were there any performers in your family?

Peter: My grandfather was a violin player and accordion player, so he would play at parties, and he was a good joke teller, but he never did it commercially. He always had the same joke. It became funny to hear him tell the same joke over and over again. We knew it was coming, and it was lovely actually. You let someone who loves being in the spotlight do the same thing over and over again – as long as they do it with passion.

EL: Can you tell me the joke?

Peter: It's a well-known joke about two Jewish guys who find out that Hitler is going to drive down a certain street. So they decide to hide in a corner, and when he drives down the street they're going to kill him. They wake up at 6 a.m. because they know he's coming in the morning. They hide out, and its 6:30 and Hitler hasn't shown up, and then it's seven o'clock, it's eight o'clock, nine o'clock, ten o'clock, he hasn't shown up. Eleven o'clock, they're getting nervous, and at finally two o'clock, he still hasn't shown up, and so one Jew turns to the other Jew and says, "I hope he's okay." That's the joke. *[Laughter.]* You haven't heard that before?

EL: No, I haven't. That's a good joke.

Peter: I wish my grandfather was alive. I'd call him and tell him someone hasn't heard that joke.

EL: So you liked to do things alone.

Peter: I was in a rough neighborhood; as I said, I got beaten up a lot. I loved plays and I loved television. I loved the Three Stooges. I wasn't a big fan yet of the classic silent comedians, that didn't come until I got into theater, and really I didn't care about Charlie Chaplin. He didn't touch me. I liked the Marx Brothers more, and the Three Stooges. They were my idols. I loved those shows. And Jerry Lewis.

Inspirations

EL: At what point did you become interested in being a performer?

Peter: I was studying sociology at Temple University in Philadelphia, and during the last year of school, to supplement my income, I became a tour guide at the university. I pushed myself to do that because I am very shy and I wasn't good in front of groups of people. My roommate had this job, and she said, "Just try it." So I tried it and I got the job. I would meet incoming and transfer students. Every week it was a couple of hundred, and I would show them how to get around the university. So I was in the spotlight. That was my stepping stone to being in front of people. It was nice to be telling people what to do rather than being told what to do. I liked that. And then one day I was walking around Philadelphia on the pedestrian walkway, and I saw a magician doing some tricks. It was incredible. I loved it right away. He was doing these close-up tricks. He was making this red silk disappear. He had these sponge balls that would disappear, reappear, and he would captivate 50 people in 15 minutes. I loved the tricks and I loved that whole process of stopping strangers and creating what we call an audience. (I don't know what the definition of an audience is, one person or two people?) This guy had 50 or 60 people. I loved that there was a wall of these people who were interested in what he was doing. No one was telling them to stay, but they wanted to. And you could hear their reaction, of course. They were laughing and applauding. Maybe applauding is something we learn to show our appreciation, but laughter is an instinct. It made me realize they felt good. You can't laugh unless you're feeling good. He was doing magic and comedy, and it was amazing. Then the best thing was that he got paid for it. He would pass his hat and collect it. I counted: it was always between 30 and 50 dollars. Because people were immersed in what he was doing. So I watched him for hours that day, and he realized that I was watching him. We started to talk a little bit, and I asked him, "How do you do that trick?" He said, "Can you keep a secret?" I said, "Yes." He said, "Me too." Ha! Nice set up! So I asked him to teach me, and he said, okay, for a hundred dollars he would teach me some of his tricks, and tell me what books to read. That was a fortune to me. But I was so into it, I took out my life savings, and three hours later I could make a cigarette disappear in my hand, and I knew some basic magic tricks. What he didn't realize was how ambitious I was. Chris Capark, that was his name, Chris Capark. He must have really influenced me. I ran into the magic shop and I said, "Do you know Chris Capark?" Of course. "Give me his tricks. I want the silk. I want the balls. I want the rings." And he said, "Look kid, you can't do this act." And I said, "Look, you're a salesman. You can't tell me what I should do, now give it to me. Are you going to sell it to me?" He said, "Actually I'm not, because Chris is a friend of mine, and if you're going to go and rip his act off I'd rather not." I liked his integrity. He was a good man. I said: "I'm going to buy his tricks and do them my way. Does that work?" So he took my money and gave me the tricks, and, like an idiot, I started to do my show a few yards away from Chris. Chris had to stop his show in the middle, come down, and say, "What are you doing?" And I said, "I want to play." And he said, "Do you not understand? It's a territorial thing. You don't do my numbers, and you don't invade my space. Or wait until I'm finished." (Can you understand now why I was beaten up in school?) So I narrowly avoided getting beaten up, and I learned to wait my turn. He had a prime spot. I started to learn about playing the street, away from cars, the right background. I listened to his advice. He watched me and even helped me to do what I was doing. Sometimes you have to copy the best guys, the great ones, and get it in your body and mind. Then you have to change it, or you get a reputation for stealing material, and not being original. That's a whole other topic that I hope you ask me about later.

In ten minutes I was making more money than in a day at the university. I told my mother, "I'm going to play on the street tomorrow." My mother said, "No you're not; we're paying for your education. Working on the street is begging." I said, "No, it's performing. There's a distinction, and I'm proud." My mother watched me with tears in her eyes. She was very uncomfortable. A nice Jewish boy goes to law school. Her Jewish boy worked the streets and moved to Germany.

I performed. I couldn't stop. It was so much fun. It got me in trouble though. I applied to a fraternity, a German one, because I couldn't believe the Germans would hate me just because I'm Jewish. I wanted to prove that wasn't true. And I got in. First Jewish guy in the German fraternity, but they threw me out after I started performing, because the fraternity is about one for all, all for one, and that wasn't me. I was out performing for myself. I was doing bar mitzvahs. Then I was hired by an outdoor market to play on the weekends. I met these two guys – one's a juggler and one's a musician – they say, "Hi, we're Penn and Teller, we perform here, and now we're sharing the space with you because we have to." And they went away for one weekend, and I stole Penn's ring routine, and people were laughing, and I was making money. They came back and said, "We heard you were doing our routine. Peter, if you were not our friend we would break your legs. You can't do that. How ridiculous. You think we won't find out? They're our fans." But they were laughing. They said, "Don't do our stuff. Do your own stuff." My own stuff? I didn't believe that I could develop my own stuff. I was just doing it by accident. It was my hobby.

But I got better and better, and little by little I discovered my own stuff, by accident. I would forget a prop, and people would laugh. I had a way to meet people now. After a show everyone wants to meet the performer. I was 19 years old, and I took a backpack and traveled through Europe. I went to 12 different countries, and paid for it myself; I started with $300, and came back after four months with $2,000.

I went back to school and completed my studies, regretting I hadn't studied theater. After I finished I went to Switzerland, and I worked really hard performing on the street. It was a beautiful time. I saved enough money to live in Paris, so I went there to study with Marcel Marceau. But by the second day, I'd started talking to performers. René Bazinet, in particular. And I realized I shouldn't go to Marceau, I should go to Lecoq. But I didn't have money to go to Lecoq, so I went to study with Etienne Decroux for three years instead.

During that time I hardly learned French. Decroux hated that, but he moved me up through his three levels. It was incredible, like studying mathematics with Einstein. I loved it. It was the first time I was excited about education. Every Friday night we came to the school where he would lecture about the philosophy of theater. He would come and say, "Any questions?"

I met other mimes. I met Daniel Stein. He influenced me a lot. Decroux taught me all about technique, and Daniel taught me how to play with it. I didn't feel free to move on stage until I met Decroux. And it wasn't until I met Philippe Gaulier that I learned how to be ridiculous, how to find the joy to be an idiot on stage, which totally contradicted the style of Decroux and Daniel Stein. I realized there are no rules to creation. Each time you write a show, there are no rules. It's up to you. You can borrow from different art forms. My goal was to be an entertainer. So I was free to mix styles. I took a lot from mime and pantomime. I took some ideas from other artists. I changed it. I faked it until it became me.

EL: Was there a time when you felt you were doing clown?

Peter: First, when I was in mime school, I wanted to be a serious actor. I wanted to do Shakespeare in a different way, that kind of thing. But most of the time when I was on stage people laughed at me. Because I would forget choreography. I would forget a lot of things. Forgetting, you look like an idiot. But I represented everybody, because we all have flaws, and I guess that's what comedy is, showing what it is to be honest, an honest way of showing what it is to be human. So I stepped away from wanting to be a serious actor, and moved into comedy. People had asked me before, was I a mime? I wasn't a mime. I was just performing on the street without talking because I didn't know what to say. But that's not mime. And that's a misconception generally, if you perform silent you're a mime, or if you put on a red nose and big shoes you're a clown. Of course you need a lot more than that, you need about seven years of studying. I think to be an artist you need seven years. In fact there are so many bad clowns because of that assumption. Someone puts on a red nose, and everyone gets a bad reputation.

EL: Why seven years?

Peter: If you look at most of the artists who are great, they have told me it takes seven years to gain a base. I hate to say it, but there's no shortcut. You have to do the work. Clothes do not make the clown. You have to experience life, and have ideas, and build technique. The best clowns today, besides being clowns, they are very good actors. So every good clown is first a very good actor. It doesn't work the other way that every good actor is first a good clown.

EL: So you were in Paris.

Peter: I kept getting hired as a comedian. Roman Polanski hired me one year to work with him because he saw me performing on the street. So I auditioned, and I got the job as a servant in the play *Amadeus*, and we performed it in the oldest theater in Paris, on the Champs Elysées. So my schedule was full. In the morning I worked with Decroux; in the afternoon I went to the opposite side of the world of theater to study with Gaulier; then in the evening I worked with Roman Polanski. What an honor. Plus I had a rich girlfriend. There I was riding my unicycle on the Champs Elysées from one place to the next.

Techniques

EL: How do you build a show?

Peter: By finding the game between me and the audience. If you see my show, it is an accumulation of games that I enjoy playing, and that have survived over the last 35 years. So is it the same show? Yes and no. Some things I've been doing since before you were born, and some things are a few days old. Here in Avignon I start the show lighting a match and I end the show lighting a match. That developed a few days ago. That's the fun. No one has the right to tell me how I do theater. If they don't like the idea that something has been in the show for 30 years, sorry, go next door. It works for me. And I'll keep doing it as long as it's fun. If you don't have fun the audience will feel it, and won't like you. They'll eat you, and I don't want to be eaten. I enjoy being on stage with my ideas, in the moment, looking for the game of the moment. And the audience will tell you. They suggest something, and you play off it. The last few months I've enjoyed playing with the sounds of the audience. The most common sound is coughing, they go "ugh, ugh." It's an international phenomenon. I try to find the minimum I need to elicit laughter. You need technique and ideas, and you marry them on stage.

EL: How did you develop the coat hanger bit?

Peter: I was in Freiberg a couple years ago at a showcase. There were a lot of people there, and I knew half the people, a lot of friends, people who knew my show. So I didn't want to do the same show. I was backstage, three minutes before I had to go on. There was a coat hanger there, and I asked the people backstage if I could use it. I took it on stage, hanging myself on it, rolling myself in, and it got immediate laughter. I buttoned my button, and, hanging too heavy, I broke the button. My head fell. It got big laughter. I didn't know why they were laughing. Later my manager told me how it looked. So I played with this for a few minutes, and kept it. Developed it. It's a dance. I have music, choreography. This is how I have created 80 percent of what I do, by accident. Putting myself in a room with objects, not trying to be funny. When I try to be funny I'm not. I put myself in a universe with no conflict, no problems, and do one simple process, like hang a coat on a coat rack, but there's just one problem: I'm still in the coat. I try to be boring. Funny things happen by accident.

EL: You wanted me to ask you about originality and stealing. What about this duality of it being important to take from the best and make it your own, but also to discover by accident?

Peter: I don't like it when people take things from my show, especially things that I've taken from other people. That'll read nice. I think I have a reputation for taking stuff, and I think many artists do that. Most won't admit it. I think if you take something from someone else, you're saying you really love what this other person is doing. It affected you. But you shouldn't, because you ruin it for that person in a way. You ruin the surprise. If you tell the joke too many times to the same audience, they're not gonna laugh anymore. Which is true and it isn't true. I do a lot of things in my show people have seen many times, and they come to see those things. If I change a lot, they ask for the old things. Sometimes we laugh even when there's no surprise, when we know what's going to happen. We wait for that moment, and we expect it, and we want our expectation to be satisfied. That's one theory; another theory is of course you break the expectation – that's the formula for comedy. That's the beautiful thing about comedy, you can't nail it down. There are no guarantees. You don't know if something's funny until you play for an audience. How do you know if you're funny? If people laugh. And if they don't laugh, that can be funny too.

There are a few ideas in my show I've taken from other artists. There's one from Kenny Raskin, who deserves a lot of credit. There's a number with an invisible man. I was invited to the West Virginia Mime Festival, and in the evening following my performance, there was a performance where I saw Kenny Raskin. I was sitting next to a woman, and we were both amazed by him. I took this idea, and later developed this routine, and she did too, the woman sitting next to me. She did it with magic. I didn't catch up with her until 15 years later, or with Kenny until 20 years later. He had heard that she and I were doing his number, and he wasn't too happy about it. I heard that Kenny once said that he liked the way I was doing it. I didn't call to confirm that, but I like to think it's true, because I changed it. I think I own it now.

I think it's pretty amazing how successful I've been with the combination of my own stuff and the stuff from other people. I guess I'm lucky I'm still alive.

EL: *[Laughs.]* It all goes back to grade school.

Peter: It all goes back to the fact that I'm a fast runner.

EL: What does it mean to fail?

Peter: On stage, in a theater, I think you want to be vulnerable and stupid. With your pleasure to be stupid. Not embarrassed to be an idiot. A little bit dumb, loveable, naïve, and warm. (In the real world you don't want to be stupid.) It's your reaction to failure that tells us a lot about your humanity. Do you run away from that failure to something you know works to make people laugh? Ultimately, I think you have to do that, because if you stay in the failure too long we'll feel sorry for you. And we don't want to feel sorry for someone too long. We want to see someone in the shit, to see that something you thought was funny was not funny, and in that moment we want to see how you get out of it. Do you feel sorry for yourself because the joke didn't work? That reaction tells us a lot about you as a person or a clown. I say person or clown, because you can choose to play yourself, or you can make an intentional step aside to play another character.

EL: Yesterday there was a moment you mentioned to me.

Peter: There was a moment with a music box. It's the only instrument I know how to play. I play it like I'm really proud to play it. I stand up to get applause, and yesterday there was no applause. So I sat down. It wasn't played properly.

Not to say it should have worked, but just that the timing was off. If it's not done in the right way, it doesn't get the result. In that moment when I played the song and no one laughed, it created a certain tension. It's my job to relieve their tension so we can breathe again, and we can go on with the show. If I don't handle it right, you're not going to trust me, and it will be more difficult to go on and have fun. It got too heavy. My comedy is light. I was in the shit. It didn't work. I sat down. I knew the next thing would get a laugh, and I'd be rescued, but I didn't want to be rescued so fast. So I sat and I breathed. Breathing is important, because if I don't breathe I'll get tense, and the public emulates the actor on stage. If I'm smiling, an internal smile, they're smiling too. If I don't breathe, they don't breathe. In a moment of tension, we stop breathing. In that moment, I just had to exhale, and they did too. It wasn't the funniest moment, but we had an unspoken negotiation that we could continue with the fun.

You have to love your audience. "Go politely through life," Decroux used to say. If someone yawns, don't be defensive, instead, think, "Oh you're tired, let me get you a pillow." Be naïve.

Philosophy

EL: When your son died, and then you started to work again, what changed?

Peter: I realized that even with the deepest pain, you can still come back. It made me more sensitive to the moments of life, because you know life, like a candle, can blow out from one moment to the next. I was with my son having a pizza, and at the end of the pizza, he wasn't there anymore.

I started to appreciate the moment. Everyone says that, but I experienced that myself, to be in the moment with people you love, to cherish it. I wanted to express it to the world at first, but you know who cares about my suffering less than me? Everyone. No one says life is going to be easy, and everyone overcomes hardships. I wanted to put it in my show, but that's not fair in a way. People are not coming for my personal tragedies. If you feel too much sympathy for someone, it doesn't work. I couldn't find a way, until one day I did. And for me it's cathartic. Long story long, I was walking in the woods with my son Luca, and he said to me, "Poppy, what happens when you die?" He was four years old. "If you die, what happens to me?" I just wanted a nice light walk. So I said, "If I die what happens to you? You go to mommy." He said, "What if mommy dies?" I said, "If mommy dies, you go to grandpa and grandma." "And what if … " So I said, "Luca, you know, it's all going to be okay." "But I don't want you to die, poppy." "I'm not gonna die." We were walking, and I could feel he didn't like my answer. Then I tried again. "You know what? You see the leaves, how they're moving in the wind? If I die … " – as a father, I wasn't really confident in what was coming out of my mouth, but I thought "Let's see what happens" – "If I die, you come back to the woods here, and when you see the leaves waving, that's me. That's my soul, my spirit, waving to you. So you can always find me in the woods." He was looking at the trees and he was smiling, and I thought, "That's wisdom. I did right as a father." I couldn't know that six months later he would die. The night he died I couldn't sleep, I went into the forest, and I watched the leaves. Even now, in a naïve way, I look at a tree, and what makes those leaves move? I think, he's here. I wanted to take it on stage, so at the end of my show, I wave. Because I didn't get to say goodbye to him. And some religions stipulate that we're all connected. So if that's true, if we're all connected, if Luca exists in each person, I wave to each person until the last one who leaves. That way I get to wave to him.

Laughter and comedy should not involve pain. It is a celebration of joy. And here I am dealing with this experience, and I like that very much.

When I did my first show after he died, it was the first time I put that pain out of mind. Just to find the game of the moment, to be in the present moment. I was able to have fun again. In tragic moments we feel comedy or humor is taboo, and I think that's wrong – I think it can be the best medicine.

EL: Do you think that's the role of the clown?

Peter: I know most clowns think it's important to have clowns. I sometimes think clowns are a luxury, but it's nice to have them around. Would we survive without them? It's in us to find comic moments in life. We need to laugh. It's part of us. You take the clown away, then the clown in you comes out. There's a clown in each person that's dormant. You see a clown on stage and think that's special. That's only because you don't listen to your own clown. You haven't brought that to the surface, and you're happy someone else is doing that job for you.

Are clowns special people? Or is every person a special clown? You need people like me who help bring these questions to the surface. To find what is inside each person.

The role of the clown is to keep people laughing.

To clown is to have hope that things will end the way you want them to. You hope to get the girl in the end. You hope that you will be loved. I think love is important for the clown. He steps on stage and wants nothing more than to be loved by his audience. Without his audience, he doesn't exist.

I don't think clowns are so necessary. Comedy is what's important. In any group of two or more people, we always look for the laughter. Laughter is very important for groups. You don't need to go to school to learn that.

12 David Konyot

Figure 11 David Konyot. Photo by Andrew Payne

David Konyot (born in London, England, 1947) is from two of Europe's famous circus families, the Konyots and the Fossets. He was brought up in show business, working as a song and dance man in the '60s. He quickly established a successful career in variety and cabaret until in 1972 he starred in London's West End in the long-running hit comedy *Pyjama Tops*. Moving back into circus in the mid-1970s, he became one of the top ringmasters in Europe. In 1981 he combined the role of ringmaster with the role of the white-faced clown in Germany's Circus Barum. Since 1985 he has led his own musical comedy act and is also an innovative and award-winning reprise clown.

David talked with me in his London home. (EL)

Origins

Circus comes from two sides of my family. The English side goes back about 700 years. The German side, the Konyot side, my mother's side, which is a Hungarian family, goes back to the mid-1600s with credible evidence. My great-grandmother on this Hungarian side was a Blumenfeld, which is one of the biggest German circuses, and we traced her back to Emanuel Blumenfeld, who was a wandering vagabond and jester in the seventeenth century. And then sometime in the early 1700s another Blumenfeld had six elephants in Würzburg. So we know the history of the family. I was the first one to come out of the family and get a job in what we call "city street," a private job.

My father was a brilliant clown, but bringing up kids ... Not his forte. My parents divorced when I was 14, and my mother sent me to boarding school, which I ran away from. And where did I run? To a circus! My uncle's circus, a little circus in Wales. Had two horrendous years. My father was a very good animal trainer, elephants especially, so it was immediately assumed that I knew everything about elephants. So there I was aged 15, supposedly training this elephant in a little circus in Wales. Elephant knew more than me, I have to say. That lasted a year and a bit.

I'd never thought of doing comedy, and apart from my father we had no history of clowning in the family. They'd all been riders or acrobats or circus directors, but it had always been the serious side. Comedy had never been part of me, and I don't think I was particularly funny at school. I wasn't the typical thing: "I was bullied at school, so I made everybody laugh ... " I *was* bullied, mind you, I was little, and from the circus. In the playground I got the living bejeezus kicked out of me because I was different. But I don't remember being a Woody Allen, being funny to get out of a tough situation.

At 15 I left my uncle's circus, went back to London, found my mother, and decided I was never, ever going to work in circus again. I left for ten years. Went into theater, went to stage school. Again, not a thought in my head about doing comedy. I'd discovered books, and I read everything I could. John O'Hara and Steinbeck and Shakespeare ... I'd read the back of a cereal packet. It just absolutely got me. Went to dancing school, got a partner, did a dancing act. Our first date was the Palladium in Edinburgh in the variety show. We were a song and dance act. But I also got dragged into doing parts in the comedy scenes and was told that I had perfect timing. I still wasn't that bothered. But after six weeks of six different shows, there were maybe 12 or 13 different comedy things I was involved in. Still, I was more interested in the song and dance thing. I wanted to do that.

There was Roy Castle, and, of course, Sammy Davis. They were my two idols because they did everything. I saw Sammy Davis do the gun-spinning routine with the greatest line of all time: "If I wasn't good at it, I wouldn't do it." Yes! So I started to learn gun-spinning. I shamelessly copied everybody I could find. And I did impressions. Again, not comedy, just voices and actions. In 1966 I went to Morecambe for a summer season on the end of the pier in a theater, and, again,

I got involved in the sketches there, but not as a comic, just as a feed. At the end of that season we split up the dancing act, and I went out on my own as a singer, playing guitar, singer-impressionist, tap dancer. Soon found out that when you work the nightclubs in England you have to do 45 minutes. Well I wasn't a good-enough singer or guitar player to do 45 minutes, so I started putting gags in to fill up time. And I realized that what I'd been told about timing was right. It was just … The timing was there. I knew how to hit the punchlines. I could deliver a gag properly, without stumbling, and I could self-edit in my head. If the audience changed, so did I.

So over the next, I suppose eight to ten years, I carried on. Gigging in clubs, big nightclubs. I was part of a whole generation. Some of whom are now hugely famous in television and theater. In a way, we changed comedy. We got away from mother-in-law jokes. We started doing stream-of-consciousness – way before the '80s when it became the next big thing. I worked a lot of clubs in London, did some television, ended up in a show called *Pyjama Tops* in the West End, which was wonderful. And during that time, the only contact I had with circus was a man called Michael Austin, a friend of mine who I'd grown up with. One night, I was working at the Star and Garter, a nightclub in Leicester Square, and I got a phone call. (Like, when you say you get a phone call: there were no mobile phones. This was a phone on a wall.) It was Michael. I hadn't heard from the guy for about three years, and he said, "I don't know if you're interested, but I'm taking a circus out. Want to come with us?" And I said, "No. Never going back to circus again, never gonna do it." But I did agree to go up and see him that winter. It was in Birmingham, I stayed the weekend. While I was there, the ringmaster, Michael Gordon Howes, got laryngitis, and Dicky Chipperfield said, "You're a bit of a talker. Just do the announcements because Gordon can't." So Gordon's daughter brought me out her dad's red coat, which was about three sizes too big, and handed me a microphone, and I went out and I announced the show. And it was alright. There were people there I'd known when I was a kid, and, you know, it was … alright. So I did the next two or three days. Then I went away, but I came back the following weekend because there was a girl in the show, a Hungarian girl, who I quite liked. And out of the blue, Dicky Chipperfield said, "You're good at this. Why don't you come and ringmaster for us?" And I said yes. Never hesitated. Didn't even cross my mind to say no. And that … I will never know why. But that was the decision. Totally irrational. And I keep looking back and thinking, "I've never regretted it. Ever."

I did that for six years, seven years. Working in Germany with Circus Barum, doing circus world championships, ringmastering in Holland and France. And started putting shows on, because in those days the ringmaster still put the show together. Met people who had known me when I was a kid. Even though I'd been away for ten years, it was like I'd been away for ten minutes. Nobody gave two monkeys that I'd had a hugely successful comedy and television career. Nobody gave a shit. "Oh, yeah, fine. You're back." That was it.

While I was at Circus Barum I met Francesco Caroli. We were working toge-ther in a show, and Uncle Francesco said, "You should be a white-faced clown, because you're too funny to be a ringmaster." I thought: "Yeah, right. That's what I'm gonna do. I'm gonna cover myself in sequins and white paint. Yeah ..." I wasn't crazy about house clowns. Family acts could be too old-fashioned. They'd have one that was very funny, and the rest were not. And the one who couldn't do subtle was usually the white-faced clown. But then I said, "Well, what if I sort of ringmaster and white clown together?" I'd seen Sergio do it at Monte Carlo the year before. And I thought, "We could do that." Next year we opened the show with just a pin spot on my face, as the white-faced clown, and I introduced the show in the three languages, and then the spot pulled back and I had the full ringmaster-style sequins and shit everywhere. And everyday in Germany that got a big "Oooooh" from the crowd. For the first half I ringmastered, and in the second half I put the white-face clown costume on and we did the entree. That was very successful. I got a lot of interest from other places. And finally Tony Alexis, who I'd known since he was about ten, told me "I'm gonna split with the family," because he'd married a German circus girl, "and we're gonna start a new act together. Do you wanna come with us?" And I said, "Yeah." Another spontaneous decision, just like that.

And for about two to three years we took European circus by storm. We never stopped working. We were all young, we were all cool, and we were different. I got involved in the action. I didn't just stand there in the white face looking good. We did karate! And then it went to Tony's head a bit. We were the Tony Alexis Trio, which I'd agreed to, but after we became very successful, he had a new prop made and it said "Tony Alexis and Company." And I said "Woah! Part of being a trio, I don't mind, but I ain't 'and company!'" So there was a difference of opinion and we split. And then I got the Cardinalis, the two boys Francisco and Negliomo. We teamed up and went to Hong Kong for Gerry Cottle and we did *Island*, and around then I thought, "This isn't going anywhere. I could be a jobbing white clown, but nah – I don't want to." So I got my own act together. Awful makeup. Awful costumes, by nowadays standards. But it lasted a couple of years and it was successful. By that time I could play about 14 or 15 instruments and I had my knowledge of comedy that I could build into any act, so it always worked, but to varying degrees of satisfaction for me. And then in the early '90s I started working with my current partner, and she pushed me in a different direction. Very clever. She saw something in me that I hadn't seen. "No, try it that way. Try it that way. Change the costume." Thanks to her, the costumes became a lot more classy. We got rid of the wigs. We got rid of all the gags that everybody else was doing – the hairy legs and the crying eyes and all this stuff that traditional clown acts did – and we went in a totally different direction. The act became a lot less prop-oriented and a lot more character-oriented. By that time – this was early '90s – I'd seen Peter Shub, I'd seen David Shiner, I'd seen a lot of these solo clowns and thought, "That is just so cool." So I tried to get my own style, and we've been doing it since then. We had four years in Norway, five years in Ireland, three years with Zippos ... Everywhere we go we end up staying. But it's always fun trying to find something new. You never stop learning. Much to my wife's annoyance. It's like stand-up. You have the order of your gags, and you'll find something new, and you go, "I like that. That's funny. Put it in there." Brilliant. Gets a laugh. Now, most people would leave it at that. Not me. "Take it out. Try it there. Works! Not as well? Okay, put it back. Try it there. Oh, it works better there." I'm constantly messing. And her biggest complaint with me, she says, "You do a gag, and it gets brilliant laughs, and then you never do it again!" I say, "No, but I can always go back to it!" It's that thing of constantly changing, constantly improving, constantly putting a new gag in, and once you've got one that works, put it in the library. It might come out a year later. I did one two days ago that I hadn't done for about three years, but suddenly – it was right, the time was right, bang. Out it came, out of the library, I did it. That's the fun of it. Every day I say, "What can I do today? What can I get up to?"

Inspirations

My father. When I think of clown, I think of my father. When he went in the ring, woah. The guy was magic. And I see a lot of me in him, the actions in my memories. I just remember him being funny and inventive, and it was an amazement to me that it was so different from the man I knew outside. Here's a little philosophical psychology – I think maybe I wanted him to treat me the way he treated the audience. Because he treated the audience beautifully. Very, very good clown. Maybe, I don't know, I've never thought of that before.

Influences, not so much. Nobody that I've really copied. There are people that I like, but nobody I've really copied. Thinking about Slava – I've seen his work, and I go, "Woah. I couldn't do that." That slow, that patient, that takes some balls. Jigalov, excellent. David Larible, some of the stuff he does, very good. There's an Englishman over here called Tweedy, worked with Ringling Brothers with me. He is sensational, off the wall. He's got a pet iron called Keith. He drags the iron around on a lead, and it's just so surreal, you know? I think if anything, it would be the Monty Python influence. Coming out of left field, I try to do that more than traditional clowning. I like to reference everything. With a big clown act, I reference anything from the Teletubbies to Aida or Rigoletto, Elvis Presley … A lot of it is very, very Monty Python. I love Billy Connolly. Ya know? This guy, he thinks sideways. And that's what, in a weird way, that's what I try to do in the clowning. I try to think a little bit laterally. Don't go there because everybody goes there – try something different.

My wife and I disagree violently on Chaplin. But you know, that's me. When they said Chaplin did a hundred takes, I wanna see the first one because I guarantee the first one was the funny one. After that it was all fine-tuning. "Oh, maybe the arm should be there instead of there, maybe the head should turn … " No! The first one, that's the funny one. That's the one that comes from the heart, and that's the one you do.

I laugh at different people. I love Jigalov, who's absolutely mad, but I know somebody who works with him who says he's a fanatic. He stands in front of a mirror and practices each thing. I don't do that. I don't practice. I don't rehearse. I was driving to a show with my wife's cousin one year, who's a very good clown, and in the car on the way he's going, "What do we do?" and I say, "Don't worry about it. Just follow me. You'll know what to do." You know? I can't rehearse. I just go, "I'll do that." I don't know if it's adrenaline or what it is, but it's as soon as I walk on, I'm not nervous, which has always frightened me. Never, ever been nervous. I hear people say, "Oh I throw up," and I can't wait to get on. It's like an adrenaline rush. So far, I can't remember being outrageously wrong. I know what to do. Whether that's institutional memory, whether that's generational, whether that's nature or nurture, I honestly don't know. But the day that fails me, that's when I'm gonna give up because then it becomes hard work.

Techniques

I always say, "Let me go out first. I'll do a warm-up gag." I do a conductor gag which I try every circus I go to. We're working with Charles Knie this winter, and I'm gonna try and do it there. I did it with Barum last year, two years ago. Every show I'm on I want the first five minutes. Give me the audience for the first five minutes. After that, we're away. Because I can judge it, and I also know when to come out and go, "Okay people. Roller skates on. Put the foot on the pedal." That's when they're not interested, they're there for different reasons, or it's too hot or whatever. I don't try to change an audience. They've come for whatever reason they've come for. If they've come to be entertained, we'll entertain them. If they've come just to sit down and get out of the hot sun then we'll do what we've gotta do. I don't force it.

The act is different every day. It is. That depends solely on the audience. The timing might be different, one part of the act might be more emphasized than the other. It starts off with a traditional opening. Me and my daughter – she's in it now – play "Hello Dolly" on the saxophone and the trumpet, which is the traditional "Here come the musical clowns." After that, the traditional stuff goes out the window because that's when my wife and I start with what's basically a double act, which goes for about five or six minutes. We do a lot of talking in it, but if we're abroad, we'll cut it down to a lot more mime. Then it becomes a whole bit with the instruments, in and out, in and out with the different instruments. My daughter interrupting on the drum. That turns into about eight minutes of total mayhem. Then it settles down again, and we go into a little sort of mini routine, and then it's the finale. And the structure has always been the same. The gags change. How we do it changes, where we do it changes.

I'm not so keen on clowns who take people out of the audience. That's the worst thing. If you're taking somebody out of the audience to make you funny, give them half your wages. Saw a circus last year in England that had two clowns. Both very good, very well-known clowns who obviously didn't get on because they did nine reprises between them, and out of the nine reprises, for eight of them they took people out of the audience. I don't like taking people out of the audience and making them look silly, and if I see one more clown bring four chairs in the ring and sit four guys in it and take the chairs away, I will probably go and buy myself a gun and become a sniper. Because it's just horrible. Whose was that originally? Whoever did it originally did it better.

We've died a couple of times, but I tend to be very analytical about it. I don't expect too much from an audience. I don't go out expecting to be brilliant. I'll go out and do what I've gotta do. Although there is something I've wanted to do for years. Backstory to this: years ago Barbra Streisand was in *Funny Girl* at the Prince of Wales Theatre in London, and I went to see it with my aunt. And there's a scene where she auditions and she sings off key, and for a singer to sing off key purposely is bloody near impossible. But she did it. And the woman in the row behind us said, "Well, I don't think much of this Streisand woman. She can't sing in tune." And I thought, "Well, in the context of not getting the gag, kiddo, you just got 10 out of 10." But it led me to thinking, and over the years I've pondered, "I wonder if I could go on and purposely not be funny?" I've talked about this with my brother. Because the thing we want to do is write a sort of sociological paper about circus audiences. What makes a good audience? How, why do audiences become a living organism? In our last show, I did the warm-up trying to remind people that they are in a live show. They're not sitting in front of their televisions. They're not playing their Xbox. This is live. It's happening now. And what happens depends on you. The louder you clap, the more you enjoy it, the more you cheer, the better we become, because that feeds our adrenaline. So think about that. But I was wondering if there was any way I could go out and be bad with a good audience. And I've thought about it, I've talked about it with my wife, I've talked with my brother, and I don't think I could physically do it. The button would kick in. I wouldn't, I couldn't let myself do it. Of course I've died on my ass a load of times, and no excuse. (I've got a big folder that's called "Shit happens.") You're not going to be perfect. A lot of people come out and blame the audience. I'll always know if it's really the audience. There used to be an old gag, a comic would come off stage and say, "Well, they're a singer's audience." And it's true. Some circus audiences come to see the jugglers. They come to see the animals. They come to see the flying trapeze. Not everybody comes to see the clowns. Most people don't, in fact. So you've gotta do the extra mile anyway to get them on your side. Sometimes the whole show won't go well, and you go, "Ok, forget it." It happens with the biggest shows, ya know? It happens everywhere. Bad day at the office.

But now … I know it might sound terribly pompous, but I'm good enough now to know that I don't fail. I don't put myself in a situation where I can fail. I can't remember ever truly failing because I never put myself in that position … There's a lovely line in a Jack Lemmon film called *Tribute*, he's a press officer, and he gets cancer, and he talks to his son and he says, "I never had the courage to fail." And that's always haunted me. I've never put myself in a situation where failure was a probability. Having the courage to fail. I love that line. I often think to myself, "Have I cheated myself in a way by not putting myself there?" But I look back at what I've done and I go: "I've done quite a bit." I've done more than most clowns have done. And I've diversified in a lot of ways.

Should I have pushed myself further? I don't know. I really don't know.

Philosophy

Most important thing in the world? Not the nose, not the makeup, the humor …
It's the court jester. You are the one who's allowed to comment. You are the one
who's allowed to criticize. You are the little boy who tells the emperor he's got no
clothes on. Every society has to have that, and every society does. In the old days
it was the witch doctors or the shamans who did it, not necessarily with humor,
but somebody has to tell the truth. The English kings always had a jester that was
allowed to tell them the truth. They were obliged to tell them the truth. They
would dress it up with a cap and bells and be funny, but there was always the barb
at the end. And everybody had to have that. Every society needs it desperately.
Even China's got clowns. Totally different. I mean, they're very old-fashioned.
We worked in Hong Kong, and they like bangs and falling on your bum and
throwing water about. They're into that. Not very good with subtle stuff. But
every society – it's the release! The funniest, the greatest, *the* greatest line I ever
heard – and it's one that I quote and I have in the back of my head all the time –
Jack Benny said it. He was on an interview show over here. He was being interviewed by one of our best interviewers, a man called Michael Parkinson, who
said, "Mr. Benny, I've got to ask this," he said, "because if I don't, it wouldn't be
right," he said, "but it's the crassest question you're ever going to be asked: What
is the secret of comedy?" And Jack Benny said, "In many ways, comedy is cruelty.
Very cruel," he said, "Look," he said, "I see nothing funny in a woman walking
down the street and slipping on a banana skin and falling on her ass." Pause.
Long pause. "Unless it's a very fat woman." The pause! Benny was the only one
who could do it. I couldn't do it. Benny let that go for what must've been 20
seconds, but he was so cultured. He knew that the audience knew there was
gonna be a pearl at the end of it. So they were waiting. That timing. Normally
the timing would be 1–2–3–punchline. He let that go and go and go, and there
was this silence. And the audience knew something good was coming, and
Michael Parkinson knew something good was coming, and then, "Unless it's a
very fat woman." Woooom! Explosion of laughter. It is cruelty. Every society
needs the truth-teller. And if the truth-teller comes as a serious philosopher or as
a serious man, they won't believe him. They will believe the clown. And the
harder life gets, the more important it becomes. And I fear, on a larger scale, I
fear for the future of most Western democracies because they are forgetting their
clowns. And the clowns, or the comedians, have forgotten their role. Comedians – George Carlin, Billy Maher, Connolly – they're philosophers. I mean, if
Socrates and Aristotle and Plato were alive now they'd shove a punchline in at
the end; they'd put a gag in somewhere. You need to. Because it brings your idea
down, and it brings the people's perception up to the same level. If you quote
Hegelian philosophy at an audience one or two of them will get it. They might
appreciate it. If you do it and fall on your ass in a tub of water, the impact! "OH,
I get it now!"

That's the beauty, and that's the elegance of comedy. That wonderful, wonderful finesse of the slice with the stiletto. And it's funny, but you know it's gonna

hurt at some point because it's true. That's the deep side of it. And I suppose, I've got to this point in my life, drives my wife mad, that I keep saying, "I want to leave some sort of legacy." And she reminded me of an Irish journalist about, must be ten years ago, he said, "How many people do you think you've entertained?" And I said, "Well, I don't know. I honestly don't know." He said, "Work it out. For 45 years, you've never stopped working." And he worked out I've entertained something like 17 million people. I went, "No, no that's wrong. Go back. Do it again." He did, and he was right, and I thought that's bloody amazing. "Okay. Alright. That's not too shabby." What a thing to have done. Making all those people laugh. Not bad. Not a bad way to go.

In England, the audiences are, by numbers, not very good. We've played to 19 people and 20 and 25 people. And I learn more from that than I learn from a full house. When you've got 19 or 20, you feel more of a responsibility. They've actually come out. You really gotta work hard. And you learn more. If I've got one person laughing, then I know the rest of them are there as well. And that's lovely. That's nice. That's a nice way to be.

Comedy's going through a funny stage, I don't know. People aren't doing political comedy anymore because politics is taking over too much of your life. I remember growing up, and you voted for politicians once every five years, and then they left you alone. They don't leave you alone anymore. I look around the world, and I don't see leaders. I see men saying, "Where do you want to go? I will take you." That's not what I want. I want people to go, "We're going there. Follow me." And politics is too invasive in your life. There's too much going on in it. And too many people are getting hurt, and too many people are getting killed by it. And I don't see an end. I wish I could do more. You look at what's going on in the Middle East, you look at what's going on in the Ukraine – you can't make jokes. Not even the Woody Allen one, "Comedy is tragedy plus time." When you can't laugh at it, there's no solution. And you look at Gaza and you look at Ukraine and maybe there's never going to come a time where you're gonna be able to make a joke about it, and that's terrifying. That really is frightening. Because where are clowns and comics gonna get their material from? This is just irrational violence. And there's no funny side.

Of course clowning will survive. But I think circus in England has a problem. I think circus in England has got a shelf life of maybe another generation. The families have left. I look at my generation, the kids who were born in the circus … And I'm back in the ring, but very few others are. And the next generation down – my daughter may stay in it, but I think she's gonna go down the theatrical side. She's gonna go a different way. My other daughter's in it because she's a singing ringmistress, but she'll get married and leave. The majority of new artists are coming from circus schools, where they've learned how to do their act, but they don't learn the tradition of the act; they don't learn the history of it.

Comedy will always be there. But it will change; it will evolve. Clowning will change. There's coulrophobia now, so the clowns are putting less makeup on, which I don't think is a bad thing. I think that had to change anyway. You have to be more yourself. There will be less unfunny clowns! There are too many unfunny clowns putting makeup on and thinking they're funny. That's the biggest problem. You have loads and loads and loads of reprise clowns all over Europe, not necessarily funny. They fill the space. They fill the gaps between the acts. They're not funny. Some of them aren't anyway. So I don't know.

Again, it depends on the politics of the world. It depends how the world goes and if they have time for us. The minute they stop having time to laugh, then it gets serious. There's nobody laughing out in Gaza and nobody laughing out in the Ukraine. If the world stops laughing, then you're in trouble. Then you're in trouble.

13 Dimitri

Figure 12 Dimitri. Photo by Rémy Steinegger

Dimitri (born in Ascona, Switzerland, 1935) decided to become a clown at age seven. He appeared as Auguste with Circus Medrano in Paris with the famous white clown Maïsse. In 1959 he appeared for the first time in a program of his own, in Ascona. He soon went on tour throughout the world, including three times with the Circus Knie. In 1971, together with his wife Gunda, he founded the Teatro Dimitri in Verscio, Switzerland, and, in 1975, they opened Scuola Teatro Dimitri, a school for performing arts. He was awarded the Grock Prize in 1973, and appeared with New York's Big Apple Circus. In 1995 he was inducted into the International Clown Hall of Fame.

Dimitri sat down with me to share some stories at his theater in Verscio, Switzerland. (EL)

Origins

EL: When did you first experience clowning or circus in your life?

Dimitri: By chance my parents were artists; not in show business, but they were very open to theater, to circus. As I remember, every year I went to Circus Knie, our famous big Swiss Circus. Naturally, when I was five or six years old, I remember the animals and the atmosphere, but the greatest souvenir was when I was seven years old, when I saw for the first time, consciously, a clown, and his name was Andreff. I was so impressed by this man who could make the audience laugh, and he was a good musician, and a dancer, and a little bit of an acrobat. And I asked my father, "Does he do that all the time, a full-time job?" And my father said, "Yes, you see this man is an artist, like I am a sculptor and a painter. Many people don't know what I do the whole day, but we have to work and to practice and develop ideas. You see how this man is a musician, he has to rehearse every day. It is a profession." I said, "Wow, this is a profession, to be a clown. I want to be a clown like Andreff." This was very important for me because I had already discovered the pleasure of making people laugh – my companions, my friends, but also my parents, adults, or teachers in school (for me the biggest success was when I could make a teacher laugh). I always knew where the limit was. As a child, when you find you can make people laugh, you have the tendency not to know when to stop. But already I had this barometer that told me: "Now I'd better stop, otherwise they will not laugh anymore, but they will yell." This, for me, was the important moment. So when I was bigger I asked my parents, "I want to become a clown. How? Can I go to Russia to circus school?" And they wanted to help me to realize my big idea. This was wonderful, to be born into an artistic family.

EL: Did you find that your parents shaped your own perspective on art?

Dimitri: My parents suggested I should learn a craft profession, so I learned pottery, and I became a potter. I took an apprenticeship, but during that apprenticeship I also learned music and acrobatics and dance.

EL: What kinds of performance did you experience as a child?

Dimitri: In Ascona, where I was born, they didn't have a theater, but many tourists came there, and sometimes in a hotel they would make magic shows, and it was interesting for me to see the relationship between the audience and the magician. But also very important for me was the marionette theater. As a child I saw all these shows – my father also sculpted marionettes. For me it was fascinating to see the puppets come alive. This is an incredible phenomenon. You see a wooden head, and when you see a movement – crying, or being sad – you believe he has tears. And when he is laughing, the same. He is wooden, but your imagination can project the emotion, the sentiment, the mood. As a child I couldn't really analyze the reason I was so impressed, but later I studied the magic of the marionette, and I think the actor or even the clown can learn a lot from the marionette.

EL: When did you begin to study clown?

Dimitri: I couldn't really study clown because there were no schools for clown. But I knew for my dream of clown I needed many elements. I needed music, dance, acrobatics, puppets, eccentric juggling … So my aim was to learn as many things as possible. The clowning I learned by myself, doing little sketches. Let's say when there was a party, a birthday, I'd say, "I can make a sketch for you." Then I would study the reaction of the audience. When they were laughing I thought, "Not bad."

I invented pantomime sketches. For example, a boxing match with two people, one stronger and one weaker. This was even before I had ever seen a mime. I had heard that mimes exist who tell stories without words or objects. I thought, "I want to try that," so I invented it. I was fascinated by the idea to express myself without words.

It is still my dream of the clown that he has multiple talents. But the panorama of possibility of the clown is so big. You can be a clown on a wire, a clown without words, with words, a juggling clown, a musical clown. When I had the chance to be the student of Marcel Marceau and to be in his company, I found out what many people didn't know – he was also a very good comic, Marceau, he really had a comic talent. Even if he was a mime and had many tragic sketches, he had moments quite like a clown.

Inspirations

EL: You said Marceau and Grock became heroes for you. What about them was so magical?

Dimitri: Today I am almost 80, and my aim is just what it has always been: to be a clown. This is the motive of my life. But I thought, to be a mime, to express your feelings, to communicate without words, would be an important beginning for me. So I went to Marceau. At that time he didn't have his own school, he made individual courses lasting three months. I took one of these courses, and at the end, he said, "I need someone like you for my company because you are a good acrobat, and I want to create the pantomime *The Little Circus.*" So we made it. There were about ten people in that company, and Marceau performed with us. This period of my life was perhaps one of the most important. Imagine the show in Paris: the first part was the pantomime company; the second part was Marceau alone. I was always in the wings watching him. How did it work? How did he become such a success? How did he impress the audience so much? I wanted to understand that secret of that great genius. How did he make the audience laugh? Even now, looking back, I remember I thought it was astonishing. Without any object, any words, nothing, he could make the audience laugh. He could impress and touch them. And then one day he said, "You know Dimitri, I know you want to be a clown, even though you came to me to study pantomime. Let's be sincere and honest, like friends. You will never be a very good mime. But you will be a very good clown." When you are young, and you have an aim, a dream, and somebody like Marceau says that … For me it was the greatest day of my life!

And then Grock! Grock was my idol, my great great master. When I was 17, I saw Grock for the first time in his own tent. I was so impressed. He had an interesting system. He had no animals in his circus. He was a pioneer – this was in 1952. He had a juggler, a singer, an acrobat, comedian – no trapeze – and then the second part of the show was Grock. Always with his partner, never alone. I was so shy I couldn't even ask him for his autograph. Even now I watch the films of Grock, and although there are so many famous clowns living and working in the world, there is no one who can compare to him. Others may have specialties that may be better, but when you take the whole personality, there is no one better than Grock.

EL: Can you describe why?

Dimitri: This is a phenomena that is so difficult to explain. It's a mysterious thing. But my opinion is that Grock had this quality of naïveté, like a child, and yet at the same time he was very smart. And he had very few and simple dialogues. When the partner says, "What is your name?" He says "Jack-ck." How? "Jack-ck, with a ck-ck!" Then five minutes pass, and again he says, "Ck," and the partner says, "What was that?" And he says, "Well, I had one more." It seems so silly, but when he did that you had to laugh. It's so simple. This was for me incredible, that it is possible with such silly, simple dialogue to make the audience laugh. It was never vulgar, never primitive, it was always naïve. Then the most important thing for him was that he was a brilliant musician, really a virtuoso in piano, violin, saxophone, concertina. And many people don't know that he composed over 300 pieces of music.

Though, yes, I had the opportunity to meet all the famous clowns, Charlie Rivel, and the daughter of Fratellini. I also know some members from Cavallini. All the clowns you will have in your gallery, I know practically all of them. I like them, appreciate them.

And this is a question for you: Why are we so few? There are hundreds of thousands of pianists, and actors and dancers and musicians. Why are there so few clowns?

EL: This is your interview, not mine. But it is an interesting question. I don't think that there are necessarily so few clowns. I think there are a lot. But I think that as we go through time, how they look and where they appear changes.

Dimitri: Perhaps it is this. That's a good answer. You can also ask, why are there less women clowns? I saw Nola Rae once; she's interesting, she is poetic. Then there is Gardi Hutter. She has never been in America, but she is now very famous in Europe. She makes solo shows, and has been in Circus Knie also. She's very funny.

Techniques

EL: How do you train now as a clown?

Dimitri: The acrobatics are important. You know, when you learn this kind of discipline you have to practice every day, so this was part of my life to practice every day, the somersault. I made this until I was 55. I did it every day, practiced every day, and then one day I said, "Okay I've finished the somersault." I could do this until I'm 70, but it was a very important decision, because when I will stop to practice, I will not do it on stage, and I will not do it again. At that age, after a couple of years without practice, I will not do it again.

But then I discovered that you can easily leave the acrobatics. I move; I am still quite flexible. I do not make acrobatics, but every day I practice my physical form, my handstand. I don't use it on stage, but I do it every day because it is a good training.

This is the acrobatic part. The music part, this is known, unfortunately you have to practice otherwise it doesn't sound good. This is my daily training. Then the little moment when I am juggling with the ping pong balls, I also have to practice that.

EL: In your training, certainly there are skills – acrobatics, music, and so on. Do you feel there are other aspects, psychological or philosophical, that are important to practice in another way?

Dimitri: This is a good question. Even if I am not in a good mood to practice, I have to do it, and I do it. And every time I do it, with motivation, I have a good feeling afterwards. It is a kind of philosophy to practice, to take care of your physical form. You have to be grateful you have a body that works. You could be paralyzed or sick. When I was younger I used to think, what would I do if I was blind? Okay, I thought, it will be difficult to paint, but it will be easy to sing, or to tell stories. I like to invent stories. It's the same thing with makeup, your preparation before a show, it introduces a kind of meditation – you enter the personage, the character of the clown. These are my two important philosophic moments: practicing and training, and also getting into makeup and putting on the costume, entering the world of the clown. On stage I try to forget all the problems from my private life. I try to be better, to make the audience laugh. I am grateful and thankful I have my health, my chance, my audience, success. I never forget all the artists who are very good who don't have success. It is sad. It is a kind of destiny, but what can you do?

EL: What does it mean for you to "be better"?

Dimitri: To be better technically – to not make a mistake, to play musical instruments accurately – this is normal. But for me, it refers much more to the interior attitude. To become better is to come closer and closer to my dream about the clown. I still have a dream of a clown, a perfect clown, who is like a child. He only has to come on stage and you are touched. My dream is that the audience falls in love with the clown and has the desire to embrace him. This is also reciprocal. I can't embrace 200 people, but I can love them back. When I feel they love me too, there is a giving and taking and giving and taking. This is, for me, what it means to become better. And to fight always against routine.

It's okay to have a routine when you juggle. It has to work. When the ball falls down it is a mistake and it is not good. But my dream is to be a clown whose heart is naked on stage. To give all that I have. It is not always possible, but there are moments on stage. This is our spiritual acrobatics: to be like a child on stage, innocent, naïve, but at the same time to be so smart that you know what you are doing. But when it becomes routine, in other words, when you make it mechanically, and people don't laugh, then you didn't have your soul, your heart in it. This you must fight.

I have to tell you an incredible true story about Grock.

His friends said, "Listen Grock, there is a clown in another city who copies you. He has your costume. He makes your jokes. You should prohibit it." Grock said, "Let me look at him." And he went to see his rival's show in disguise. He put on a fake mustache and glasses, and a hat, so nobody would recognize him. And he watched that show, and in fact, his friends were right. The other clown did all of Grock's gags – same violin, same trunk. But nobody laughed, the whole show, nobody. And Grock came back to his friends, and he said, "Let him do it! He does not have the soul." You can be inspired by another clown, or another artist, but when you are inspired you have to make it your own. Only then can it work – perhaps.

Marceau said, actually, there are not so many ideas. The secret is in how you combine them.

EL: One of my favorite bits of yours is with the beach chair. How did you develop this routine? Where did it come from?

Dimitri: In one silent movie from Chaplin, there is one little moment on the beach or in a boat ... I don't remember ... where he has some troubles with a chair. This was perhaps ten seconds long, but it was enough to inspire me. I said, "Okay, let's try what can I do with a chair. With a beach chair." And so the act was born. And I have done it the same for 50 years. Actually the same. I couldn't make it better. I like to do it because people are laughing a lot, and that is the greatest pleasure for a clown, when the people are laughing! But it is not so easy, really, because you can also hurt your fingers. I have to practice.

EL: Can you talk about a moment when you experienced failure?

Dimitri: When I experienced ... ?

EL: Failure. When something ...

Dimitri: Goes wrong! Ahah. Fortunately, mostly it is only small things that can happen. Maybe I forget something. Usually the audience doesn't even know it. But I have my technician and he is sitting there in the booth, and sometimes he will say to me, "Why did you play so terribly tonight?" And I will say, "Ja, ja, you are right." Then I go home and I practice more ...

But the most terrible thing for an artist is when you have a blackout. This is terrible. Many people think you can only have a blackout with text, but this is not the truth. You can have a blackout with mime, with music, clowning ... Months ago I was doing my performance and I made one thing happen too early. And then – I can tell you the truth?

EL: Yes.

Dimitri: After the banana comes Pierrot. But when I got there, I said to myself, "Wow! I made that already! I was supposed to do it now. How can I continue?" And I was waiting backstage for a long time. My assistant said, "What happened? Are you sick?" And I said, "No, I had a blackout." What a terrible feeling.

EL: You mentioned that Grock always had a partner. And at one point you had an act with Circus Knie, and you had an elephant as your partner. (I notice elephants in your museum upstairs, everywhere.) And also you worked with other partners, people. Is there something different about clowning in these circumstances?

Dimitri: Even if I have an elephant or a partner or people or a company, I am still my clown. I am still the same, alone or not. Naturally, if you have a partner you have many possibilities for funny situations. But I have to go back to the time of Marceau. When I saw Marceau, I dreamed about making a solo show – like Marceau, but as a clown. Actually, I was perhaps the first clown to make a solo show – truly solo, on stage as a clown. Excuse me this vanity!

Philosophy

EL: You were born just a few kilometers away. And you've traveled the world and lived in Paris and in different cities, but you've come back to this place and built your theater and your school and your family and your life in this community. Do you know why?

Dimitri: Well, in one of my first little books I say, as a joke naturally, I say, "I am the best clown from Ascona." And then I say, "You know why? Because I am the only one!" I was lucky enough to be born in a great country in a marvelous area. But you know, when I was young there were no theaters here. Nothing consistent, no companies. And then it was such a challenge to open a school here. I was fascinated to create something new like this. But I never wanted to make a clown school. It is a theater school, especially for physical theater, and we teach also clowning, but not only that. And perhaps this is important to say: I don't really believe in a clown school, actually … *[Laughs.]* It's dangerous what I say now … You can't learn it. You must have it and then you can perfect it. You can learn skills and techniques, because when you have a talent, you can develop it, someone can help you and make it great. But when you don't have the talent to begin with … Well. For this reason, in our school, somebody can become a fantastic physical actor, you know, but not everybody who studies here becomes a clown … Some, yes, some who have the talent, but not all.

But I think family is very important. I work with my family. We have shows together. When my children were small, we began to make jokes and practice together, and I learned a lot from them because children are so … Actually we clowns can learn a lot from children. Not only from our children, from all children. And now we are five of us. Masha, Nina, the grandchild Samuel, myself, and a woman clown, an Italian, she's the partner of Nina. And my children criticize me and suggest things. They say, "Papa, why you don't do that anymore?" Or, "Why you do that so often?!?" They are sincere with me, you know, honest. And I think I am fortunate. My wife is like this too. My family never gives me false compliments. They always say, "Oh, this is not good, don't do that," or, "This is very good, continue!" I would die if I had a wife at home who would always give me compliments. "You are the best," and "I love you, you are great!" This is terrible, terrible. Then you live in an illusion, not reality.

EL: What do you believe is the clown's role in society?

Dimitri: Optimism is one of the most important things in the world, especially today. So, I think it is silly to say it, but we have a mission. When I think now. Reflecting. Our family, we clowns, we are important. I think we are really important.

I receive so many letters from people who say, "You gave me a moment of joy and happiness and laughter. I could forget all my problems, and you gave me humility." May clowns always have such reactions from the audience, from the children and the people that are in problematic situations. Even the healthy ones have the necessity for joy and laughter. I never forget that we are privileged. I live in Switzerland. We have no war. We make a good living.

I have friends from Spain who founded Clowns Without Borders. They go into difficult situations in countries at war, and they make clown and circus shows to give some joy to those people. I'm also good friends with the medical clowns Michael Christensen and Patch Adams. (I even worked with Michael Christensen at Big Apple Circus.) And this is also an important part of our profession: that clowns go to the hospitals for the children and make them laugh a little bit. So, to conclude, I say that the humor, the laughter, when it is pure, it comes from the heart … and heart is the most important thing in that world.

And then I think always about Saint-Exupéry, the great writer from France. He wrote *The Little Prince*. There is one sentence: "On ne voit bien qu'avec le coeur." "You can only see well with the heart." This is the essence and this is also the greatest part of clowning, of good clowning. The heart … The laugh. Of course there are many kinds of laughter – sadistic laughter, diabolic laughter – but pure humor, pure laughter, this brings health to the world. I think.

14 David Larible

Figure 13 David Larible. Copyright Roncalli

David Larible (born in Verona, Italy, 1957) is a seventh-generation circus performer of the Travaglia family. He received both the Gold and Silver Clown Awards from the Monte-Carlo International Circus Festival, and in 2007 he was awarded the Grock Trophy of Imperia. From 1991 to 2005 he performed as the star of the Ringling Bros and Barnum & Bailey Circus. In 2006 he returned to

Europe to perform with Germany's Circus Roncalli, and is currently on tour as the star of Circus Knie. He is often referred to as "the clown of clowns."

I met with David under the big top on tour with Circus Knie in Lucerne, Switzerland, before a matinee performance. (EL)

Origins

It's very difficult to remember my first image of clowning because I am born in the middle of them … But I remember the clown stuff that was in my family's circus in Italy – my mom's family. I was probably four or five years old, and I remember they used to do a gag about shoulders. One time I was in the first row of the public, and one of the clowns takes me and puts me on his shoulders, marching around, and he puts this helmet on my head. And I was so proud of myself, you know, because I was feeling like I was part of the act. So that is really my first memory about clowning, about this universe. I call it my universe. I don't call it a world. To call it the world of clowns is, I think, really reductive. It's a universe.

Sometimes people ask me, "Oh, David, you know so much about the circus, who teaches you? Where do you learn?" And I realize that most of the things that I learn, I learn at dinner, at the table. Because you know, you're small, and everybody is eating all together … And I remember my father speaking with my grandfather, with my uncle about things, and all this information gets in your brain. When you're a little kid, your brain is like a sponge. You're assimilating everything. So there are things I know about circus. For me, it was a very important part of growing up. I think every clown comes from a different story, a different background, and I don't think that my background is better than another one. It was just for me so natural, to grow up among circus people. Sometimes it felt like I was living in this court of miracles. Where I was a little kid, and I was backstage and sometimes I would just be chatting with this con-tortionist, and she was totally upside down, and she would look at me and her two feet were past her shoulders, and she talked with me so naturally. "Hi, David, how are you doing today?" Or speaking with a man that was 35 years old, and he was exactly as tall as me, but I was six or seven years old – that was my universe. And slowly I started to know, to love this job that's not a job, but a form of art that's not a form of art, this way of living that's very difficult to explain to people. Sometimes a journalist on a TV show will say, "Describe to me in five words the circus." I say to him, "Describe to me in five words God." But then I say, "If I have to be simple, I will be simple. This is the circus. You have a ring, and you have someone sitting, and you have to fill both. That is the circus. You have to fill the audience, and you have to fill the ring with talent and art." That's it, as simple as that.

I personally believe it's not the person that chooses the clown, but the opposite. It is the clown that chooses which person it will go in. We are possessed by this entity, by this spirit that is like God – a positive entity that gives us this out-of-control need to make crazy things that create laughter in the people around us.

And yes, I have it. For me it was so natural, this process, this choice to say, "That's what I wanna do. This is gonna be my life." When I announced this to my father, he was not so crazy about it. Not because he had something against clown, but because, in circus families, normally you follow the step of your father, especially at that time when I was little – we're speaking about 50 years ago, when there was no circus school. Your school was your family; your teachers were your father and your mother. So my father was not a clown; he was a great trapeze artist and a great juggler, but not a clown. My grandfather was not a clown. My father, at first he thought it was like, you know, a child thing. Children, one day they wanna be a football player; the next they wanna be an astronaut. But then I think he saw in me something real. A real desire. So I don't know if he does it to discourage me or to educate me, but he starts to say to me, "Oh, you wanna be a clown? Great. You think in the circus that is the easiest job?" Because some people think that, you know. Some people think that in a circus family, if you have four or five children, the child that is a little bit fat and is not talented enough to be a juggler, okay, well, he's gonna be a clown. But my father made me understand that the truth is totally the opposite. Clown is a job that includes all the others in the circus. So he says, "You wanna be a clown? That's not a problem. First you're gonna go to music school, and then you're gonna go to ballet school." I say to him, "I don't wanna be a dancer. I wanna be a clown." But he was so smart. He understood it. He understood that ballet could give me this control of my body and also this harmony in my movement. This is very important. We mustn't forget that clown is like a visual art. So it's very important that you have a harmony in how you do it. And after ballet, he sent me to music school, because it's a big tradition in Europe, the clown has to be a good musician. From Grock onwards, every clown was a great musician. So when my father saw that this was really what I wanted to do, then he started to truly help me, to be on my side, to work with me, really hard. And he says to me, "Start with something else. Clown is the end of a process, not the start of a process. You cannot be a clown for 12, 13 more years. You're cute because you're small, but that's not a clown, you know?" And he made me understand what a big responsibility comes with the fact that you name yourself, "I am clown."

We were playing in Circus Nock, in Switzerland. My father used to do a trapeze act and I was part of it. Three or four months after we started the tour, the clown – there were two clowns, there was a guy and his wife, the only two clowns in the show – the main one broke his foot. There was no way that he could perform. He was out. Now in the middle of the season, of the tour, it's very difficult to find someone. So they said to my father, "Mr. Larible, can you please do a little something, a little clowning, till we find somebody? Because we have a show tomorrow … " Of course my father said, "Yes, we can do it." For my father, nothing was impossible. Everything was easy. Everything was possible. So he said to me, "Okay, now you get your chance. Let's go."

And that was it. I had a little kind of costume. In a couple of days we were ready. My father played the saxophone. I played the trumpet and other instruments, so we put them together. Honestly, it wasn't the greatest act that was ever performed, but we had clowns in the show. And the replacement clown never arrived, because Madame Nock thought that we were working pretty well, and that every day we were improving. Of course my father went to them and said, "When is the clown gonna arrive, because we've performed for two months!" And they said, "You know, we think it's good the way it is." So my father said, "Okay, then you have to pay me because I will not do it for free." Of course they laughed and they reached an agreement. So they offered us a contract to come back the next year with the clown things.

Then we were engaged by Circus Krone. And they asked me to do a solo act, which I created, and it got longer and longer, and the people liked it, until a TV producer came to see me and said he wanted me for a series about circus. He asked me, "David, do you only have one act like this, or you have many?" "Oh," I said, "I have many." Not true. Was totally a lie. But sometimes you have to bluff. And he said, "Okay, well, for our next series in March, I need you to do eight acts." "Okay." So we signed the contract. My father said don't worry, we will do it. So my father and I, we started thinking about all the traditional acts. Riding, and things like that. We pulled it together, and I did it, and it was a success.

At this time I asked Circus Krone to give me 15 minutes before the start of the show. Nobody ever did this. But I asked Miss Krone, and she liked me a lot, and she said to me, "Tomorrow you will do it. I will come and watch. If I like it, it stays. If I don't like it, it goes. Don't be offended." Well, of course, it stayed. So I had 15 minutes to work with the audience. I started to create things. I still have a newspaper at home, and a reviewer wrote, "If you want to see the best thing in the show, you have to come 15 minutes before the show." And that was for me a big thing.

After a year or two, somebody invited me to the circus festival in Monte Carlo. They wanted me to support a couple of famous clowns, do some of their dirty work while they performed their act. And I discussed it with my father, and he said, "Look, you have nothing to lose. Nobody will know you before the festival and probably nobody will know you after the festival." And I thought, when you have nothing to lose it's always a good deal. So I agreed, but I asked that in every show they leave me at least one act where I can be alone in the ring with nothing. They agreed. I was the outsider, supporting these two big clowns. And to make a long story short, when they announced the prize, I won the Silver Clown, and they didn't win anything. I had the audience from the first day. From the moment I came out, I had them with me, and they didn't. They never empathized with the crowd. From that day ... To win a Silver Clown in Monte Carlo, it was really a big deal. Ahead of me were only Popov and Charlie Rivel with the Gold. From one day to the next I went from being Mr. Nobody in clowning to having an agent who wanted me to go there and there and there. And the rest is history, the contract with Ringling Brothers, and all the rest.

Inspirations

I was probably in my twenties – 21, 22 – I was doing an act in the circus with my father – I was an acrobatic, juggling dancer. And I played in the same show with

Charlie Rivel. And of course it was great. I never missed one of his acts. And you learn, you learn by watching. But you also have to be very careful when you watch, when you admire somebody, because the tendency is to copy him. And that is the biggest mistake that the clown can do. At the beginning of your career of course you have to do it, because you have no other way to go. It's much easier to copy somebody. At the beginning of my career I copied all these great clowns – took some things from one, other things from the other – because I had no material, no repertoire, and I didn't have a clear vision of what I wanted to be or what I wanted to do.

But you have to understand in the early stage that you can be inspired by somebody, but to carry on copying the material is a suicide. There was a moment where my father stopped me from watching Charlie Chaplin because unconsciously I was starting to move like him. And you cannot do that. If I'm a painter and I start to paint exactly like Picasso I will go nowhere, because everyone that sees it is gonna say, "This is a copy of Picasso!" You are not an artist once you copy somebody. Stasis is the big risk. When you admire people, try to be inspired by them, but at the same time don't copy them. It's very important that a clown understands these things. You have to try to analyze, analyze what you want, but at the same time find the right balance with your instincts. Then you experiment with things. That's why I say it's a collage. You take away a piece, you put a new piece in … "Oh, this is great, this works really well for me. I'll leave it there, and then I'll try something else. No, this doesn't work for me. I'll take it out." There are some acts that I do – my opera act, for example, I've done it for 20 years now – and I still find little things to change because it's never finished. Until the moment you present it in front of the audience, it's a work in progress, you know? It's not a movie that you finish and don't change. Your masterpiece; you have to present it and redo it every single night in front of somebody. So you must change it. I really think you should never be totally happy with your act, because that gives you the stimulation to work on it. And if you don't do that, you become like a puppet that makes the same movement every day until the movements become fake, and people know. There are some clowns that work in this way, you know, you see them today or tomorrow, it's exactly the same. But I think that takes away what is the real meaning and the soul of the clown, and that is the spontaneity, to be able to give every show something different because you are different. We don't feel the same everyday. Your feelings are mixed, and you have to express this, so you will not perform the same things. For me, that's the artist. But you need a big element of humility. Sometimes success can be dangerous. Very dangerous. Because to have around you people that tell you that you are great and that you are the best and to have people give you prizes … If you are not a very balanced person, you start to believe your press release, and that's when you are in big, big trouble because that's when you think you are good enough. And we are never good enough. We cannot be good enough. In one of Chaplin's movies he says, "We are all amateurs. We don't live long enough to be anything else." That phrase should be in every clown's dressing room.

Techniques

Circus is very difficult. Because of the ring. Thinking about it, you never have your butt covered in the circus. Doesn't matter which position you take. You're gonna have someone watching your back. So you have to know how to express yourself even to the people who watch your back. And there's another thing. In the circus, because it's a circle of things, the audience that are on one side see you in the middle, but they also see the people on the other side. So if somebody from there stands up and goes to buy cotton candy or go to the toilet, everybody can see it. So in the circus you have to learn charisma. You have to be able to say, "I'm here. Watch me because I'm here." It's a great school. It's a great performance school.

Let's be honest, anyone can buy a costume, some shoes, put on some makeup, and look like a clown. But I can buy a white coat, a stethoscope, and put on some glasses, and that does not make me a doctor. To be a doctor, you have to go to university; you have to study; and this is exactly the same with a clown. Dressing up as a clown, it's easy. Being a clown is really very difficult. And I have to tell you the truth, I think only 10 percent of people that stand in clown shoes are really clowns. It's not only about talent. A good clown has to be a very intelligent person. You have to play dumb, stupid, but you have to be a very, very smart person because there is a mix of spontaneity and preparation that is extremely difficult to combine. If you are too spontaneous, you forget about the technique, and if you're too much in the technique and you think too much, you forget about the spontaneity. It's a collage. A clown is a collage, and every piece has to be in the right place. It doesn't come only from one thing, because I know a lot of guys, they have an unbelievable talent, and they have the potential to become great clowns, but they never do it. Why? Who knows? The talent is there, but there is some other element that they are missing.

One time I worked for three months on a new gag, and it was complicated – I needed to build some props and things, so there was like a lot of process, and really, I was dedicated. In my head I said to myself, "This is gonna be great!" And then came the day when I presented it. Now when you present a new gag, it's never gonna work perfect, but even then, if it doesn't work so well, you see the potential. You say, "Okay, something is there. I have to work it, I have to change it," and you know what to do. But this gag – I presented it in front of an audience … People were looking at me … And there was nothing to save. Nothing to save. Really. I worked months and months and I had to throw it all out. I was so frustrated.

And then sometimes, the opposite. Twenty years ago I was doing a gala. I was improvising, and it was very hot, and I drank some water, and to make people laugh, pppht, I spilled the water. And I saw a little kid was laughing when I did this, and then I started to improvise, and I took the kid, and I gave him the water, and we started to play, and it became what it is right now. And this one worked from the first day. It was born and it was all ready, in 30 seconds! You know, clowning is not a perfect science. In clowning, sometimes two plus two makes ten.

And sometimes five plus five makes two. That's why you have to find the right balance between analysis and inspiration. And you learn much more from a failure than from a triumph. Because it's not often you stop to analyze a success. If something works, why do you have to analyze it? But if you fail, then you analyze. You stop and you start to think, why? Why doesn't it work? And this teaches you a lot.

Success is like somebody that comes and punches you in the face. If you're a smart person, you say, "Well, come here, I will manage you. I will manage you. You are the success; I manage you, and I will kick you back." And this is very important. Because success, it's the same thing as failure. You mustn't let it affect you too much. We all fail – big flops! Everybody has that. But with age, you begin to understand, you know what's what. Experience – that's the best thing in the world. But, of course, what they say is true: You learn much more from a failure than a triumph.

You cannot look for the poetic. You cannot say, "Okay, now I will write a poem." No. You write something that comes from your heart. And then, "Oh, shit, this is a poem!" This is exactly the same with clowns. There are clowns that try to do poetic things. But in the end, poetic is not in what you're doing. It's in you. It's in how you do it. Some clowns can be poetic by spitting water. And some will never be, not even with the best situation, not even with a moon that's calm.

There are two different kinds of laughs. Stand-up comedy can make you laugh – speaking bad about a politician, it's funny – but it's not a laugh that makes you feel good about yourself. It has an aftertaste, this kind of bitter aftertaste. And then there's a genuine laugh. You laugh, and it's funny, that's all. It's just funny. And it comes from your stomach, and it makes you feel good. When the laugh is finished, that's when you feel the difference.

I gave a definition of clown. I said, the clown is nothing but a juggler of feelings. The feelings that are inside of a human being are so many, there is no end to them, and the clown tries to touch everyone. The clown, if he does his job in the right way, can really reach that, can really reach to touch that. People ask me, "David, what do you want the audience to take home at the end of your show?" I cannot pretend to know what they want. What I can do is give everything I have in my repertoire, in my heart, in my soul, because this is very important, you know. Soul is something that is very important for a clown. There are clowns that touch you. There are clowns that are very funny, and you go and see them, and you laugh, and you admire them, but they don't touch you. And they are great clowns. And there are others that reach the soul. It's a little bit like singers. You know, there are singers that sing and they have a wonderful, beautiful voice, and you say, "Wow." And then you listen to Tony Bennett, who has everything *but* a great voice, and this guy touches your soul.

What I realize is that I do things now that I could never have dreamed of … That I was afraid to do before. These days I can stay still and stare at somebody for 30 seconds without moving, and people start to laugh. When you're young, you think you have to do something in every moment … You think, "I'll lose the attention! I'll lose the attention! I need to do something! This silence, I don't like the silence!" And you don't realize that the silence is just the prelude to what will happen. But this is experience. If I could have the experience and knowledge that I have now with the body I had when I was 20, my God.

But the good thing about clowning is that you don't need your body so much. I'm flexible, I can still do things, although of course I cannot do flips and things like that. But the good thing is you don't need it so much. That's what I learned from Marcel Marceau. Marceau, if you see his early shows and his late shows, you will realize that he transfers all the movement that he was doing with his body to his face. That was a big lesson. So I started to transfer a lot into my mimic expression.

It's a fascinating job, a fascinating art form. One time I was in Charlie Rivel's dressing room, and he said, "David, you wanna be a clown. It's a great job, and I have to tell you something. I still learn something every single show." And that's what it's about, I think. This knowledge that it's never ended, it's never finished. It's the constant search for perfection, knowing that you'll never reach that perfection because it doesn't exist, but what is wonderful is to see how close you can get to that bitch!

Philosophy

Fellini, in his movie *I Clowns*, he asks whether clowning has a meaning in modern society. He made that movie in, I think, '67. I read an interview with Grock, I think was from the early '50s, the same question. Sixty years later, we are here, and we are still thinking about clowning. I think clowning changes its role in society. What was clowning in America right after the Depression is different from what is a clown right now. But for sure people are always attached to clown. And they love clowns a little bit more when there are difficult moments. I was in Ringling Brothers in '91 during the first Gulf War, and it was not a nice moment. Everybody was afraid, could it be like another Vietnam? And I saw how people changed. After the show. They went from one day saying, "Oh, you're great. Oh, that was so funny," to the next day saying, "Thank you." That's something I don't forget. The day after the war began we had an opening night in Birmingham, Alabama, and the reviewer there said an interesting thing; he wrote "For two hours David Larible had the audience forget about the war."

Probably that is the role of the clown – to try for a couple of hours to make us forget our problems. I say that what I want is to take them on a trip. That was always my intention. To a place that has no place in a time frame that has no time frame. And when (or if) I reach that, then I really think there is a meaning in what I do. Because I think it goes farther than just entertaining a family with a couple of kids. Clowning has to be more than that. Now, whether we reach this goal … Whether we are successful or not … History will say. But that's what we should try to do.

There are people, amateurs, that love to be clowns, and they do a great job. They go to the hospital, they go to the orphanage, they go to the birthday party – they do a great job. But we have to separate them from the professionals. From Slava, David Shiner, Peter Shub, Barry Lubin – these are not Ringo or Dingo or Banana. They are two different things. I don't say that the amateurs are bad. They do something they love, and they put their heart into everything, but it has nothing to do with clowns. One of the Fratellini said something beautiful once. He said, "Clowns are a very rare entity." There were never many great clowns in the same moment in history. We have great clowns in this moment, this era. We have them.

In Europe there is a big crisis in the theater. There is less and less theater because there are less and less people who go to the theater, and this affects the young clowns who are just starting. Because you need the space to present yourself. Of course, if you are a famous clown you have no problem because you are offered engagements all the time. But I'm thinking of the clowns that are coming out now. They need good places to perform, good places to establish themselves. And there are less and less of them. So I think one of the problems that's being encountered right now is that. How can we give these young, talented people a place to grow?

You don't say, "I play the clown." You say, "I am the clown." Not like an actor. An actor is an actor. Today he plays Henry the Fifth, and in one month he will play Cyrano. One time he is a murderer; one time he is a priest. Different roles. Clowns: they always play themselves. Chaplin was a clown. He always played the same character. Keaton was a clown. The Marx Brothers were clowns. In today's world, Roberto Benigni is a clown; he is always the same character. So that is the difference. A clown can play a situation, of course: maybe he is the king, maybe he is the cook … But he will always play his own character. They are two totally different, separate things. An actor plays a character created by somebody else. A clown doesn't play – he *is* the character, and he creates himself.

You always have to leave clowns with their freedom. You cannot tell a clown, "Come here, walk this way, step there!" You cannot do that. You can only give him a situation, and say, "You come from here, here you find this, and then you go away. But do it however you want to do it." Only like that can the clown give you his best. So you have to know about clowning to direct a show with clowns, because if not, it's really difficult. Sometimes in the past I have had problems with directors that directed the show and they told me, "David, do it this way." I said, "I cannot do it!" "Why?" "Because it doesn't go with what I am." "Why can't you do it!?" "Because I'm not an actor." I have to feel comfortable in what I do, and if I don't feel comfortable, I will not do it because I will do it very badly and the show will stink. That's the bottom line. There are a lot of people that confuse clowns with actors. Jimmy Stewart was a great actor. But he played the clown, and he was a horrible clown. It's true! It's true, and I'm a big fan of Jimmy Stewart. I saw all his movies. He's an unbelievable actor, but then he had to play the clown in *The Greatest Show on Earth*, and look at it! It stinks. It's bad. It's really bad. You cannot play the clown. It doesn't matter how good an actor you are.

We have to progress. We have to tag along with the time. But at the same time we must not lose the spirit of the clown, that was there for hundreds of years and should be there also in the future. I'll tell you why. This world changes so much. My father used to tell me that in the small circus where he was performing in the '40s, when the clown came out for the first time, with the big shoes and baggy clothes, he just stepped into the ring and people start laughing. Now that doesn't happen anymore. After all, in the street you see people that are dressed much funnier than clowns, with green hair and makeup … That's fine. It's society, and we have to accept that. And other things – my kids, on their smartphone, they can connect with YouTube and watch the best clowns ever. They can see pieces of Popov, Rivel, Grock … So it's much more difficult these days to surprise people. Before, clowns and the circus were amazing just because they came to your town. But now, to amaze people who are surrounded by all this modern technology, you can do it only with the one element that technology will never have, and that is your soul. Your smartphone may be smart, but there is no such thing as a soulphone. I think that's what clowns have to do. They have to be very careful to always work with a lot of soul and feelings. Don't be afraid of feelings. Don't be afraid of this sweetness that the clown has to have. If you do it in the right way with the right sweetness, it becomes loveable. Clowns have to be loveable. That's it. A clown has to be loveable. Because at the end that's what we want. The acrobat wants to be admired. The animal trainer wants to be applauded. The clown looks only for love. He doesn't care about the applause, the admiration. He just wants to be loved, that's all.

15 Oleg Popov

Figure 14 Oleg Popov. Photo by Hermann Liemann

Oleg Popov (born in Moscow, Russia, 1930) is also sometimes called the "Sun-shine Clown." He was given the title of People's Artist of the USSR in 1969, and his fame extended to Melbourne, Australia, where he was called King of Moomba. In 1981 at the Monte-Carlo International Circus Festival, he won the Golden Clown award. His role as a clown follows the tradition of the Russian "Ivanushka," a clown who fools other people and is also teased himself. At age 75, Popov was invited to perform at the thirtieth anniversary of the Monte-Carlo International Circus Festival.

Oleg spoke with me from his home in southern Germany. (DB)

Origins

In 1940, I went to the circus for the first time with my father. I was about ten years old, and I was really happy because the clown gave me a balloon as I was leaving. It was a big gift for me. I took that balloon for walks. I slept with it. Finally the balloon popped, but the circus never died.

I loved acrobatics, and when I was a young man I attended a sports club called The Wings of the Soviets. I studied acrobatics there. Nearby, there was a circus school. The students came from the circus school to this sports club, and they taught us. So I made friends with them, and then they dragged me to their circus school. The next year I entered the school as a student. I already had friends there – so it was like coming home.

I continued as an acrobat. We were a trio, but sadly one of my partners had an accident, hurt his spine, and died. After that it was just the two of us. And then I started to rehearse as an eccentric, working on the wire, working alone. Eccentric is not clown, but a comedian. Very close, but not the same. So I graduated with this eccentric number that I created.

About a year and a half later, there was a program in Moscow, a gathering of circus artists who were under 25 – a showcase. We all came to show our numbers. That's where I met Karandash the clown, who saw my number and really liked it. He invited me to tour with him – to have that number as part of the tour, and also to apprentice with him, and appear on stage with him. I was both his assistant and his partner.

When the tour with Karandash ended, I went to Samarra. There was another clown working in the circus there, his name was Pororikov. He had an accident, fell down and broke his rib, and so the circus was left without a clown. The director of the circus came to me and said, "You worked with Karandash. While Pororikov is in the hospital, can you step in for a week?" I had no costume, no shoes, no wig, no nothing. What to do? He said, "Don't worry, tomorrow we're going to the hospital to visit Pororikov." So we did. Pororikov was lying on the bed, and the director said, "I'm so sorry this happened to you. I'm so sorry. But what do you think if this kid, if this young man steps into your shoes this one time?" He said, "I don't mind. Let the boy be in my skin for a little while and try it out." The director said, "Well, we only have one problem." "What?" "This young man has nothing. No makeup, no wigs, no noses, nothing. … " So Pororikov found his keys, and gave me the keys to his makeup room in the circus, the backstage room. He said, "Go there and find whatever you want." I was very grateful. This gave me the chance to really select what I needed. I worked there for a year. But that first night … When people asked me, "Oleg, did the public like you?" I could only say, "I was so worried, I couldn't see the public." These were my first steps.

Inspirations

When I was six or seven, my mom gave me money for ice-cream, but instead of getting ice-cream I ran to the movies, and I watched Charlie Chaplin. Whenever she would give me money for ice-cream, I would run to the cinema. I loved Chaplin very much; for me, he was the icon.

All young clowns, of course, have figures that they refer to, but ultimately all clowns are very different, so there's no stamp. We all have different characters. Chaplin is part of the lineage for everyone, but over the years, this kind of extraneous influence starts to peel off, and the clown, the authentic clown emerges that is very original. Making a perfect copy of someone is not the achievement – the achievement is finding your own unique voice.

Techniques

"The Spotlight" is my signature number. It comes from the classic number where the clown comes onto the stage with a broom. I first saw this when I went to the circus with my dad. The clown is sweeping, sweeping, sweeping, and, all of a sudden, the lights go off, and a spotlight appears. And he starts to sweep the spotlight, and he catches it, and he puts it into his pushcart, and he takes it off stage. But I have a slogan – it's my motto: "If you're doing someone else's routine, you have to make it better than it was." I learned this from Charlie Chaplin, who said, "In every reprise, there has to be a reason." You don't smack somebody in the face for no reason. You have to know, why did you smack? You have to have that motivation.

So this is my version. There's a spotlight on the stage. I find it. I sit down under it. I decide to have my breakfast. The spotlight moves aside, and I'm left in the darkness. So I decide to go toward the spotlight. I find it, and, again, I sit down, and again the spotlight moves. Now I'm chasing after the light for a while. Finally I catch it – this is all in pantomime – and then I fall asleep under it. All of a sudden there's a whistle, a police whistle, and I look up. "Okay, I have to move, right? I'm in the wrong place." I get up and I start to walk away, and now the spotlight follows me. And I see that it's following me, so I collect it again in my hands, and I put it into my bag, and my bag lights up. I walk with it, I'm leaving, but then I change my mind, because I'm not egotistic, and I want to share it. So I take the light out of my bag again and I throw the spotlight into the audience, and it lights up everything. The song "My Way" is playing throughout the number. I still do this number. When I come onto the stage in the dark, the ovations already begin. And whenever I meet people, periodically they will ask me, "Are you going to be doing the spotlight number?" They are nostalgic for it.

My way to create is through mistakes and trials. Trials and mistakes. Some people are really afraid to create new material. I'm not afraid at all, because when it's a flop, when it doesn't happen, I know that I will analyze it, figure it out, ask the question, "What am I doing?" And the next time it will happen. I'll make it work. If you're afraid, don't go into the woods.

Philosophy

I decided at one point that there are different kinds of laughter. In one kind of laughter, the people are laughing hard and rolling on the ground. In the other kind, people are smiling. What I value the best is the smile. Because the smile remains in the heart, while the laughter is easily forgotten.

There's a photo that I really love. I'm wearing a yellow chapiteau, and I'm peering through some curtains, just peeking through. I wrote a little poem about it. "I'm looking at the world through the circus."

Here's my suggestion for young clowns: they need to learn how to make their own props and all of their entourage of things for clowning. When I was 14 years old, during the war, my mom sent me to work in the printing shop for the newspaper, and this became very vital and useful for me. These kind of pragmatic sides to clown are very important. You have to become very good at some things that are simply housekeeping. Nobody is a man who doesn't know how to work a machine. So here is the test that I suggest. Bring a plank of wood, hammers, and nails, and then make a competition to see how long it takes each clown to put a nail into the board. One minute, two, three, four, five, or twenty. It's very important! My teacher of eccentricity, he would always send me home with homework. He would say, "Okay, here is a broom. Come back tomorrow. Bring back numbers, something funny. Here is a pen. Here is a pot. Bring back numbers. Here is an apple. Bring back numbers." And it had to be something funny. It was consistent work with simple things like that.

Now I have to go and walk my dog.

16 Bello Nock

Figure 15 Bello Nock.

Bello Nock (born in Florida, 1968) is a seventh-generation member of the Swiss Nock circus dynasty who began performing at the tender age of three. Known as "the World's Greatest Daredevil," he has been described by *Time Magazine* as "America's Best Clown," and is famous for his terrifying stunts, both in the ring and at venues such as Madison Square Garden, the Rose Bowl, and even the Statue of Liberty. Bello was the first performer to have a show named after him by the Ringling Bros and Barnum & Bailey Circus. He has performed regularly with the Big Apple Circus over the course of eight years. *Bello Mania*, at the New Victory Theater in New York (2013) was nominated for a Drama Desk Award. His 2014 spectacular, *The Ultimate*, featured Bello performing 15 death-defying stunts in 15 minutes.

Bello chatted with me in his home and training center in Sarasota, Florida. (EL)

Origins

Ezra: Let's jump in.

Bello: Great. I'm silent comic, but I'm never at a loss for words.

Ezra: *[Laughs.]* Perfect. So when did you first experience clowning or circus?

Bello: I come from seven generations of circus on both sides of my family. From the Italian side, my mother's side, the Canestrelli Circus, who are still very popular. There was circus, but also more. They were in theater, opera, music – more on the theater side. My father's side, seven generations, still going strong, Circus Nock. In 2010 it was their 150th anniversary.

Ezra: Wow.

Bello: So seven generations of lineage on that side. They were more strictly circus, but daredevils also. So I experienced circus at a very young age. I can remember it very clearly. I can remember being three years old and being on Disney On Parade. It was before there were ice shows. There were five segments to the show. The only thing that I cared about was the Dumbo Circus. I can remember watching it everyday, from the front, from the back, working with a guy named Buck Nolan, who was the tallest clown, 7'8" or something like that. Really tall guy. There were a whole bunch of clowns in the day. Very American-style clowns. No acrobatics. It was a different world of clowns back then. But that's what got my attention, and I probably performed two dozen shows throughout a year. I was the baby in the burning house. There was a facade. It looked like a whole house, but it was just plywood. It was a set. There was a deck up top, and there was just a ladder to get up to the deck. So there was a guy who was basically the clown in drag, and he had a baby, but it was a doll. And he would say, "My baby, my baby!" And all the clowns would run over to the big trampoline with a tarp. Well, they had me climb up there. He's holding me, "My baby, my baby!" We're running around on this deck, no railings on the back. I remember this very vividly. No railings, but there was a ladder to go down, and at three years old I just remember the timing of it. "Okay, ready? Down!" He told me "Down!" He picked up the baby. He threw it down. They caught it. And in that amount of time I had to climb down the ladder, and it was probably two stories high, maybe even three. I climbed down the ladder, and went out underneath this vinyl, and then climbed up there so they could throw me up and down on the little tarp to show me off. Then, you know, "Hey, I made it," bah, bah, bah, bah, bah, little dance, bunch of nonsense was what it was. Chaos. Now, here's what's funny. I remember what I did, because it was choreography. It was fun. It was attention. And then, the next morning there was an 11 a.m. show. And no one's ever up early. So I can remember looking around, and the show's going on, and I'm worried because they forgot to paint my face. They were like, "Kid, kid what are you doing?" To this day the only nightmares that I have are being late for a show, or late for an act. I hate to say nightmare. They're my only dreams that are ...

Ezra: They're startling.

Bello: Startling. Yeah. Well, here's what's funny. It was in St. Louis. That night, I wouldn't let them take my makeup off, because I knew I needed my makeup for the next morning. I didn't know how else to tell them I needed to be ready! So I woke up ready the next morning, and my makeup was smeared all over my pillow and my face, but I was ready to go, because I had a show to do.

Ezra: Were you interested in clown as a child?

Bello: Let me tell you about a photo. I was six or seven years old. We were at home, on hiatus. We were in Florida. All my brothers and one cousin. They all have the most embarrassed look. You look at it now, it was '70s clothes, we looked like the Brady Bunch, except one kid in a clown costume, in a perfect clown pose, in the middle of the day, in Florida. It wasn't halloween. We were home. I can only quote my mother, "What was wrong with your eyes?" I can tell you what I was thinking. I asked to have a costume like the guy who was on the billboard outside Circus Circus. All I wanted to be was the guy on that billboard. I didn't want to be someone they saw when they came into the circus. I wanted to be the guy that got them inside. Hence all the outside daredevil stunts to get people excited about circus.

Inspirations

Ezra: Did you have any formal clown training?

Bello: They say that to be an Olympic athlete you need four things. Talent, a good coach, access, and drive. Drive is the only thing you have control of yourself. The rest is given to you. Those middle two are what I had – access and a coach. I was never forced to carry on the circus tradition. They just said I had to try it ... for 30 or 40 years. Then I was free to try anything I want. I wish I was kidding. There was an expectation.

The access was amazing. I had a unicycle before I had a bicycle. I had ADD, and I was dyslexic so I wasn't so excited to read, but I had a wire – and I was excited to move. So my parents would say, "Walk the wire ten times." Then I had a challenge. (They taught me to be creative; I had to earn to play outside.) I would have to juggle 100 times without dropping, things like that. I had access at such a young age, the coach, and the circus arts. What I also learned, as the youngest of four boys, was that if you're going to be a juggler, you better be a great juggler.

Ezra: Do you think of yourself as a clown, or as a daredevil who does comedy, or something else?

Bello: As you grow up, your audience gets bigger, but there's no audience more important than your family. As the youngest of four boys, all three of my brothers could do a one-arm handstand, run across the wire, and all that, when I was just learning. All my life was a practice class. My dad would say, "Show me something." They would walk the wire forward, backward, etc. I realized I wasn't as good as them – yet. My dad was already drooling at the brother who could do something amazing. I knew they would step up on the wire and get across, step up on the wire and get across. To get my dad's attention was the most important. So I walked up the three steps, tripped on the first step, then reached for the pole, lost balance on purpose, all to get his attention. He was the audience, and when I got his attention I had succeeded.

Different clowns have different abilities. There are musical clowns. Dimitri played in the Big Apple Circus. He is an unbelievable clown. He plays more instruments in a day than you can imagine in your whole life. In his act, he picks up his first instrument, okay. He picks up his second, wow. He picks up his third instrument, the audience is amazed. I come from an acrobatic family. That's my genre. My abilities are second nature. After that, it's about face time and doing an act for the audience. It's 80/20. Most of me is with the audience, and intuitively I'm able to do the skills.

People say there are three types of clowns: the white face, auguste, and character clown. I think I've created a fourth style. I can be all three of those, but I also can be an act. I can bring personality to that act. The only other person who could do it was David Larible, when he could be there throughout a whole show, and do four segments where he was the theme. For me, the show can be about my clown, but I am also the high-wire act, the wheel of death, and the sway pole. P.T. Barnum said, "The clown is the hook that you hang your circus on." But you also need that spectacular act, the cannon of death, the act that tops it all. Well I can do that. That punchline, right before the end, that's what I bring to the show. "We like him, we care about that guy, now he's the guy up there?" Unlike most acrobats, if you get to know my guy, there's an emotional connection.

Am I a clown? Am I a daredevil? And what is the mix? It depends on who I'm talking to, and it depends on where I am. It's like Bill Irwin. You say, is he an actor or a clown? When he's an actor, he's an actor. When he's a clown, he's a clown. I think I've been successful on both sides. It's just a genre. It's what I do. I don't know what comes first. If you said, what do you call yourself? I don't know.

Techniques

Ezra: Do you have a favorite act?

Bello: Trampoline is my favorite because everyone can relate to it. Everyone has jumped on a bed when they get to a hotel room. Just that fun feeling. You've seen it in cartoons. Basically I have a WWF wrestling match with the trampoline. It beats me up. But I get up, wipe myself off, and go at it again. I love that backstory, even though I never tell it. In eight minutes, it throws me off 20 times, and then I beat it, then I get cocky, and it throws me off again.

I love the sway pole, the high-wire, once it gets high off the ground. When it comes to doing the real life-threatening stuff, everyone who does that takes themselves real serious. "Don't laugh at me, I'm the star of the show, drumroll, silence, so serious." I never wanted to take myself so seriously. Think about that little kid trying to get his dad's attention. Silence, drumroll … "ACHOO!" Was it funny? Was it embarrassing? Look at Charlie Chaplin. Funniest guy around. He made you cry. He made you think. He brought different emotions, not just ha, ha, ha. So in my act – yes, it's daring, going up high, there's the high-wire, it's dangerous … But we don't need to explain that. But what if I trip when I'm there? "If he trips, what is he doing up there?" You know, it just hit me: If people didn't fear the consequences – falling, getting booed – would we try the high-wire, climb that pole to change a light, forget the lightbulb? We would. If we lived in our dream world. If gravity, embarrassment, failure didn't exist. That's what I think Bello as a clown doesn't know.

Ezra: Tell me about an experience of failure.

Bello: There are so many! I think this is what puts me in a different place than most clowns. Eighty percent of the time my feet are off the ground. So it's the flip side of any other clown, because if my comedy isn't funny, I still have people's respect because my feet are still 30 feet off the ground and I'm doing something life threatening. So in a way there's no room for failure. Can it be better? Yes. But some people hang on to something that they didn't get right. I don't. When something doesn't work, okay, show's over, fix it next time. Move on. I'm a failing perfectionist. I know what perfection is. I know I will never achieve it, but I will always try.

Ezra: As a clown, what is perfect?

Bello: At the Monte-Carlo Circus Festival. I was 40 years old. I did an introduction act. I did my trampoline act. I did an audience participation act. Then I did the wheel act. I came down, they sent me back in, and I never dropped character, even when I was taking a bow. Now I know how to take that stuck-up, aristocratic bow. But I was in the circus as a clown, in the ring, taking a bow as a clown, and they said, "Now, the performer, Bello Nock." They sent *me* back to bow, not the clown. "The performer, Bello Nock." They wanted me to take a normal bow. I didn't do it. People started to stand up. The little kid in me came out, the clown, the character didn't know why. I knew why, but I was the clown. Even when I got the trophy, I never stopped, because I wasn't there as the person. I was there as the clown. If I'm there as a performer, as me, I'll take a bow. But right then, I was the clown. When do you break character? You don't. You suspend belief. You are an illusionist. That's my mentality.

Ezra: What's your perspective on originality and stealing?

Bello: Very touchy subject. I have a lot of friends on both sides of it. Stealing is stealing. When you go back to the generation of a very young David Larible, Bill Irwin, Barry Lubin, there were no computers, no email, no Facebook, no Google. You had to go to a museum to see even photos. So you didn't, you couldn't look at what someone else was doing to do it yourself. My whole life I've heard of Popov. I have a very famous uncle who was a clown who did two acts, Pio Nock. He did bells and a high-wire act. Bill Irwin brings him up. David Larible brings him up. He was a loveable old clown at that time. He was a guy they looked up to. But the work wasn't accessible in the way it is these days.

Someone told me, facetiously, if you see one person do it, and you do it, it's stealing. If you see two people do it, it's research. That was joking. But the whole thing about being a performer: an artist creates, a performer performs. On *American Idol*, you're going to hear that same song. But as good as they do it on their best day is not as good as Mariah Carey did it. When you can create, you will be known as Dolly Parton, Whitney Houston, Mariah Carey. Otherwise you're just a singer, and you will never get past that cap, past that limit. Like with guitar. Teach me how to play guitar, not how to play that song.

If you want to be a clown and you go to Google, you'll never be more than a copycat, a likeness. You will hit that cap. As hard as it is, you will never grow. You will never be respected, not from the people you took it from. It would be arrogant, foolish for me to say that we don't all take inspiration. If someone ever says as a clown, "I never stole anything," hmm. Have you watched a Charlie Chaplin movie?

My secret weapon is my wife. We've been married 26 years. It takes a pretty secure person to marry a clown. She came up with a couple of important questions. Number one, why? If you don't ask why you are doing something, don't do anything. Even if you have success, why? You have to have that in there. Then she asked me, why do you need all those props? What can you do with nothing? That's how the William Tell act came to be. Her challenging, her asking why, is vital to every creative act I make.

Going back to failure, when do I fail? When I'm talking. If you ask my wife, "When do you get afraid for Bello?" "When he has a microphone." And I've given her reason time and time again. So that's it. I fail when I have a microphone.

Philosophy

Ezra: What role do you think the clown plays in our lives?

Bello: No matter where he is – theater, film, circus – the clown is who everyone wishes they could be, if only they were without fear. You know the top three fears? Fear of heights, being laughed at, and being in front of an audience. I tackle all three. I make people laugh at me, up high, in front of large audiences. Letting someone laugh at you is giving them good medicine. You're like a doctor. I believe not every clown is for everybody, but the clown, in society, is who everyone wishes they could be, if not for those fears. They won't admit it. I think everyone sees themselves in a clown. You know the movie *It*, the scary clown? There are people who see themselves in that clown. There is a clown for everyone.

Ezra: What do you see as the future of clowning?

Bello: In the '90s Kenneth Feld closed Ringling Brothers Clown College. He said, "It's a business move. At the same time, I can only give placements to ten a year, but there are 30 who come through Clown College. Now I'm creating clowns for the competition, for other circuses." What he was saying was, there was a surplus. There was a surplus of people who knew how to put on makeup, show up on time, go on tour, etc. Life has changed, because there used to be a time when you only would see a clown in a circus. Now you see a clown on the street, on a cruise ship. You will find clowns, or comedians, in the strangest places. So now there are clowns in more places. Then there is whatever the word is for being afraid of clowns, whatever that is. People say, we don't want the clown, but we want the funny guy. Blend in, don't wear a costume, but be the funny guy. So there are more genres and more places to work. There are millions of clowns. Mexico, clown society is unbelievable. Japan, unbelievable. Europe, a lot of clowns. How many funny ones, how many successful ones, creative ones? Whatever the genre is, how many are professionals? And this is important, just because someone is paid to do something, doesn't make them a professional. The difference between someone who is a professional and someone who gets paid to do it, there's a big gap. I don't think it's dying. I think it's just changing. Back in the day if you asked Red Skelton, what are you? "I'm a clown." Whatever you call them, whatever genre, there will always be clowns.

17 Angela de Castro

Figure 16 Angela de Castro. Photo by Julia Guimares

Angela de Castro's (born in Rio de Janeiro, Brazil, 1955) widely acclaimed clown shows include *The Gift*; *My Life Is Like A Yo-Yo*; *Only Fools, No Horses*, a show about the Shakespearean fools; *Laughing Matters*; and her clown opera *Alleluia*. She has been recognized in the UK and abroad, receiving a Laurence Olivier Award (UK), the Golden Nose Award (Spain; best show, *Slava's Snowshow*), and fellowships from the NESTA Dreamtime Fellowship, the Arts Foundation, and the Royal Scottish Academy of Music and Drama. She is internationally recognized for her research, performing, and teaching on the art of clowning.

Angela sat down to share some stories with me in her London apartment. (DB)

Origins

DB: When did you first come across clowning or circus in your life?

Angela: I was 12 when I started in Brazil by accident. I wanted to be a writer. I started to write things when I was very young, 11, and my mother thought that was a bit weird. So she said, "Well, there is an amateur group here nearby. Why don't you go there to be with other people?" So I went, and that was my first contact with theater. I started working as an amateur. Everything was a series of accidents. Five years later, there was this girl who wanted to do an audition for a professional production, and I went with her because the theater was opposite my house. I just went with her, and there was somebody missing – they wanted to do a kind of workshop audition – so I did the workshop with them, and I was offered the part. My friend didn't get the part, but I did. So it was the end of the friendship and the beginning of my career.

And that ended up being an amazing production because it was a children's play, and it was in the middle of the Brazilian dictatorship. We had 25 years of dictatorship, and, at the time, all the theaters were closed, actors in exile, people disappearing. There was a lot of censorship in the arts and everywhere. It was horrible. So this play was written by a political journalist, and he'd done a kind of allegory of the situation, disguised as a children's show. (I didn't know; I was completely innocent in the middle of this whole thing.) And the director was a very good director, the best in popular theater, so by chance I ended up in this master production. And that's how I started in professional theater. And the director took me under his wing, and I started doing a lot of work. (I wanted to go to a drama school, but I didn't get in, but it was good, because in the end, three months later, I got a call to do another play instead.) So all my training was working. Different workshops, private courses that I paid to do, like voice, or ballet, or dance, or movement, and music, and working with good and bad directors, good and bad productions, and that was my formation.

I was always a bit different, that's the thing. This concept of the fourth wall and ignoring the audience, that had never felt right to me. I always thought it was very rude to ignore the audience. People pay to see you, people are looking at you, and you're pretending they're not there? So somehow there was this very elemental sense of clowning, and I think some of my directors liked it. They didn't stop me, you know? They didn't say, "Don't do that." And so, I started doing counterpoint. You know, a few people go that way, so I go there. People go down, I go up. And it worked.

Then I landed in a very big play. It was the first time that there was physical theater in Brazil. It was a director that had been influenced by Pina Bausch and Peter Brook ... In the middle of the '70s. And we traveled all over the world. Four years of touring. And this thing about me being different was really starting to bother me. At this point I'd already had a few years of a career, already had a few awards, and this and that, but I still didn't like to be a protagonist. I preferred small parts, parts that didn't speak very much, so that I could develop as my own artist. And all these little things ... When I look back, I say, "Oh my God, this is already clowning." But I didn't know it at all. And when I was doing this big play, I saw a show that changed my life in a festival in Freiburg. Everybody was talking about this little show that was off, off, off festival, wow, one o'clock in the morning, blah, blah, blah. There were quite a lot of big names at this festival, but the show that everybody was talking about was this little show. So off I went to see it. And there was this guy. (I forgot his name, I never remember the name of this guy.) It was just one man, two chairs, and one parcel, a brown paper parcel. And the whole show was about passing the parcel from one chair to another. That was it. There was a bit of lighting, a bit of music, nothing else. And in the end, everybody was really overwhelmed. There was something about it that was amazing, and no one could say what that was. I came out of the theater, and I asked, "What is this? I never saw such a thing." And I heard a man say, "Oh, this is clowning." I said, "Bullshit, that's not clowning. There is no red nose, no wigs. That's not clowning." "Oh, yes, it is! It's the base of the clown. Think about Chaplin, and Laurel and Hardy … " He went on and on, talking about a lot of people, he said, "Think about Fellini and about Giulietta Masina, she is a brilliant clown," and blah, blah, blah. And that's when I understood. I said, "Oh my God, that's what I am." I went back to Brazil, and I said to everybody, "That's that. I'm going to leave this play, and I'm going to pursue clowning."

DB: What happened next?

Angela: People said, "Go to the circus school! Somebody will teach you!" I was 25 at the time. I went to the circus school, and the guy said, "Oh no, we don't teach this, and by the way, you're too old." So I started working on other productions, stage productions, but at the same time, I was looking for clowning. Whenever I heard that somebody had been in Europe or knew what I was talking about, I would take my little bag and go to see if this person could teach me anything. I spent a few years like that, three or four years just traveling and looking and trying things. And then I opened my company in Rio. Because I thought, "If nobody else is doing it, I'm going to do it. I'll do it myself!" I teamed up with a very nice guy, a very quirky director. He had a group that was circus theater already, so we created a company, and we started doing plays, and the plays were good, and there was an element of clowning, but it was very circus-like, too extravagant for me, and wasn't quite the line of clowning that I wanted to pursue. It was very successful. The first show played for a year in the same theater, six days a week, two shows a day. The second year we did another show, very successful. But by the time we started doing preparation for the third production, I was feeling very uneasy. I knew what I wanted to do, and time was going by, and this wasn't it. And everybody said, "Ah, you're crazy. You're crazy! You're successful! You're making money! Why do you want to change anything?" And I said, "I may be crazy … but I'm going crazy because that's not it. And I'm not going to settle for something that isn't it. I know what I saw and I know what I feel." I was losing it. I booked myself to go to a health spa because I thought, "Well, if I do a little bit of treatment, a bit of yoga, some meditation, a bit of therapy, maybe I can abstain from this obsession." It had become an obsession. Remember, at this point there were no books on clowning, no videos, no DVDs. In Brazil there was nothing.

While I was waiting to go to this place, somebody called and said, "Look, de Castro, do you want to go to Europe? We're going to do this play, and we want to invite you to do it. We know you don't like to be a protagonist, but it's a protagonist role, and you can clown." I said, "I'm not very well, I'm about to go to this spa," and they said, "Cancel it! A trip to Europe doesn't come every day." True. So I went to Portugal and France, spent about ten weeks touring, and then I came to London to visit a friend of mine who has nothing to do with the theater. She's a doctor. I just came to say hi. I was feeling better. And I remember, we were sitting in her kitchen, she opened a magazine, and she said, "You know, this clowning stuff you keep talking about. There is a course that is about to start in two weeks' time. Why don't you stay? It's only ten weeks." I said, "You're crazy. I don't speak any English. I don't know anybody. I don't know where I'm going to live. What about my car? What about my house? My cat?" And she said, "Oh, just stay. When are you gonna get another chance? Stay with me." So I stayed to do it. And so that was an amazing experience for me. I was 31 at the time, with a few years of a career already, and I had to be very humble about everything because I didn't really know anything. I wasn't prepared to be in another country. I didn't speak the language. I didn't know anybody. So it was a kind of rebirth for me, and I was happy.

I'll never forget the emotions I felt when I came through that door for the first time. You know when you're going to do a workshop and you come in and you don't know anybody, and nobody knows anybody, and there is that kind of awkward moment? But when I came in to this workshop, I saw everybody, and I saw the look in their eyes, the spark in their eyes. They had eyes exactly like mine. Eyes of wonderment, of inclusiveness. I had found what I was looking for for so long. Six years I was looking for that, and that was an amazing experience in my life. I'm still friends with some of them. For 28 years. So I stayed. And I had to do all those cleaning jobs and work in restaurants and this and that. But I was happy.

Inspirations

DB: Who was your instructor?

Angela: My teacher was an amazing woman called Frankie Anderson. Many people studied with her. She was the woman to study with at the time. It was brilliant; I ended up doing six months. But in the end I was going to go back to Brazil, to my company, when I got a call from a circus theater group that was looking for a woman clown. So I went to the audition just to see how auditions were done here, because really, I didn't see the point of doing anything here. My English was still shit. So off I went, and it was a very funny audition because I couldn't understand anything that was going on. The instructions were, "Bring an instrument and bring loose clothes." Look, if you don't really speak English, you take everything literally. Loose clothes means clothes that are too big. Loose. So I arrived in a massive T-shirt and massive pants. "Bring an instrument." Well, I have a horn, one of those bugles, you know, so I took that. And I spent most of the audition hiding, because there were ten other people and they were very good. They played saxophone and trombone and this and that. They did magic and juggling … Amazing women. And then it was my turn. And the director said, "Can you do some acrobatics?" I said, "No, better not. I twisted my foot." "Oh," he said, "Well, play your instrument." And then I said, "Well, you didn't say I had to know how to play it. You said *bring* your instrument, so I brought it. Here it is. Didn't say I had to play it. I don't know how to play it." And he said, "Oh. Can you sing?" And I said, "I can hold a tune." "Okay, so sing for us." Me and my good ideas: I decided to sing in English. The only song I knew in English was "Happy Birthday." So off I went singing "Happy Birthday." I sung it in different rhythms, styles, samba, opera, rock'n'roll, heavy metal, cha-cha-cha. Then I decided to sing in Portuguese. And then I translated from Portuguese to English. Basically I spent half an hour singing "Happy Birthday" and laughing at the same time at the absurdity of it. And the guy offered the job to me! That's how I ended up here. I called my business partner in Brazil, who had just been offered a job to be part of the comedy department of a big television channel in Brazil, in Rio. So we dissolved our company. He became a millionaire, and I became a missionaire.

DB: Did you continue to work with the group you had auditioned for?

Angela: Four years. The Mummers and Dadas *Mummerandada* Circus Theatre Company. And in between tours, that's when I studied in mime school with Desmond Jones, in London, and all the workshops in clowning I could find, and commedia and masks, you know, doing it. By the time the Mummers and Dadas *Mummerandada* finished, I already had my own solo show. I had developed my own clown persona. Souza. He has been with me ever since, along with my second persona, Silva.

It was around this time that Frankie Anderson called me, and she said, "I need you to be my assistant because I have to run a two-week course, but I can only do Mondays and Fridays. I want you to fill in for me." I said, "Oh, no, I can't. Who am I?" "No, you can do it!" So I did it because I felt that I owed her a lot, and I wanted to help her. That's when I discovered how great it is to teach and how much you can learn when you teach. It's a way of keeping the research going.

DB: Was there anyone else who powerfully influenced your understanding of clowning?

Angela: Yes. Pierre Byland.

DB: Can you tell me a little bit about that?

Angela: What I understand now is that the older you get, the more mature you get, the more you understand about clowning. When we're young, we think that we know – we are eager to know, and we are eager to go out and do it. But actually, we don't know as much. We don't have the depth or the maturity to understand or to be able to play with the necessary simplicity to convey the true dimensions of feelings. I met Pierre twice, and I immediately connected with his way of teaching and his understanding of clowning. Gaulier and Pierre Byland are equally important, in fact. They were partners, so they were two sides of a coin. With Gaulier it was about the discipline you needed to have, and the clarity that you need, there is no bullshit. No bloody bullshit. And with Byland, it was the simplicity that was in it. And also what he said to me that I can never forget, when the penny dropped, the second time I met him, in 2002: he said that clowning is not a technique, but a state. A state that you put yourself in, to be able to play, or to create, or to be. It's a state for you to be: the state of clown. And that, for me, is simply the essence of it. There are many lines of clowning – the circus clown that has its own tradition, the clown-doctors, the clown-priests, all the spiritual clowns, mimes, musical clowns, acrobatic clowns, theater clowns – which are all different, but no one is better than one or the other. They all live in this state. I understood that suddenly. When Byland said that, it was the most clear statement I had ever heard. It's not something that you can learn technically. It's something that you have to put yourself in it. A different intelligence.

So for me, Byland and Gaulier are really big influences. But then, there are others that I never met. For example, the work of Giulietta Masina. I used to repeat the same moment from her movies, over and over again to see how did she go from here to there? What is she thinking? Because the camera is right in front of her, she couldn't bullshit. The work of Fellini and the imagination, the why not, what if, why can't I? To develop the clown's intelligence and not your own intelligence – that is the most difficult thing for people to understand. You don't create a character. "Oh, my clown's gonna be like this, like that." No. That is not a clown. That is a character you are creating. A clown persona – you don't know what's going to happen. You just go with it and see where it takes you. Like Einstein said: "Imagination is more important than knowledge." You can't be pressured, or anxious. You can't say, "Oh, I want to do a clown show, and it has to be an hour and a half." I never know how long my clown shows will be. I haven't a clue. I'd much rather have a brilliant five minutes than a boring hour and a half.

With Slava, it was – artistically – a very brilliant meeting. Think about it: a man from Russia, from St. Petersburg, and a woman from Rio, suddenly meet in London, and their clowns belong to the same universe. This metaphysical universe that has these concerns about the condition of human nature. I never worked with Nola, Nola Rae, who I really like. I worked with Sue Morrison, who I really respect. Each one contributed something, even the ones that I didn't like. Have you read Philippe's book? It's wonderful! It's a really wonderful book, you know. It doesn't make any sense at all!

Techniques

Angela: The thing is, my show became very famous somehow. I took it to Edinburgh and lots of people liked it. People started saying, "What do you teach?" Somebody took me to a university, and I start doing it because I needed a job. And I worked with The Right Size, and a lot of odd companies. I did many small shows, street shows, here and there, and I kept my show going, and then the workshop starts picking up. I taught a two-day workshop, and after a couple of years it became three days, after five years it became five days, and so on. I started developing a way of teaching that I thought was important for people – for people who don't want to bullshit anyone.

Then Slava came to London, and Nola Rae recommended me to him. When I first met him I didn't know him, I didn't recognize him, and he didn't tell me what he was doing, either. He didn't speak much English. I understood that his troupe was a group of clowns, friends of Nola Rae who were arriving in London who didn't know very many people. That's what I understood. So off I went to visit them. A social meeting, I thought. Certainly I didn't know it was an audition. Slava is a very tricky man, you know? So at the end of that visit, he explained his situation, and he said to me, "Do you want to do it?" Do what?!? But I was free at the time, and I thought, "Why not?" He had a series of numbers, and so I created what today is known today as the Green Clown in *Snowshow*. The clown is green because the coat I got was yellow, but Slava said, "Oh, you can't be yellow. Which color do you want to be?" I said, "Green," because green and yellow are the Brazilian flag.

So I become very popular here. I opened the Why Not Institute when I finished in *Snowshow*. Many people come to do my workshops, people from all the disciplines. Writers, advertisers, people from the corporate world, therapists, voice coaches, actors. And the courses became very, very popular. The government created an organization called NESTA, the National Endowment for Science, Technology, and the Arts, to support people who have their own research, and I won one of those fellowships to pursue my project "Clowning in the Modern World: What Clowning Has to Offer." Somehow I became an academic! But I am not an academic! I don't have a degree!

Clowning is pretty much a way of life. You know, it's not a job. It's not something I put on. I don't have any security; I didn't settle, you know, like many people of my age are doing, or they start teaching in schools and have a bit of security. I don't. I have none. I don't know what my next job will be. I haven't got a clue.

DB: I'm curious: what happens when you make a show for yourself?

Angela: It's complicated.

DB: Where does it come from, and how do you develop it?

Angela: It doesn't have a rule. It's all very much by accident, very organic. For example, my first show is called *The Gift*, with my clown Souza, and it came from an idea of being romantic. It's a very simple show. It's not innovative or anything. It's a well-known subject. A clown has a date and he has been stood up. Everybody knows that; there's no novelty to it. It came from the fact that I was living here in London, and Brazilians are very romantic. We are over the top. But I didn't speak any English at that time, so I didn't know how things happened here when you made a pass at somebody. In Brazil we sing songs, we send messages, we give presents and cards and this and that and la, la, la, and so I was like that. And in Brazil, if you go out with somebody, say you start dating and going to bed with somebody, and after a few meetings you want to go steady with this person, you go to them and say, "Will you marry me?" And that means, "Would you like to go steady?" It's also kind of a compliment: "I like you so much that I would even consider marrying you." There is no malice. It's lighthearted. "Oh, would you marry me?" So I wanted to say that to this girl I was dating. I wrote it on a piece of paper, put it under her pillow the morning after, and off I went. "Will you marry me?" Oh my God! This girl was out of there in no time! And my Brazilian friends said to me, "Oh no, you can never do that! Are you crazy? It's not like that over here. Blah, blah, blah." So I could never be me, you know. Because I was too much. I was over the top, and people would say, "You can't do this. You can't do this. You can't do this." So I wrote the show, *The Gift*, where this clown is completely over the top. I wrote it in half an hour – sat down and wrote it out. I wrote it in '87, but I wasn't ready to play it till '91. Because my clown, Souza, wasn't ready, and I wasn't going to spoil my show. It was too precious to me. I don't have this need to do a show. "Do a show!" No, I want to write! It's precious to me. And that's what people don't understand. They want a result. But my clown wasn't ready, and, until he was ready, I didn't do it. The first time I played was at the Edinburgh Festival in '92. And I won an award immediately with it. And then I started touring. The show is still on; I'm still doing it. I keep changing it. Different versions. So that's how it is. It's clown led.

One of the questions that people ask me a lot is: "How come you have more than one clown persona?" I have Silva, Souza, and the Green Clown from *Snowshow*. How many can I have? Because usually people have just one. I reply, "Well, it just comes to me. I give space to them." And so when I am in this mood here, or that mood there, something comes to me. That's what came to me. How many people I knew, how I have a ballerina, a fat ballerina. I really like *Fantasia* by Disney, and the people that dance so gracefully. I used to be very fat. I was 18 stones. Then there is Silva, who came in one day. I was running a workshop in Australia, and I decided to improvise something, and suddenly I was so different: jumping, shouting, being very bossy. (I don't shout. I don't run. Not like that.) So that took a day to create, whereas Souza took four years, and the ballerina took four months, and the *Snowshow* guy took three weeks. It just comes.

Each clown represents different things. Souza is a guy who comes to say that to be romantic is okay. To be metaphysical, to be poetic, to be philosophical, is all right. The Silva guy comes to say that to be bossy is okay. The ballerina comes in to say to be fat is fine. And the *Snowshow* guy is the only one that has a low status. He's very below zero; he represents the people without land. The refugees. The people that don't know where to go. The homeless. The hopeless. That was the time of the Balkan War. At night, I used to sweep the floor of the corridors of the theater because I wanted to understand – it was the first time I created a clown that was from the outside in and not from the inside out, and I wanted to know why he was so slow, why he followed the other clown, why he was low status. Why did this clown have no spirit, why was he hollow, with no soul, just a shell? There I was every night, sweeping the floor, trying to find out, giving space for this guy to exist in me. And one day someone translated a review of the show for me. We were in Poland, and in the paper it said that I was Slava's sidekick. And I never heard this expression before. It was the first time. I took it literally. A sidekick is a kick in the side. I said, "Oh, this just shows how people can see the truth." And when I was sweeping (wearing my costume and everything), I kept remembering sidekick, sidekick, and then I thought about a dog. When I lived in

Rio, there was a butcher shop near my house. Not hygienic at all, the meat hanging there and stuff. And there was a dog that came there. No one liked the dog. He was dirty, full of hurts, and scars and stuff, bleeding, covered in mosquitoes, and he was always right on your leg. He would come on your leg and look at you, wanting something, a bit of love, and we all used to kick this dog. And then, somehow I understood that my dog-clown went behind Slava because he was following the yellow, and the yellow is a warm color, so he was following the warm color. And I looked down, and because I was fat, I couldn't see my feet! I got a Coca-Cola bottle, the two liters kind, cut it in half, put cardboard underneath, put it in front of my shoe, and put a sock on it. That's why my shoe became so big. And the hat that I had found went like this, and then my coat went like that, and then the shoes went like this – all very clear angles for a very big audience. And then I went to the dressing room and started doing the makeup, and that's when it came out. I started thinking about a movement called The People Without Land in Brazil, and I kind of understood them. Everything fell into place. So that's what I mean about being in a certain state. You put yourself in this place where you don't know what's going to happen, you are blank, and you are patient, and you wait until you understand or feel something you don't expect.

Recently I started developing a clown angel, who comes to say that to be spiritual is okay. And he came from something else as well. I was in a kind of new-age bookshop and I opened up a book and it said, "Imagination is not the end of reality but the beginning of it." I said, "That's true!" I bought the book, started reading the book, and got hooked. And I read another book, another book, start collecting angels and wings and this and that. I was just enjoying it, learning about something new for me, without any prejudice, without any agenda, just receiving it, enjoying it. And then one day I heard a voice in my head, "Oh, you have to do a dance. Do a dance with your wings. Outside." I said, "Oh, crazy. I'm not doing it. This is crazy!" Then one day I did it, and then after that I realized, why not? It was this special magical moment, really. My house here is full of steps, and I did this dance in my backyard, and then I went to the very top floor and looked down at the woods, and I put out some candles; I prepared the space. It was kind of a ritual. And I thought it was so beautiful, and I said, you know, to be spiritual is okay! It's all right. So he became a clown angel called Hallelujah. It's not religious. It's just spiritual. Now he exists. He has his own body and his own ideas. It's not an act. It's not a performing clown. It's a walkabout, or somebody that just exists, like Silva. He doesn't have a show. He's just himself.

DB: He's just there.

Angela: He works as a car park attendant in festivals. Or he is a stagehand in a cabaret. But he doesn't have a number. He doesn't have a show to do. Souza is a performer. Rusty, he's a performing clown, and the ballerina, as well, all the performing clowns. But Silva isn't, he's just himself, and same with the Hallelujah guy. And that's how I create. I sweep the floor for hours and see what happens. I walk, I walk, I walk. Miles. For years. You know, just walking with the guy and writing to him. He writes back. The ideas come like this. And then I have a go. If it sticks, it's a good idea. If it doesn't stick … I created a show called *Laughing Matters*, where I only laugh. I just laugh all the way through. It's about 20 minutes long; I just laugh. And then I have another show that's called *My Life Is Like a Yo-Yo* that's autobiographical. It's an hour and a half of speaking. And then I created another one called *Only Fools, No Horses* about Shakespeare's fools. Each one of them takes time. I'm not a machine that is creating, creating every season. It comes to me slowly, but then they stick to me for a very long time. *The Gift*, it stays, you know, for years now. It's very sweet. It's vintage, a classical theater clown show. I always say to people, "Don't expect it to change the world! You'll get out of there feeling good." So that's it.

Philosophy

DB: Are you aware of why you think clowning is important, why it matters? Is that a conscious thought for you?

Angela: I think it's very important. At the beginning it was pretty much an impulse. "I have to do this." And there was no question about it, and for a very long time I didn't want to know about acting. But now I realize that actually the acting helps a lot as well, and I also think there is a new kind of actor and a new kind of clowning. There is a very contemporary clowning that crosses over with physical theater and the physical actors. So my clowns don't always have noses, a red nose. I can be clowning in many circumstances, in many ways.

I don't do it for the money. I do because I have to do it. It becomes a way of life. It's what I have to do. I think clowning is never going to die because it is the basis of everything in artistic terms. Many actors come to my course because they want to refresh. They want to remember the basics. I think clowning reveals your humanity, when you perform with such honesty and such simplicity and you're not scared to expose anything.

Although people have terrible prejudices about it. We are demoralized; we are not taken seriously. "Oh, it's just a clown." They don't recognize the work, or they don't call you to perform as an actor because you're not an actor. And you have to deal with this kind of prejudice, discrimination, ignorance all the time. But that's how it is. What can you do? I just deal with it. It's very difficult, isn't it? Because you have to make your audience feel more intelligent than you are. So therefore, you make yourself stupid for your audience to feel intelligent. And then they feel better about themselves. You put yourself in this position to represent people's mistakes, or people's difficulties, to expose that. But it's you. You're also human, so you have to deal with yourself as well. My question now is why so many clowns kill themselves. With Robin Williams and, you know, I know so many clowns, *good* clowns, the *real* clowns, that are depressed, very, very depressed. I don't know if it's a kind of sensibility that we have, or how much we give of ourselves all the time out there for whoever comes.

But I want you to know that every day I am grateful to have clowning in my life. Every day. Sometimes it's very hard. I also get depressed from time to time, sickly depressed, and I have to go and deal with it. It's a life of constant struggle to survive, survive artistically, survive mentally, and to have to deal with it day by day, as well. I think clowns live in two worlds. The world of "day by day," and the world of the imagination. It happens that the clowns are in both worlds at the same time. I am, right now. I'm talking to you and I'm also thinking, "How beautiful is this, what I see out of the window … The shape of the wood of my desk … Oh, that is nice … " You know what I mean? And I'm thinking, "Oh my god, what am I gonna do next week?" I live like this all the time.

It's not always funny, you know? Last year I went to Nepal. I went to work voluntarily to train people for the circus, and that was a very humbling experience because some of them were children who had been abducted, trafficked to work in the circus in India, in China. A foundation from the UK had rescued them, brought them back to Nepal. So I went as a volunteer to train them. It was really an amazing thing to do. I've never done any charity work before. That was the very first time. I've never been to Clowns Without Borders. I train clown-doctors, but I never actually did it. So that was very humbling, and I enjoyed that.

You know, we're not many. We're all getting old. But what would the world be without clowns?

18 Geoff Hoyle

Figure 17 Geoff Hoyle. Photo by Terry Lorant

Geoff Hoyle (born in England, 1946) is a founding member of the Pickle Family
Circus, where he created beloved clown Mr. Sniff. He performed as a clown in
Cirque du Soleil's *Nouvelle Expérience*, and originated the role of Zazu in *The Lion
King* on Broadway. He later created several critically acclaimed solo performances
including *Feast of Fools*, featuring masked commedia dell'arte characters; *The Con-
vict's Return*, about taking *Feast of Fools* to Broadway; *The First Hundred Years*, an

improbable history of comedy; and *Geezer*, a highly physical comedy about what it is like to grow old.

Geoff took a few minutes to talk shop with me in his San Francisco home. (EL)

Origins

EL: What was your first experience of clowning or circus?

Geoff: Oh, I thought you were going to ask me if I was still alive … Just as a preface, I should tell you, I don't consider myself to be a clown. I consider myself to be a physical actor who works in a spectrum of performance styles, of which clown is one part.

I can't put my finger on a specific event, but I have a vague memory of seeing clowns on television. Charlie Cairoli, the Cairoli Brothers, working in the Chipperfield Circus, or Bertram Mills Circus, or Blackpool Tower Circus in England when I was growing up. I don't remember being that impressed with what they did, even though one thought one should be. Sort of a grand old tradition.

It was only much much later that I came to clowning, after theater training. That I came to see who the great clowns were. The same kind of investigating that Fellini did with *I Clowns*. I became aware of clowns like Rhum and Pipo and Grock, or even Victor Borge, through to vaudeville and variety and musical comedians, which is my real influence. It wasn't really circus clowns, more variety performers.

EL: Were there any performers in your family?

Geoff: They didn't perform professionally, but they performed all the time. A large extended working-class family. They were always doing stuff, always making fun of each other. The circus tent was the dinner table. There was a lot of wry, survivalist humor, which came out of the post-war generation of my parents and uncles and aunts. Also they imitated working-class comedians.

EL: Was there a point when you knew you wanted to be a performer?

Geoff: My first inklings toward performance were both a means of survival in the schoolyard and in the classroom, and a means of obtaining affection from friends and family. I would always imitate variety comics, and get a laugh from my family, and my mother would usually say, "Isn't he awful?" which would mean, isn't he great? The moment that I would point to: my Latin teacher was reading the story of Theseus and the minotaur, and I started acting it out, and she beckoned me to the front of the class, and she read the story, and she said to the class, "He's going to act all the parts." I then acted the story of Theseus and Egeus, his father and the minotaur in Chaplinesque pantomime. I was her PowerPoint presentation as it were.

Inspirations

EL: Did you go to drama school?

Geoff: As a working-class kid from northern England there was no possibility of even getting into RADA (the Royal Academy of Dramatic Art) because it was basically an old boys' network of middle-class people. It wasn't until much later, after *Look Back in Anger*, Pinter, kitchen sink dramatists, when theater started to open up to the drama of the working class. There were very few places to go. So my option was simply to go to university. John Russell Brown had started a drama and theater arts department at Birmingham. I was one of ten combined honors students to be admitted, so I combined my drama/theater arts course with a course in English language and literature, which was very useful and had a lot to offer, though it was completely academic, and it meant doing a massive amount of reading, which I never did because I was too busy being involved in student and department theater productions. At the end of my time at Birmingham, I had had a clear division in my thinking of high art (or bourgeois art) and low art, popular performance. Most of my teachers at Birmingham were into high art, and I'm not making a judgment on that, it just wasn't as interesting to me to be a chorus member in *Agamemnon* by Aeschylus as it was to write my own play about the Profumo Affair, which was a musical send up, using established songs and rewriting lyrics to explore the absurd farce of the Profumo Affair – spying and national security secrets being betrayed on the pillows of Whitehall officials to the Russians. This was very exciting to me, and part of this came because one of my mentors had worked with Joan Littlewood, who ran the Theatre Workshop and had communist sympathy in the post-war era. My mentor and teacher, Clive Barker, was a member of her company. We were very excited because he was a teacher who came from the profession. He was an actor and a writer and a director. He had written a book called *Theatre Games*, which actually sits on my desk at this very moment. He introduced me to Brecht (although I'd skirmished with Brecht already), Theatre of the Oppressed, Story Theatre, and non-play-structured, non-middle-class theater forms. He saw theater as a weapon. The theater I wanted to do was based on irony, popular comedy, working-class comedians, comedy that had a political ramification and a stance, which was subversive, iconoclastic, and absurd; all the things that great comedy can be, pillorying the powerful, pillorying the pretentious, the pompous, and the rich, because by definition their wealth abuses a great mass of people, and causes great disparity in people's ability to reach fulfillment and enjoyment. That's where clowning comes in much much later. I was doing *The Entertainer*, not Iago.

EL: What brought you to Paris to study with Decroux?

Geoff: I went to Clive and said, "I'm graduating in three weeks. What do I do now?" He said, "You can move. You need training. Go to the master." I said, "Who's that?" He said, "Etienne Decroux. Telephone the French embassy. They give money to foreigners." And so I did. And it was Lecoq or Decroux, and Lecoq was three times the price, and being a true Yorkshireman, which is one step below a Scotsman, I went to Decroux.

EL: *[Laughs.]* What was important for you in your work with Decroux?

Geoff: It was rigor. Discipline and mastery. Even though I didn't know it at the time, I was working with a twentieth-century legend. He had done amazing performances himself. He was a mad genius. It was like sitting at the foot of Leonardo da Vinci or Michelangelo. It was also the setting. I came in one day and said, "There's a demonstration outside." Decroux replied, "Against us?" And I said, "No, no." It was 1968, and the streets were erupting, so I was there for those days, and they definitely had a big effect on me. I mean, I was 19, 20 years old in Paris in 1968 studying mime. Come on, that's a mythic thing.

I also did acrobatics with a guy named Tudor Bono in Gymnase du Cirque. I watched Jean-Louis Barrault in his production of *Rabelais*. I remember going to Avignon. We saw Grotowski's company do *Apocalypsis Cum Figuris*. We saw the Living Theatre. These were important moments in theater history.

EL: This moment in Paris, between 1968 and '72, has generated many of the heavyweight performers of the last 40 years. Did you have a sense of why this entire generation of performers developed? Was something happening that was unique that generated this explosion of artists?

Geoff: Wow, that's a big chunk of history. We were just there doing our thing. "Go to the master." The French government was giving out money.

EL: That must be what it was. The French government gave money to artists.

Geoff: Right! They were! Either through incredibly arrogant pretentiousness, or generosity of spirit, or a combination of the two. They gave money to foreigners to come and study their art. One of the lines in my show *Geezer*, in the middle of a demonstration, I say, "The French government is paying me to riot against them." There was culture happening in France that is no longer viable. It was the time. We were just doing our thing.

Techniques

EL: How do you frame yourself as being or not being a clown?

Geoff: I consider myself a comic actor. A living cartoon. That's what I try to do.

EL: How did Mr. Sniff develop?

Geoff: When I created Mr. Sniff, it was first a drawing. There's a book called *Acrobats and Mountebanks*. Larry [Pisoni] had been trying to track it down for years. When we were in London I took him to this antiquarian bookshop that specialized in children's books and theater books, and lo-and-behold they had it. There were lots of drawings and pictures of comedians and clowns, commedia dell'arte spin-offs. One had a long coat. So we thought maybe this guy Mr. Sniff would have a long coat. I had done an audition for Larry where I wore a long coat, a street performance with gloves with no fingers, sort of a hobo, a bit like Chaplin taking the dress of the upper class and parodying it by giving him no shoulders and baggy pants. And then we put a bowler hat on, because we were doing hat tricks so I needed a hat, and a red nose, a long red nose, which was somewhat obscene, very commedia, almost a Pulcinella nose, but no mask – and he would sniff. He would sniff everything. I've always had that as a personal thing. I have an intense sense of smell. So in the style of many other clowns, I used my personal attribute to create a slightly strange character. Larry wanted the coat to be a circus coat because we were doing circus, so we settled on a yellow coat, a black hat, and I decided he wouldn't actually wear any pants. He would just be wearing long underwear, and striped socks. (Again, a concession to circus. Clowns have to have striped socks.) I had to wear big shoes because Bill [Irwin] and Larry had big shoes, not that I particularly liked them. And he had a cane, in the Chaplin concept. He could hit people with it, and he had a swagger. This stick gave him some power with which he could demolish pretension and annoyance. And he could take other people's sticks and destroy their sticks. And I did this drawing of him. I put him in a long union suit and this long coat. He'd forgotten his pants. You know Einstein never combed his hair; well, Mr. Sniff forgot his trousers, but it was cold so he put on his coat. And he needed his hat because he did hat tricks. And he had his cane. And he went out in the world, and what he saw was Larry and Bill. They say the same about Chaplin. He didn't arrive fully blown with his costume. It developed over years. And then one day suddenly there was the little tramp. These things arrive because we accumulate. Mr. Sniff is an accumulation of all my uncles, and my dad, and my mum, and my aunties, and geezers I saw in England growing up. And he always has a dewdrop on the end of his nose.

EL: Is Mr. Sniff a clown?

Geoff: Yes, he's a circus clown, but he's also a character. That's what makes him more durable. He has a whole way of looking at things. He's not a happy clown. He has moments of happiness, but he has great sadness and a sense of dilemma. Most effectively, he has moments of contrariness, and he's angry, and to bring that to American circus clowning is this whole different thing, I think. Larry had this deep melancholy as this old fat guy, and Bill had this reckless grace, but he had an angry side which I found so refreshing. We were using real emotion, and trying to represent images of real life, not just happy clowns.

EL: Is there a sketch from Pickle Family Circus that characterizes this kind of material?

Geoff: The one that comes to mind is "The Three Musicians." But that one doesn't have Mr. Sniff in it. It pre-dates Mr. Sniff. One critic referred to it as earth, fire, and water. It was elemental. My character was called Bushy Beard because I had a beard at the time, which was a holdover from when I had done street performance as a geezer, with painted glasses on his face like Bobby Clark. Bill was Willy, and Larry, I think we called him Fatso. (We couldn't get away with that now.) Larry had a fat suit on. He pulled out a tuba case, in it was a pocket cornet; lots of jokes about laundry, and too-high heat in the laundry. I played the trombone. Bill played the big base drum with a cymbal on top. And we all had Italian accents, because it gives that level of strangeness, of distance, a dreamlike quality, and also outliers, someone from a foreign land, in exile, an immigrant. The main idea of the sketch was we were three musicians from the circus, we were going to play a song, and everything went wrong, everything conspired against us. In classic form, the clown is battling the tyranny of things, and battling objects, and battling the tyranny of structure, and laws and rules, rules of physics and rules of authority. I mean, how many times is a great silent comedian trying to outrun the cops? That's what it's all about. And the musicians win. Everything goes wrong, but eventually they play the tune. They win. By cooperating. But I don't think we ever intended to do a moral tale for children, family values clowning. No, no, no. We were saying stick it out, we gotta do this, pressure's on, what do we do? "Another fine mess you've gotten me into … " "Where are we going? I don't know." That's it. "Where are we going? I don't know." Put your trust in unknowing, uncertainty. The greatest wisdom is embracing uncertainty.

EL: Have you brought any old material back recently?

Geoff: I've done "The Three-Legged Man" recently, which has become a signature piece. The work is a continuum. Every time it's the same exploration. You use similar tools in the exploration, not always exactly the same. You want to get down to the core. And that's the journey. You want to get to some deeply affected truth about life and its difficulty, which is ultimately, ironically, crowned by death. The fool outwits death to a degree, or at least he's not afraid of death. I have a piece called "Dance with Death" where I dance with a skeleton. It's the conundrum of life, how wonderful life is, and at the same time what a disaster, and how do you mediate that? It's not just a fool, a clown. It's a poet, a painter. We're investigating. Nietzsche said, "We have art in order not to die of the truth." And that's what we do. We're in dialogue with death and reality. And it's serious business. It's hilariously painful, decidedly, a means of surviving the worst pain. We are all ultimately fools, and we don't have a solution.

EL: Why do you personally do this work?

Geoff: It's always initially to make people laugh. I love laughter. You can't die when you're laughing. You can laugh and then die, but you … if you're laughing, you're alive. It's a way of beating death. I want to make people laugh. I want to make people feel close to each other, feel equal, feel that we're all just animals, and we better get used to that fact. And we all have blood and bones, and life is short. And how do you cope? I guess there's a deep vein of depression, sadness, and melancholy in my comedy, which gives it a bit more weight or irony. It's a fight.

EL: With "The Three-Legged Man," how have you experienced its evolution over time?

Geoff: Originally, I had to do a bit for a benefit for the Pickle Family Circus. I didn't know what to do. I pulled out a book by a man called Patrick Page. It was self-published. It was called *150 Comedy Props: How To Make Them, How To Use Them*. It had a bunch of pictures of clowns in red noses. The book was only in black and white. It was perfect. And one of the pages had this three-legged man bit. He said if you wanted to, you could probably make a little dance. I thought, ahah! I put it together, and started doing moves in front of my mirror. I thought, this is paydirt. I started developing different moves. I happened to hear on the radio the tune "Flamingo." It's an old jazz tune. It's very smooth, very loungy. I started playing around. I would just improvise. At that benefit I put that tune on, and I went out there and improvised. I had these bits I'd worked out, these bravura moments. I'd named them, the Bell Ringer Swing, the Braiding, the way choreographers name their bits. I knew I'd put these in. So I would wander around the stage as a ballroom dancer who takes the handicap of having three legs and turns it into an advantage, and have this raucous finale, and then finish up with braiding. I'd know I need to get to that point in the music and do that bit. You just start fitting the bits together where the music is. Eventually it got sort of choreographed by default, by investigation. It's called rehearsal in regular theater, but I did it in performance. I always say I rehearse in performance. It honed down to fairly specific things so I could actually write it out. Now, when I go back to it, I get very frustrated because I can't remember a transition from here to there. But I have to get the inner part right. He's a character. It's not just me doing a bunch of moves. He's a guy who develops throughout the dance. He starts kind of tentative, embarrassed, and then he finds he can actually do something, "Oh this is fun, wow," and I'm off! It's a piece of theater, not just a series of funny bits.

EL: As you prepare to do it again now, how is it different from when you first performed the routine?

Geoff: When you revive something, you revive it in the light of what has happened since the last time you did it, in terms of your work and your life. There may be things you can augment; there may be refinements you can chisel out of the raw wood. You can chisel something out here so it links with something. You get better at your carving. The difficulty is that often you want to put in too much carving. You don't trust the basic instinct. The initial instinct is the best; it's actually subconscious. You start messing with stuff and it's not as good. It loses its rawness, it's interface with your own subconscious impulses.

EL: Can you think of a moment of failure in performance?

Geoff: Sometimes I'll come off, and they'll say, "Wow, that was two hours of substantial performance." And I'll think, well, I missed that one thing, that 1-percent thing; it ruins it for me. And I'm constantly struggling with that. When people say it was a great show, my tendency is to say I didn't get this, or I didn't give the audience that. It's actually disrespectful of the person who said it's a great show. It questions their assessment. I think it feels like a bit of a betrayal by you of yourself. It's usually a lack of trust. An attempt to overdo it well. There was a wonderful article by Malcolm Gladwell called "The Art of Failure: Why Some People Choke and Others Panic" in *The New Yorker*. He draws the difference between choking and panic. Panic is where you don't trust your instinct enough. Choking is where you don't trust the information you're getting enough. One comes from the inside; one comes from the outside. I think if you're a performer, opening night, and if you know someone in the audience and you try to impress them, it's not failure so much as missteps. You start betraying trust in what you've developed. If you do what you are supposed to do modestly and without having a secondary agenda, consciously or unconsciously, then it becomes graceful, and you do what you do.

Philosophy

EL: What is a clown? And what is the role of the clown in society?

Geoff: There are two meanings to the word "clown." There's the limited meaning of circus clown, which is what most people think of in America. "Oh, you mean Cirque du Soleil." That's what they think, or Ringling Bros, and that's the clown, which is the clown that comes out of the European tradition, but magnified with American optimism. It doesn't have the same kind of social context and irony that the early imports to American clowning had, like Otto Griebling. He had a bit where he was trying to deliver a block of ice. It was a walkaround piece, and he couldn't find the addressee. He starts out with this big huge block of ice, and eventually gets it to the addressee, and it's an ice cube. There are implications around that. But later clowning, clowning that relied on props, because of this three-ring-spectacle-bigger-is-better idea, put restraints on the original commentary of clown, of the great clown dynasties of Europe, and Afro-European clowns as well.

The other side of clown is a philosophical idea, which is the subversive presence in a structure which has to be broken with anarchy, which is encapsulated I suppose in the classic duo of the Elegant and the Auguste. The Elegant representing structure and authority can also be the state, capitalism, the media, it can be your boss. And you see that thrust in different places, on *I Love Lucy*, *The Honeymooners*, *Jack Benny*. The underdog fighting the top dog and trying to break the structure. Nina Simone sings, "I wish I could say what it feels to be free. I wish I could tell the great love I have." The great oppression. It stops you from being capable, from finding your worth, your identity, your value, and being able to share that with people. And the clown is constantly asking, why is this the case? So the clown in some philosophical way is also a cynic, subversive, but also behind every cynic is a romantic who says, why is it like this? So a lot of clown work uses non-structured reality, to break the structure of everyday perception. The easiest example of that would be dreams. You can look at Artaud, Theatre of the Absurd, Beckett, all of those use clowns.

EL: What do you see as the future of clowning?

Geoff: I don't really see clown as a thing. I think that's a result of the desire of the media to box something up. Remember the whole thing about New Vaudeville? I tell people I'm an old vaudevillian. There was vaudeville. It was a market. There was circus clowning, and that was a market. There are things you want to do in a circus ring as a clown, there are traditions you want to honor, and keep alive, and transform, and adapt. Why are there clown conservatories? Why are there clown schools? What's that all about? You get a diploma of clowning. Do you take it to the Starbucks of clowning and ask, can I get a job here? It doesn't make any sense to me. You gut the whole idea of comedy as commentary. You become a conformist. You're commoditizing the idea of commentary and art through performance, through story, interfaced with live audience. Theater, a lot of the time, it's about monetizing, or celebrity, and conformity. And also, because of the competition, it's about massively virtuoso and life-threatening performance. You can't box it up and say, "What is the future of clowning?" It's like saying, "What is the future of weather?" We don't know. Weather is weather. I mean, what is the future of the human condition? We could talk about that, we could have a seminar talking about the future of clowning, and it would be really not much fun.

EL: Your son Dan Hoyle has become established as a solo performer as well. In terms of stepping into the future or carrying on tradition, thinking about the philosophical side of clown that you described, what do you feel you have passed onto him?

Geoff: The first thing that springs to mind, and he probably got more of this from his mom, but maybe also from me, the first thing is compassion. He's massively compassionate. And the second thing is curiosity. Curiosity and compassion about what makes people tick, what their stories are, how they got to be where they are, what they do about facing the day, how they handle life. He takes that, turns it around, and makes that into art, into commentary. So the cynical, romantic clown does have compassion and curiosity, and I think that's what Dan has in spades. More than me.

19 Bill Irwin and David Shiner

Figure 18 Bill Irwin and David Shiner. Photo by Gregory Costanzo

Bill Irwin (born in Santa Monica, California, 1950), after graduating from Ringling Bros Clown College, performed with the Pickle Family Circus for three years. His long and varied stage career has included his highly acclaimed clown-based solo shows *The Regard of Flight*, *Largely New York*, and *Mr. Fox: A Rumination*, as well as Broadway appearances in *Waiting for Godot*, *The Goat*, and *Who's Afraid of Virginia Woolf?*, which earned him a Tony Award for Best Actor in 2005. He is a Guggenheim and MacArthur fellow, the winner of many additional awards for his work on stage and screen, and an esteemed director and choreographer for good measure.

David Shiner (born in Boston, Massachusetts, 1953) began his clown career on the streets of Boulder, Colorado, and Paris, where he developed his signature style based on wildly unpredictable interactions with his audience. After stints in Circus Roncalli and Circus Knie, he co-wrote and starred in Cirque du Soleil's *Nouvelle Expériénce*, which toured the world. He initiated the Broadway role of the Cat in the Hat in *Seussical* and has appeared in several films. He teaches regularly at the Theater Akademie August Everding in Munich and conceived and directed *Kooza* for Cirque du Soleil.

Irwin and Shiner met in the early '90s on the set of *Silent Tongue*. Within a few years, they had created and premiered their two-man, wordless clown show *Fool Moon*, which ran from 1992 to 1999 including three separate runs on Broadway. The production was showered with awards, including a special Tony Award for Live Theatrical Presentation in 1999, a Drama Desk Award for Unique Theatrical Experience, and an Outer Critics Circle Special Achievement Award. In recent years the duo has teamed up once again for a new clown show, *Old Hats*, which premiered at the Signature Theatre in New York. Both independently and as a double act, Irwin and Shiner are widely regarded as the two preeminent American clowns of their era.

We chatted with Bill and David in the rehearsal rooms at the American Conservatory Theater in San Francisco, where they were taking a break from technical rehearsals as they prepared to premiere *Old Hats* on the West Coast. (DB/EL)

Origins

EL: When did you first encounter clowns or circus in your life?

David: Film clowns – when I was ten. Jerry Lewis, Chaplin, all those guys. But my first live clown was a mime on the streets of Boulder, Colorado, in 1977. There was a guy there who had a mime troupe – he might still be teaching, Samuel Avital – and mime was really big in those days, you know, putting your hands against a wall, walking against the wind ... I saw a guy on the street, and I thought, "That's really cool. I'll do that." I had been building houses for ten years. I was 28 years old. But I went out into the new Boulder mall on a Saturday, dressed in clown attire – I put on some yellow pants and a striped shirt – and I started doing stuff. I was awful. It sucked. But somehow I didn't give it up because I was so enchanted by it. And then one day, I was out on the streets and a police car came through, and I stopped it. I pretended I was a policeman, and I made the real cop get out of his car, and I frisked him ... I even got into his car – in those days cops were easy-going! – and when I got out of the car there were 500 people watching me. And that's when I started improvising with people, imitating them and doing stuff with them. Then some guys came through town in the summer of '81, a couple of jugglers, and they said, "You gotta go to Paris." I realized I was due for a change anyhow, so I quit my job, and I literally ... I packed my bags and left. I think I had $500 in my pocket. I flew to Paris, got a shitty hotel room, went out the next day on the streets, and they chased me away. But I kept coming back.

Bill: I grew up in Tulsa, Oklahoma, for the first part of my life. Might have gone to the circus ... But the crux of it, for me, was early TV. Gleason, Carney, Phil Silvers. Growing up on those. I remember when we first got a TV. Sid Caesar. That stuff was on. And sometimes they put silent films on, too, as programming filler. When I was in grade school, Hollywood released "The Golden Age of Comedy," and it was all the greats from 30 years earlier – I went to see that with my family. And it was like hearing music that I already knew.

DB: Looking back on it, do you think of those early TV stars as clowns?

Bill: Certainly Gleason and Carney. And Phil Silvers, yeah. When I was in Clown College, in 1974, to keep us off the streets they would show movies. I saw a Phil Silvers movie called *Top Banana*, and it was all the burlesque stuff that he came out of.

David: I've seen that.

Bill: Physical stuff, really. Later, in the '80s, he hosted *Saturday Night Live*, and he was totally out of touch with the times. Did a joke about a cute chick in a sweater, nobody laughed. He was pissed off. But back in his time, do you remember Bilko? There's a little bit of Bilko in what we do, don't you think?

David: Yeah. And he enjoyed doing rage, as well. So did Gleason – Jackie Gleason was all about rage. He was a pressure cooker ... The audience was always just waiting for the moment when it would be released. "When's the moment when he's gonna lose it?" That was when he was at his funniest.

DB: I watched you stand in front of a roomful of fresh-faced students and say, "You wanna know the secret of comedy? I'll tell you: rage."

David: I did?!

DB: That was your opening gambit!

EL: Had there been any traces of performers in your families?

David: Crooks. Swindlers and crooks. Close, right?

Bill: Oh yeah.

DB: What did your family make of your choice?

David: Oh, they thought I was crazy. My father said, "Jesus Christ, ya gotta suitcase – ya need some money?" I said, "No, I got money." He said, "How much money ya got?" "$500." "$500! What the ... ?! Jesus Christ! Where ya gonna live? What ya gonna eat? What ya gonna do?" I said, "Mime." He said, "What's that?!?"

Bill: No, really?

David: He said, "What the hell is mime?" I said, "Marcel Marceau, you know ... " I showed him some techniques. He just looked at me like I was out of my fucking mind.

Bill: It's poignant, too, looking back. I've known David's dad ... I guess that was his way of saying, "Son, I love ya, I'm worried about ya."

David: He was terrified for me.

Bill: My mother's father was a really interesting cat. He died when I was about ten. But he was a schoolteacher in North Dakota, and he worked for the Red Cross, and he put on shows in his local town. He'd connect with the local tribal authority at the reservation and get them involved ... And my mother said that anything was fair game in the house. Her sister's new dress ... "Hey! Dad's using my dress as a costume in his show!" And my own father, when he retired from being an aeronautical engineer for 35 years, got involved in local community theater, built sets, and even was on stage a couple of times.

DB: So how did you go from getting interested to actually starting?

Bill: From the very beginning right up to today, I've always had the same feeling: "Oh, shit ... This is scary, but ... I've got to do this!" Even when I was in grade school, when I was supposed to write a report, I'd want to do a monologue instead. "Could I do a monologue?"

David: Samuel Beckett!

Bill: No, even worse – I wrote them myself. Rip-offs of Bob Newhart. Then I got involved in school plays and musicals, and I studied theater in a variety of colleges – UCLA, then I transferred to CalArts, and from there I went to Oberlin. So I was in the collegiate theater world, which bordered, at that time, on the avant-garde. And I jumped from the avant-garde into the Ringling Brothers Clown College. After that, I came to Pickle Family Circus.

EL: Were these unconventional choices? For the time?

Bill: The thing about those times – so many of us were trying to reorder the authoritarian, the vertical hierarchies – in a kind of quixotic way. When I lived in San Francisco in the early '70s, it was really Lefter Than Thou. We'd get together: "Hey, let's rehearse." So there'd be a roomful of people trying to come up with a show for a school gig, or something, and some guy would go, "I'd like to discuss everything we're doing from the point of view of Marxist-Leninist principles."

David: Really!? Are you serious?

Bill: He would totally hijack everything. The room would stop, and we'd all go, "Wow. Oh. Okay."

David: Jesus!

Bill: Oh, it was like Paris in '68. Oh, boy. Crazy. Wild times.

Inspirations

DB: Did either of you have any mentors?

Bill: Did you have a mime teacher, David?

David: No.

Bill: No!?

David: It was all by the book. Claude Kipnis on mime. I literally looked at the pictures ... And he had a flip section, too.

Bill: Really?

David: Yeah. *[Makes flipping sound.]* So I taught myself the techniques. And then when I was on the streets of Paris, all the guys who were studying with Marceau or Decroux would come by, and I'd always squeeze them for techniques: "Show me how to do this, show me how to do that."

Bill: Not so much the Lecoq people?

David: No ... I'd heard of Lecoq. I went to one of the workshops there; I didn't particularly like it ... I was very arrogant. "I'm a street artist, I don't need to study." Stupid! I wish I had, I'd have saved myself a lot of time. But I didn't really have any living mentors. If anyone, it was Chaplin – he was my idol – Keaton, Laurel and Hardy. I loved Red Skelton. Lucille Ball, I absolutely loved her. All those early clowns.

Bill: My son has gone through an intense Lucille Ball fixation!

David: There's never been a female comic like her.

Bill: I heard they didn't horse around. It was very serious on set. But how funny …

EL: Bill, did you have mentors?

Bill: While I was at CalArts I studied with Mamako Yoneyama. Also, a director named Herbert Blau, who was not a physical comedian at all. These were influential people. Herbert Blau was the one who told me about Keaton's film *The Navigator*. One of the greatest movies you'll ever see. Herbert was good in some ways, not so good in others, but he was certainly a mentor to me. He talked about the visceral nature of the intellect. How the intellect is a muscle. It shouldn't take you away from physicality – it's the access point for it. And of course I owe a huge mentorship debt – and lots of other debts – to Larry Pisoni. I learned so much from Pisoni. I remember a time early in the Pickle Family days when we showed up at Oakland for a gig. I was in big hair and red nose, so there was a lot of attention on me, but I didn't really know what to do. I could improvise with kids but I didn't really have an act yet. And Larry had to walk across the stage to shake some guy's hand, and he tripped. It just said so much. He tripped, and then he shook the guy's hand. And I thought, "Wooaah, that's a bit of useful vocabulary." One time I showed up with a bunch of props, and Larry said, "Psh, you need a trunk." So I got a trunk, and of course, very soon, I couldn't use it to carry my props because the trunk became part of the act. Larry Pisoni and Geoff Hoyle … We learned a lot from each other.

David: I had a similar relationship with René Bazinet when we were working together in Europe. We did a show together on and off for a while. René is a great storyteller, in terms of sound and movement. He has great movement. His piece, "The Crow": he tells this story about a cowboy in the desert, dying of thirst and hunger, who shoots a crow and cooks it and eats it and nearly chokes to death on it. And René does all the characters. He does the crow, he does the cowboy, makes the sound effects of the gun, the echoes … There's nothing like it. I met him on the streets. He was working with a guy named Pony, a Canadian mime. They had great routines for the street. They had one routine where they ran a race, the 200-yard dash, and they would try to trip each other up, and then it went into slow-motion. And it got more and more out of control. It was really, really good. René was one of Lecoq's best students. He came out of that school, and he took that whole form and just ran with it. I learned a lot from René in that sense, in terms of storytelling.

Bill: Then there are the people you see doing things. I went to see the Ringling show way back, and I saw Pio Nock, Bello's uncle, from the Swiss circus family. You know Bello?

DB/EL: Yes.

Bill: Well I saw his uncle, who was phenomenal!

DB: A clown?

Bill: A clown, both at deck level and with a high-wire act. And typical Ringling … The first year I saw his high-wire act, it was fantastic. And then the next year, they had him do the same act – over the tiger cage!

David: Gotta spice things up.

Bill: Exactly.

DB: David, were there clowns who inspired you?

David: First there was Marceau himself. When I saw his work, I was really enchanted. At that point I didn't actually know I wanted to be a clown. I thought I wanted to get into mime because I loved the techniques and the whole magical quality of it. You could create these illusions from nothing. But then I saw Dimitri in Circus Knie. That was the first circus I ever set foot in. 1981. He had this clown character, white face, and he had the big jacket, and he came out, and it was very simple, what he did, and it was really beautiful. That was what really set me off. I saw him and I went *[snaps fingers]* "Oh, that's it. I don't wanna be a fucking mime. I wanna be a clown."

DB: Was it the humor?

David: It was the whole thing. It was the circus. It was the smell of the animals. It was …

Bill: Was it the relationship with the audience?

David: Yeah! Everything.

Bill: It seems a million miles from, "You stand over there. I'm doing an illusion," to "Let me get in your face!"

David: "Let me get right in your face! Hit you with my head!"

Bill: Light years!

David: "I'm gonna be a mime. No, I'm not, I'm gonna hit people!"

Bill: Right!

[Laughter.]

David: But then … If we're going to talk about clowns who inspired me … Then, in '82, I saw Bill Irwin, in a video.

Bill: Oh! A grainy video, I'll bet.

David: *The Regard of Flight* on PBS. I was still in the streets. I was in Paris, and I met some woman who was doing an article for the *New York Times* about street artists in Paris. She mentioned Bill, and somehow I got hold of the video.

DB: And, Bill, had you made that recording during your time with Pickle Family?

Bill: Afterwards. Pickle Family began in '75, and I did three seasons. I was still a part of it, so I remember working on what became *The Regard of Flight* in their rehearsal space. But I wanted to work in the theater as opposed to a little circus touring in sun-baked California. And after the New York run, PBS filmed it.

David: What blew me away about Bill: he was the first guy I saw who was combining dance, theater, mime, and clowning all together. I never saw that before. I just thought, "Shit!" From then on, Bill was always in the back of my mind. I started working at circuses myself. I did Roncalli. I did a season with Knie in '87 … But Bill was always the one. I said, "That's the guy." And I saw every-body. So in '91, I was doing Cirque du Soleil in New York, and I knew that Bill was living there, and – how did I get in touch with you?

Bill: I don't know. I was going to ask you that.

David: I remember now. I found out you were in the audience. I was nervous as hell. So later I got your telephone number from someone and I just called you.

Bill: That's right. You called me.

David: And we met for lunch, and …

Bill: I would say we were like dogs in the park. *[Sniffs.]*

David: I was in awe.

Bill: I felt so dull. Remember? And we went to that terrible place …

David: He took me to lunch at this Italian place – nobody's in it. It's completely empty. We're these two guys sitting in this empty restaurant.

Bill: I thought it would be suitable, but … The part I remember is this: we met, and David said, "You wanna come see the show again?" So I said yes, of course, and I brought my mom. Now my mother was always very supportive, about my being a clown, and about theater … She ran a senior center, and we'd do fundraising for the Pickle Family and she enjoyed it all … But there was always a little bit of, "Is that what you're gonna do with your life?" She couldn't help it. Supportive, but … with a bit of reserve. So I'm sitting next to her at Cirque du Soleil, and Shiner's doing … was it the car number?

David: No, I did the camera number, with the improv in the audience.

Bill: Oh, yes! So he's doing his number, and I'm sitting there with my mother … I've never seen her laugh like that. She was in ecstasy. And I was … um …

David: You were thinking, "That guy's an asshole! Fuck that guy!"

Bill: Right! That's the thing I remember the most about meeting you. Just recently, when Robin Williams died, they played a bunch of his interviews; it was really poignant. I heard one where the interviewer said, "Jonathan Winters was an idol of yours," and Robin Williams said, "Yeah, I saw how hard my father laughed at Jonathan Winters." This is an interesting thing about our parents. They may not be the kind of influences you were asking about. But they are influences nevertheless.

Techniques

DB: David, you talked about how you started playing with that policeman and how that shifted things for you. How did that discovery lead you to your mature work, the silent movie melodrama sketch or climbing all over the audience? Was it accident or design?

David: It was necessity, because I was such a bad mime. I tried doing my little sketches and it just wasn't working. It was boring. People would walk by and I would hear them say, "Wow, this guy sucks." Literally! The shift happened purely by accident. When I pulled the policeman out of the car and I had 500 people watching me, I went, "Oh, oh! Gotta involve people." And so I started going up to people and doing stuff. In the beginning it was hard, but then I started to do more of it, and more people started watching me, and I got more and more outlandish. I wondered, "How far can I go?" The cinema routine came about when I was improvising on the streets of Paris. I thought, "Well, let me try making a movie." First I worked with just one person. Then it was two people. Then it was three. Then I got a clapper guy. And then one day in the summer of '82, I was in Avignon at the festival and I actually built a real door. So the hero guy could come through it. And the biggest gag of that whole routine, where the guy walks through the door, happened by accident. I was doing it in Berlin at some gala event, and the door was closed, and I thought, "You know, it's kinda stupid having the door closed because nobody can see the guy, and they can't see me getting upset with him." So I took out the door and just left the frame, and the very first time we did it, the guy walked through the invisible door without opening it. And then the people screamed! It was freaking gold.

Bill: I've seen that routine between a thousand and fifteen hundred times in various forms, and it's just fascinating to me how people want to be part of the story, how they sign up to the story. They serve the story. Of course it's the way David sets it up. But there's also an authority to the whole idea. It's amazing.

DB: Didn't you describe once that when you pull a volunteer out, you'll whisper some encouraging words in their ear, before you berate them publicly? To create a little bit of trust?

David: I just say, "Just relax and have a good time." I let the mask down. Otherwise, they stay closed. They need to see that moment where you're just a normal person.

DB: But you don't show that to the rest of the audience?

David: No.

Bill: I try to learn his craft. In *Old Hats* we have the audience volunteer. I'm in drag, and he's in this bizarre magician's outfit, and we bring a young woman up, and we put her in the middle of our, uh, marital anger.

David: He plays my wife.

Bill: Right. I try to touch the volunteer, to be very reassuring, maybe a little pat on the back. And then when we go off stage, I have to keep the dressers at bay, because they tend to come over right away, and it seems to me really important to take a moment and say to the volunteer, "Thank you for joining us. What is your name? Thank you so much." Then it's like a partnership or a collusion with the person.

DB: What about you, Bill? If you look at any of your signature pieces or mature pieces, how did they come about?

Bill: Some of it can be attributed to the combination of things I was interested in. By the time I went to the Ringling Clown College – I was maybe a couple years older than a lot of other people – I was already thinking, because of my theater background, about how you tell a story, how you present material. So I was good at envisioning things. But as for the clown himself, well ... When I got to San Francisco and started with the Pickle Family, I remember there was one school show we did where they gave me a trombone, just as a prop. I tried to play it, and I couldn't, of course. The kids went wild. And my instinctive response was to become afraid of them. I guess I had just stumbled upon the haplessness of the innocent clown. I realized: a) it's strong, and b) they need to be put at ease, and my being afraid of them is actually going to bring us to an equal starting point. Oh, god, did I tell you about this? Another early show with Pickle Family, we were set up in some gymnasium, and it was my entrance, and I was working with a black coat and a white cane, a fairly heavy thing; I went right out and twirled it, it flew out of my hand and hit a kid in the eye!

DB/EL/David: Oh, no!

Bill: I felt so awful. I worked on being more afraid of him than ever before. Anyway, that's where my character came from.

David: Bill is the first guy that I saw that made me think, "Holy Hell – this guy has a character!" Really. I thought, "Woah, he has a character. He has a certain look. He has a very distinct style of movement." And nobody was doing that. The moment Bill comes on stage, you know who he is, right away. And that's so vital.

Bill: I think I got a sense of that from seeing the early silents. Because there were great ones and not so great ones. Keaton, Chaplin, they were characters. So vivid. But then there were others, Chester Conklin for example. His whole thing was that his eyes would go in different directions. Bizarre and wonderful, yes – but not great. There were lesser and greater vaudeville guys too. But I think character is the whole deal.

David: From character springs everything.

EL: How did these kind of discoveries morph into full-length works, like *Fool Moon*?

David: Each one is different, of course. Bill and *Fool Moon* actually came together accidentally. We did a movie together, a Sam Shepard movie in New Mexico. And Bill and I would just be goofing off between takes – we had to come up with some clown routines – and it clicked right away, you know? It just clicked. Later, I was asked to do the Serious Fun Festival at Lincoln Center, and I asked Bill to do it, and I said, "Let's have a band play some music. We'll do a two-night gig for fun." And it turned into *Fool Moon*. Before we took it to Broadway we rehearsed and came up with some more routines. For me, some of the routines happen from just having fun and acting stupid, and others – you work your ass off to make it work. Some are a lot easier than others. You have an idea for something, and it can be torturous to get it where you want it. Some stuff you just throw in the garbage can because you know it's not going anywhere. So it's a mixed bag.

EL: When you're struggling to get something to work, do you have certain tools that you use to help you out?

David: We have the experience. All the years of experience, you know, that helps.

Bill: A shtick list.

David: A shtick list. But it depends what you're trying to do, how high you've set the bar for yourself.

Bill: And what parts of your mind you're employing. You know, *Fool Moon* – I ruefully laugh at this. We'd done the Serious Fun Festival, we had all these people interested, but I was convinced: "Guys! Guys! This can't be a mime show. It has to have some language in it." Completely convinced. So we wrote all this dialogue. I kept arguing for it, even though the band kept saying, "Uh-oh." We did it one night. The first preview. With dialogue. We even remembered some of it. My whole thing was, "We can't allow this to be called a mime show!" I was thinking from the exterior. Bad idea. Fortunately, the next day we came in and threw out all the words.

David: And then it became *Fool Moon*.

Bill: Under duress. Because the producer was going, "Uh, you know, we have a problem." Do you remember that?

David: No.

Bill: After that first preview. It was a disaster. The producer told us we had a problem. And I blew up at him.

David: I remember now! I never saw you so mad.

Bill: It was weird … I was upset. "You think I don't know we have a problem!?!" Thank God, the audience clicked in after this bad dialogue experiment was over with. The show found itself. And words were never mentioned again. Till now, 20 years later, where we have a bit in this show *[Old Hats]* where the clowns talk. Briefly. Briefly!

DB: Do you have numbers in this show that you struggle with?

David: All of them.

Bill: Every one.

[Laughter.]

EL: Is there a certain bit in this show that you've done before which has evolved into something new?

Bill: Sure. "The Encounter" is one.

David: "The Encounter," which we love doing. Two guys waiting for a train. It was in *Fool Moon*. Now it's 20 years later so they're old guys. I think it's a better version than the original because we really shrink. We really get small. It's an existential piece. It reminds me a lot of Beckett. Two guys that aren't going anywhere in life. Just thinking about the number makes me laugh. Two tortured, fucked up, lonely losers that can't get their shit together but are convinced they're doing great, life is going great for them. And they're not going anywhere, they're old. They're taking pills – they're offering each other pills for aches and pains; they're falling asleep … And they're lost.

Bill: It's a baby boomer satire, a fat satire. Then there's a number we used to call the iPad piece, but now we're calling it "Mr. Business" because it doesn't involve an iPad anymore. Samsung! Anyway, when we first created it, the stage manager and I would pray every night that it would work – the equipment didn't always function; it was a nightmare. Now, we've simplified it, and the story is so much clearer. So that's one that has definitely evolved.

David: But it's amazing how you think you have a number finished, completed – but it's never finished, is it? It's really never finished. Every night, "How can I make this better?"

EL: How can you?

Bill: Well, there's an old calculus: if you keep adding things and you don't take anything away, you're probably getting into trouble. You see that in a clown's work all the time. Add a bit, and then add another bit, and end up with a mess. So making things better is sometimes like house cleaning. You look for a clearer shape. Letting go of something is often the best addition to the piece. Leave something out. Geoff Hoyle used to say, "You can always use it for another show."

Philosophy

EL: From your vantage point as torchbearers, what do you see as the future of clowning? Where do you see it going?

Bill: There always will be live venues. We grew up saying, "Oh, movies and television will take over theater," and they haven't. They won't. Things change, but people still gather together to witness things. So I think there will always be young clowns coming up.

David: My gut feeling is there's gonna be a renaissance of physical comedy. It's been underground for a while, but I have a feeling it's gonna start to emerge. But it's a difficult art form, too. It's not something that you learn overnight. It's in your blood or it isn't.

DB: Have you seen any promising young clowns?

David: I've seen some potential people in Europe. I'm working with a guy right now from East Germany. I'm putting him in a show in the circus in the fall. I'm tutoring him, mentoring him. We do these Skype sessions. Once a week, 45 minutes. I tell him, "You gotta come up with an idea, each week, and present it to me, and I'll help you with it." And in the beginning he had no self-confidence, he said, "I don't have any ideas," and I said: "Bullshit. I don't want to hear that, ever again." And now he's coming up with these great ideas! He can sing, he can play accordion, he can play the ukulele, he can juggle … "What do you mean you don't have any ideas!?!?" How to be original, that's the question. You gotta find your original voice.

Bill: Tell them about the court case.

David: Oh right! Years ago I sued this circus. They stole my whole act; they had some American guy doing my cinema number. So we're in court, talking to the judge, and he says, "Let me look at the videos." So he looked at the video of the other guy's number. Very serious, studied it closely. He looked at mine, and started laughing his ass off. That's justice!

DB: Do you ever think about what clowning is for? What is its place in the world? Does that matter to you?

Bill: It does, very much. You think about your place in the world as you get older. I don't sleep well.

David: No, really?

Bill: Not at all. Sometimes I'll lie there and think of different shows. Take stock of my life. And that's when it comes up, "What's the value?"

David: When I ask that question, I have to ask another one: "Why did I start doing this?" It's funny: nine times out of ten when I'm teaching, I find out a lot of the students have some serious issues in life that are forcing them to get up on stage, dress up in a freakish outfit, big hats, big noses. Why do we do that? We're losers. We're messed up! I think there's always been the need for someone to make us laugh because life is so much of a struggle and so fucking painful most of the time. It's a roller coaster. And as you get older it becomes an even bigger roller coaster. You think you have time to relax and instead you're just looking at the end. At that point the cathartic need to laugh about serious issues is really important. The kind of things that would normally make us say, "What's the point? This is just too overwhelming for me. The whole experience … " Laughter is so necessary to calm us down, to make us see things in a lighter way. My mother was depressed. I think I started playing the fool mostly to make my mother laugh because she suffered so much … Plus I had seven brothers and sisters, and so there was this ritual of us acting like a bunch of idiots, especially three of us, my twin sister and my younger sister and me. We would act goofy all the time. I was also the class clown. So there was this need. And I've always loved doing it. Laughter as a healing balm has always been there, will always be there. I was drawn to the clown, the physical clown, because the laughter seems to be deeper. It's more primal than telling a joke. A joke you can forget the next day, the punchline is gone. But I always use this example when I teach. Bill is the one clown I've seen that summed it up perfectly, in one routine he did in *The Regard of Flight* where he just runs in a circle, this big run, this big stylish run, and then he trips, and he continues to run. Where's he running to? It's like life! Where the hell are we all running to? He's running. He trips again. And then he comes back around and he thinks, "I've got a great idea. I'm gonna jump over it." So he jumps over it, and he falls flat on his face. But when he falls on his face … I've never seen anything like this, and this is what drew me to physical comedy … When he falls on his face, it's primal. It's the collective suffering of humanity right in that movement. That one thing, all scrunched up. And the way he does it, and the way he scrunches up, it's stylish, it has this great movement to it, it has this quality of dance. It's not just a bad fall. It's a beautiful fall. That kind of laughter is rare. You get to laugh at the primal source of human suffering. You don't get that in a joke. You just can't. It doesn't happen. But you get that through a Chaplin, or a Keaton, or an Irwin. It's just … fuck, you can't describe it, you don't know how it happens, but it does, and that's what makes clowning, for me, such a wonderful art form, that goes so deep, the laughter. And it's not superficial, because you're always unconsciously or consciously talking about human suffering, and yet you're having fun with it. The two guys waiting for the train, these guys are in deep pain, and Bill, every time he comes out I have to stop myself from laughing because he's in agony. He's in fucking agony, you know. That's the reality, and you gotta laugh, and it's so wonderful that we can laugh at something that's so painful.

Bill: That means a lot when you tell that story about that fall, for lots of reasons. It's like a limerick, that piece. It's the structure that makes you laugh. But I realize I have to put that aside now, that particular bit. Because nowadays when I'm teaching, sometimes I'll get the knee pads on and say to the kids, "I'll show you the most dependable gag I know. Not the funniest gag I know, but the most dependable." But I can't do it anymore. The last couple times I've tried it, it was terrible. And the students look at me like this *[grimaces]* ...

David: Christ, that's sad. That's sad!

Bill: I didn't used to think about how I did it. I just went! The next thing I knew – bam, and there I was, and there was the laughter. Now I'm thinking, "How do I hit the floor?" And nobody laughs.

David: So sad!

DB: What about failure? What is the role of crashing and burning in the career of a clown?

David: It's absolutely vital that you crash and burn. A lot. If you avoid failure, you're not going to make it. I have a very good friend who is a retail guru in Germany – very smart guy – and we had a talk about failure one day, and he said, "When I hire people, I'm always looking for a person that failed at something. Because I know that person will have learned a tremendous amount from that failure. I never hire someone with straight As." In terms of clowning, whenever you're creating a new piece, one of the first thoughts you have to deal with is: "I'm afraid. This is different. Can I do this? Is it gonna work?" When we started on *Old Hats*, I kept saying to Bill, "How can we do better than *Fool Moon*?" And that was my biggest fear. But I really had to put that aside. I had to tell myself: "Stop it. Don't think like that. Just go into rehearsal and be creative and have fun, and see what happens." Because like all clowns I have to go full steam ahead knowing that when I put it in front of an audience, it may not work. The first time, the first couple of times. So can I stay the course? This is what's interesting about creativity; the only limit is ourselves. We put up the walls. We give in to the fears. So we have to go beyond our limits. How far can we go? In my case, the fear is always there, but I've found a way to live with it, and I don't let it run my life.

EL: Do you ever put the fear directly into your work?

David: Absolutely. For example, "The Hobo." I've always wanted to do a piece that was sad and funny, but when Bill and I started rehearsing for *Old Hats*, I kept avoiding it, because it was something I'd never done before. And it was incredibly painful to go through the process of playing that character – even though it's a character I've always wanted to do. So much of my own pain is in it. So I had to bring up that shit, which is not easy. But finally I had to face it, and embrace it. Stop resisting it. I was improvising one day and I did this really stupid cry, and Bill laughed. And that was the beginning. The key to the guy is hope and despair, hope and despair – and that's funny, going between the two – until it reaches a point where it is only despair. And that's where it becomes really beautiful. So human. I think it was Rumi who said, "To find God, you must be willing to swim across an ocean of your own tears." Tears of transformation and joy. Pain is the door to freedom. I'm so interested, at this point in my life, in the idea that grief and sorrow and loneliness are an integral part of the human experience. A necessary part. So, "The Hobo." It's my favorite piece right now. Remember that, Bill? I just kept putting it off until Tina [Landau, director of

Old Hats] said, "David, we're opening in two weeks. We need to start rehearsing."
Remember that?

Bill: I do.

David: Great art should elevate our consciousness. Elevate our awareness.

EL: Thank you both. So much.

DB: Yes, thank you.

Bill: Our pleasure.

David: You want to get some coffee?

20 Reflections

David and Ezra in Conversation with Phil Burgers

As we neared the end of our clown odyssey, we sought someone to turn the tables on us and pose some questions about what we'd uncovered during our conversations with 20 of clown's modern masters. Who better than the multi-award-winning twenty-first-century clown sensation Phil Burgers, aka Dr. Brown, performer and teacher, to provoke our reflections? We met Phil in Los Angeles to grapple with our findings.

PB: What are some of your first discoveries that come to mind?

David: As we went into this project, I wondered where we would find cohesion and where we would find dissonance among the philosophies of our clowns. In the end, the diversity was fascinating.

PB: What's an example of two completely differing philosophies?

Ezra: One way of looking at it is to examine the differing responses to ideas of spirituality and spontaneity, on the one hand, or definition and structure, on the other. For some of our clowns, the focus is exclusively on presence, being alive. To be in the moment is vital, and if you do anything else you are violating an essential principle.

David: Take Angela de Castro, for example. Her angelic clown doesn't even need an audience because structure is so unimportant to its development. She's very interested in the transformative aspect of clown. Like Micha Usov, clowning for her is a state of being. And it continues beyond and outside of the stage.

Ezra: Perhaps Slava has reached that point, also. He only wants to investigate what makes us happy. In any context.

PB: Really?

David: Right. Much of his recent work (he wouldn't use that word!) has gone beyond audience too. He lives his life as a clown. He lives in a clown house. He surrounds himself with a family of clowns. This has nothing to do with jokes and gags. His artistic trajectory reminds me of Grotowski's. From radical aesthetic success, to a phase of development that is no longer reliant on the theatrical paradigm at all; where performance and life blend into one.

Ezra: As for Jango Edwards, his essential concept is: "I'm fearless." The stage is the least important place for him to be. He's willing to go anywhere, do anything, far beyond what any other clown we talked to would even conceive of doing. "I'm fearless." That's what it means to be a clown for him.

PB: Off stage?

Ezra: Everywhere.

David: I think these kinds of clowns are living out a grand cosmic system of their own. It's both extraordinary and extreme. Their philosophy on clowning spills far beyond the confines of their stage personae. They believe that to clown is to undergo a spiritual transformation.

Ezra: So that's one kind of clown. On the other hand, there's someone like David Larible, who speaks eloquently about how he believes a clown is born and dies each night, that the clown exists for, and with, the audience. These are technicians, if I can use that word, who are focused on the development of performance material. As silly as it may seem to draw that distinction, it feels important. Take Barry Lubin. If a bit gets a laugh, it works. Bottom line. He keeps his philosophy very grounded, simple. "I'm there, I'm with the audience, I feel it, it connects, they laugh, I keep doing it." Peter Shub, a similar mindset. Strict with his act, especially once he's set it. Building a performance works more like a jigsaw puzzle than a stream-of-consciousness. Or Avner, who is very scientific, incredibly precise, fascinated by the identifiable ingredients of the interaction between performer and audience. Structure, to Avner, is highly significant; it's part of the joy of clowning. Bill Irwin talks about it when he discusses his most reliable gag, which he compares to the structure of a limerick. Nola Rae, especially in her *Upper Cuts* period, was extraordinarily technical. These clowns are fully immersed in the analytical aspects of clowning. If you had to summarize their philosophies, you might say they believe in the rational effect of clowning on their audience. And for these clowns, no audience equals no clowning at all.

PB: Is this the primary difference between clown philosophies? The cosmic versus the rational?

David: There are other shades of this diversity, things that show up in different ways. There are discrepancies on the role of a clown's personal life in their art.

Ezra: Peter Shub asked me to watch a film about how his son had died before I interviewed him. And then he spoke about this. He said, simply, "I'm very sad, and what I do on stage can be a lie in a way, and yes, when I'm on stage I love it because sometimes it's the only place my pain goes away. I'm putting a false image on so that we might feel joyful, to get away from our sorrow."

PB: Wow.

David: And then by contrast you have someone like Shiner who actively seeks to harness his inner turmoil in his acts. He is quite clear that rage is a huge part of what motivates him, and it's scary, but it's hilarious, because he's making fun of his own inner life. He's found a venue for expressing it that's not harmful.

PB: As clowns we have rage, and anger, and sadness, just as much as we have happiness and joy, and all those can be a part of clown.

Ezra: Yes. But is it an act, or is it real? That's where we found these interesting tensions.

PB: What about the craft of clowning? What you refer to in your subcategories as techniques, what did you discover?

David: One of the most interesting things we explored in this area was attitudes to failure. Again, there was no consensus, but broadly speaking, our clowns fell into two different camps.

Ezra: The Pisonis were very clear on their point of view!

David: Right: "No one wants to see the clown fail." That's an article of faith.

Ezra: And David Konyot admitted that he has rarely even considered anything for his act that he thinks might fail. Too risky.

David: He seemed almost melancholy thinking about it.

Ezra: Whereas we spoke to other clowns who seemed to almost rely on failure as a key tool in the development of their material. David Shiner pointed out that part of the stamina of clowning is connected to the ability to withstand inevitable failure. Put something in front of an audience, and, first time out, it will almost certainly crash and burn. Do you have the staying power to hang in there and make the adjustments?

David: Apparently the first preview of *Fool Moon* was a disaster.

Ezra: And it went on to be one of the most successful clown shows of the modern era.

David: They needed it to be terrible before it became great.

Ezra: Similar to how Geoff Hoyle discusses rehearsing in performance. He also sees that inevitable failure in front of an audience is an effective way to build material.

PB: Philippe Gaulier's teaching emphasizes the value of the flop. You have to face how bad you are. It's a vital entry point to clowning.

Ezra: I think only some of our interviewees would agree …

David: Having said that, it's interesting to note how often our clowns stick with what works. In clowning, it's possible to play a number for 30 years or more. Oleg has been sweeping his spotlight for 70 years!

PB: Is there a reluctance to try new material, because of the fear of failure?

Ezra: Well, it's rare to find a clown in a continual state of new creation. Jango, perhaps, and Slava in a broader sense.

David: Nola Rae. Angela, to a certain extent, although she still plays her old material too.

Ezra: And Irwin and Shiner spoke about the new material in their current show, *Old Hats*. They said it was torture to come up with!

David: But necessary.

PB: Doesn't the old material go stale?

Ezra: You would think it would. But take a look at Barry Lubin's water act, for example. He's crafted that within an inch of its life. And yet when you see the immediacy of the act, its freshness, the joy it brings in every incarnation – it's hard to criticize. It certainly isn't stale.

David: Peter Shub is quite unapologetic about this. He says as long as he's having fun, and the audience is having fun, then he'll play his same material ad infinitum. Or how about this: in 2008, I saw Shiner do a 75-minute solo show, a kind of greatest hits, packed with his standards. Some of them 25 years old. The impression I got, sitting in the audience, had very little to do with the tight structure of his routines (although in retrospect, I admired that too). The real experience was visceral. I felt like I was in a room with a tiger. And he was coming after me. He was coming after all of us. It was so dynamic I can still feel the effects of that evening. Nothing stale about that.

PB: What other aspects of the craft did you uncover?

Ezra: It was fun to talk about the way acts or numbers were created. There was a lot of emphasis on problems. Talking to Larry and Lorenzo Pisoni, or Avner or Bill Irwin, it became very clear that most clown routines are in some way motivated by the existence of a problem. And even if a clown did not use the word "problem" to describe their routines or shows, you could still identify it as the catalyst for their inventions.

David: Dimitri's problems taming a beach chair.

Ezra: Bello Nock taming a trampoline. David Larible trying to walk a tightrope. Bill Irwin trying to play a trombone.

David: Even Slava talking to himself on a telephone. That's a big problem. Or Angela de Castro, getting ready for a date, but not knowing what's appropriate.

Ezra: Some problems are internal – being too dumb, or afraid. Some problems relate to props – the eternal confusion of things. Some problems are social – for example the problem of human hierarchies.

David: Geoff Hoyle was very strong on this.

Ezra: Right. What to do if the boss is a jerk? How does the clown handle the problem of class? And lastly, some problems are universal; they exist in a kind of poetic dimension. Lyrical clowns, like Aziz or Micha, struggle with these.

PB: So all clown acts need a problem?

David: There's never a golden rule. But it's definitely a common theme. And a key part of the construction of many routines.

PB: You wanted to investigate the influences and inspirations on this generation of clowns. What did you find?

Ezra: A surprising number of our clowns were self-taught. Slava, for example; he had colleagues whom he worked with, but as he described it, he never had instruction. That came up again with Jango, who essentially lied to everyone early in his career, and told them he had been trained, when in reality he had no idea what was going on. He didn't study with anyone until much later.

PB: When he met Carlo Colombaioni.

Ezra: Exactly, not until much later did he take Carlo on as a mentor.

David: Shiner also didn't have a teacher. He learned it all by doing it.

Ezra: And Dimitri described how he learned acrobatics and music, and of course he worked with Marceau a bit, but he said nobody ever taught him clown – he just figured it out. Plus the Pickle Family Circus brigade spent a lot of time teaching one another, through trial and error.

PB: How does that make you guys feel as teachers, knowing that the clown might mostly come from experience?

David: Well, fortunately for us, there were plenty of mentors who *did* make a difference! Marcel Marceau was a key influence in the lives of so many of these clowns, and he actually trained both Dimitri and Nola Rae. Philippe Gaulier was very important to Peter Shub and Angela de Castro, who also gained key insights from Gaulier's erstwhile partner, Pierre Byland.

Ezra: Paris was a hugely important place for so many in this generation. Lecoq was there too; he trained both René Bazinet and Avner, and his impact on physical theater at large was incalculable. And Etienne Decroux taught Geoff Hoyle and Peter Shub. Paris in the '70s was crawling with clowns, and packed with an extraordinary caliber of mentors.

David: Plus it was on the streets of Paris that David Shiner began to build his reputation. Can a city be a mentor? If so, Paris was it!

Ezra: We could also say that the Ringling Brothers Clown College was an important "organizational" mentor too. Barry Lubin, Bill Irwin, Aziz Gual, all benefited from their time in the hothouse. And speaking of institutions, both the Big Apple Circus and Ringling Brothers' *The Greatest Show on Earth* have proved to be a vital home to so many of our clowns, including Bello Nock, David Larible, Barry Lubin, Dimitri, Aziz, and others. Without the support of those two, things would be very different for so many of them.

David: Russia has it's own history of clowning. Oleg learned at the side of the great Karandash. And both Slava and Micha mentioned the importance of Leonid Engibarov, who brought so much uniqueness to his art. Aziz Gual also crossed paths with the Russian tradition.

Ezra: But what is crystal clear throughout the interviews is the colossal importance of screen clowns; both the silent clowns of the early years of Hollywood – Chaplin, Keaton, Laurel and Hardy – and the great flourishing of TV clowns in the 1950s, including Lucille Ball, Ernie Kovacs, Phil Silvers, and others. So many of our crop of clowns wax lyrical about the influence of these greats. Slava was an impassioned Chaplin fan and used to imitate his walk when he was a young kid. Bill Irwin remembers the day that his household installed their first ever television, and what that meant to his life. Barry Lubin's father would screen the silent comics in hotels in New Jersey, and Barry would help with the projection. Angela de Castro was inspired by Fellini's films and especially the performances of Giulietta Masina. The stories go on and on.

David: I wasn't expecting the sheer magnitude of Chaplin's influence.

Ezra: There's no doubt it has been immense. Unbeknownst to him, he's been the greatest teacher of all.

PB: So teachers can make a difference, after all?

David: Well, we're not Chaplin! But we went into this project partly because we were looking for insight as teachers. I always have had that concern: what is the function of a teacher of clowning? And rightly so – some of our clowns, Jango for instance, pour scorn on the notion that clowning can be taught.

Ezra: It struck me as true when several clowns said: you can't become a clown – you are a clown or you're not. If you are, it can be cultivated, refined, and built. That resonates for me. In a class, when we see that spark in a student, we can still cultivate it, and inspire their growth.

David: Phil, what do you think about it? You teach – what's your view?

PB: I don't know. It's tricky. Maybe teaching isn't the right terminology. It implies adding something – knowledge, or experience, or skills. But perhaps in the case of clowning, the trick is to do the opposite. Maybe the teacher's role is to uncover something for the student. To help them de-layer all the bullshit that keeps them from being the clown. So that the clown can grow on its own.

David: So is everyone a clown, if only they could strip away the layers?

PB: I don't know where I stand on that …

David: Nor do I.

Ezra: We don't know!

[Laughter.]

David: It's important not to know something …

PB: You also set out to learn how your clowns entered into the field in the first place. What did you find?

David: First of all, it's important to identify the circus families among our clowns. The Konyots, the Nocks, Larible from the Travaglia family: these three families can be traced back several generations. For Bello or the young Davids, following in their family footsteps seems as though it was a natural choice.

Ezra: Although David Konyot left the circus for some time, then came back older and wiser.

David: That's true. And Larible wasn't part of a clown dynasty – he was expected to be an acrobat. But nevertheless, circus families certainly offered a simple enough route into clowning. And the apprentice model of learning – being tutored by a master – is still alive in the world of the circus.

Ezra: There's no better example of that than the education of Lorenzo Pisoni.

David: Right. From the moment he could walk, he was being taught to clown. He wrote a whole show about this.

Ezra: Then there are the clowns who had an urge to be involved in theater or performance from a young age, but didn't quite find their place until they discovered clowning. Avner was an actor and dancer at first, as was Bill Irwin. Nola was a dancer. Dimitri tried to be a mime, though he always knew that eventually clowning was the direction he wanted to take. Angela started as an actor but somehow she always felt that something was missing. Geoff Hoyle studied Drama and English at University. In all these cases, there was a general trend toward a life on or around the stage; clowning became the final articulation of this desire. (I should note, by the way, that Geoff Hoyle still thinks of himself as a comic actor, as opposed to a clown.)

David: Finally there is a group of our clowns who seemed to stumble upon the art form by accident.

Ezra: These are some of my favorite stories.

David: Mine too. David Shiner had been building houses for ten years when he saw a mime on the streets of Boulder, Colorado. It changed his life, just like that.

Ezra: The same thing with Peter Shub, who saw a street magician while he was leading a college tour to try and overcome his shyness. Bam! He was hooked! Suddenly his course was set.

David: Barry Lubin was drifting ... Not sure what to do. A friend told him about Ringling, and he decided to try it, almost on a whim.

Ezra: And Aziz Gual went to see a circus when he was 11. The clowns humiliated him, so he decided he would become a clown.

David: Most people would have run for the hills! But he told us he wanted to show them how it should be done.

Ezra: There is a healthy amount of randomness and accident in some of these origin stories. Which fits the subject-matter perfectly!

PB: So are there any overall conclusions you draw from this long adventure?

David: We wanted to explore the nature of creativity through the lens of clowning. From the beginning, we've wondered whether clowns are artisans, applying a known trade that they have absorbed from previous generations, or artists, who are prone to unusual, improbable acts of creation that are essentially unpredictable. What we discovered is that these two definitions are not diametric opposites; they exist at different points on the same continuum. And often a single clown will touch down in more than one place on this continuum. Take Jango Edwards; he's responsible for some of the most bizarre, unique, and freakish clown acts that we could ever possibly imagine (and several that we couldn't imagine!) – and yet, at the same time, he's been doing a bit where he dives into a glass of water for 20 years. Is he a revolutionary? Or a conservative? Both, it would seem. Like many of his peers, he represents differing aspects of the creative urge within his own oeuvre. And that's been a surprise.

Ezra: For all the paradoxes, though, there are some certainties. Across the board, there is an acknowledgement of the importance of having a moment that feels like it only happens for the audience on *that* night, in *that* moment, for the first time. The role of the audience in clowning is fundamental. Lorenzo talked about this; the clown's role is to bring people into the same shared experience for the duration of the show. To put down their cell phones and listen. Unlike many other art audiences, who consume "finished" art as a product, the clown audience is actually an integral part of the process of creation for the clowns who are per-forming for them. There's a lot of awareness around this. Even for the more spiritually inclined clowns, there is a heightened awareness of their relationship with an audience.

David: Phil, some of your shows are completely unplanned, is that true?

PB: Nowadays, yes. I've experimented with going in front of an audience with nothing in mind, and then seeing what happens.

David: That's an extreme case. But all of our clowns recognize that they are placing a huge degree of faith in the role of the audience. And it makes for a very particular kind of theater. In some ways, clowns are way ahead of their time, given that the current fad for audience participation in mainstream theater can be traced back, in clowning, thousands of years!

PB: What about the future of clowning?

Ezra: This is an interesting question. Most agreed that in some way, shape, or form, clown will never go away, because ultimately the definition of clown has nothing to do with whether someone is in the circus or wears a red nose. Clown seems best understood as a kind of spirit, an explorative spirit, that investigates or reveals something true about all of us, our capacity to fail, to mess up, to be humble; and also a desire, perhaps to subvert political structure or power, or to connect and bring people together. And this spirit of clown is inextinguishable. It will continue to pop up everywhere. The question is how will it look in the future? Will it continue in circuses, or will those die away as people become less interested in seeing them? Will the red nose, which, in some circles, is considered out of date or even scary, disappear? It's possible. But the important part, that spirit, is as alive and well as it ever has been.

PB: But if there are no more circuses, what will become the platform for that spirit to express itself?

Ezra: YouTube is probably the most obvious of our new platforms. Suddenly there are clowns everywhere who didn't have a platform for expression before, and now they do, and people are watching them all over the place. Maybe these new clowns, who also have exposure to all the great clowns of the past right there on their computers and phones, have a big leg up for innovation, for exploration – even if they look different from our current image of clowns. And they probably will look different because I don't know a lot of young people now who are dreaming that they want to be a clown in the circus.

David: I imagine a lot of people clowning around on YouTube have never even heard of the word, or wouldn't think of themselves as part of that tradition. Even if they're successful, the word clown may never cross their radar. But there's a big difference between comics on YouTube and the clowns in this collection, who have accumulated thousands of hours of experience in front of an audience. It brings me to a question I've been considering: are physical, acrobatic, or mimetic skills less and less necessary for modern clowns?

Ezra: That may be true.

David: Phil, have you seen clowns who still maintain a high level of physical discipline?

PB: On the streets in Europe, those kind of clowns are still working. But it's true that if you think about the way clowning is taught, things have changed. If you study clown with Gaulier, for example, the less you are capable of the more he likes it! Physical virtuosity has definitely become obsolete for him.

David: So what has replaced it?

PB: Spirit. Subverting the system. People taking the piss out of everything.

David: I'm sure these are words that many of our clowns would relate to. It just happens that they all had the physical training to back it up. It seems to me that we might be looking at a future in which the spirit of clowning continues to flourish; but the performative abilities of future clowns may not be as skilled, or as highly tuned, as they are in the current, older generation. In some ways that's a shame.

PB: Everything changes.

David: It does.

PB: So how can we help our students to uncover this spirit?

Ezra: Something happened to so many of our clowns. Micha talked about this, the "Ahah!" moment. Somewhere, somehow, they were given some kind of a permission – it feels like the most accurate word – to express themselves with this part of themselves that is their clown. It seems that each one of them received this permission, and when they received it, that propelled them in some way to change everything, to reorganize themselves around this central impulse, this clown, and what's true across the board is that the clown in them takes up a lot of space. Once given permission to exist, it explodes.

David: It follows that our role is to give permission to the clowns of the future.

Ezra: And it's not about tricks. It's about getting people to take on the challenge of becoming oneself more fully.

PB: That's quite a commitment.

David: No one ever said it was going to be easy.

Ezra: Except when it is.

David: *[Laughs.]* Right. Except when it is.

Appendix of terms

In alphabetical order.

A

Accion Instrumental, a contemporary performance company founded by Jacobo Romano and Jorge Zulueta, whose performances have generated some notoriety in France and Germany.

Acrobats and Mountebanks, an 1890 book that explores the circuses, fairs, carnivals, and hippodromes of nineteenth-century France. Written by Hugues Le Roux and Jules Garnier, and translated from the French by A.P. Morton.

Patch Adams (b. 1945) is an American physician, clown, social activist, author, and clown-doctor. He is the founder of the Gesundheit! Institute, which organizes volunteers from around the world to dress as clowns to bring humor to orphans, hospital patients, and others.

Tony Alexis (b. 1927) is the frontman of a team of clowns known as the Tony Alexis Family, and is a well-known circus artist in Europe.

Woody Allen (b. 1935) is an American actor, filmmaker, comedian, and writer whose career has spanned theater, film, television, and stand-up comedy. He has won four Academy Awards, and is widely regarded as one of the leading comics and filmmakers of the twentieth century.

Alliance Theater Company is a theater company based in Atlanta, Georgia. It is part of the Robert W. Woodruff Arts Center, and was the recipient of the 2007 Tony Award for Regional Theatre.

Jakob Andreff (1919–76) was the star clown of Circus Knie from 1941 to 1944, and performed with the Brothers Cavallini and Polo Rivel. He later toured with circuses across Europe.

Dougie Ashton is an Australian clown who performed for the Ringling Bros Barnum & Bailey Circus. He's known as a character clown who was always clowning around. He is a member of the International Circus Hall of Fame.

The Avignon Festival is an annual arts festival held every summer in July in Avignon, France. It is regarded as one of the most important contemporary performing arts events in the world.

Samuel Avital (born Morocco, 1932) is a professional mime who studied with Etienne Decroux, Jean-Louis Barrault, and Marcel Marceau. He later performed in the Compagnie de Mime under the direction of Decroux's son Maximilien.

B

Lucille Ball (1911–89) was an American comedienne, television star, and studio executive. She was the first woman to run a major television studio, and is best known as the title character on the sitcom *I Love Lucy*.

Bill Ballantine (1910–99) was a writer and illustrator of the circus as well as being a professional clown. He wrote ten books including *Clown Alley*, which chronicles his years as dean of the Ringling Brothers Clown College.

Clive Barker (1931–2005) was an English actor, acting theorist, and the author of the highly influential *Theatre Games*, one of the first books for performance practitioners that emphasized the importance of play and children's games for the actor.

P.T. Barnum (1810–91) was an American showman and entrepreneur who founded the Barnum & Bailey Circus, and became one of the most famous names in circus history despite not having entered the field until age 61.

Circus Barum is one of the top-ranked circuses in Europe, based in Germany.

Leo Bassi (born New York, 1952) is an Italian comic and actor from a circus family. His fierce style and satiric themes have made him famous and controversial, thanks especially to his shrewd criticisms of the Catholic Church. His show *Utopia* begins with a criticism of political corruption and bank abuses, deals with European history since World War One and also the story of the White Clown, a figure represented as well by his grandfather.

Pina Bausch (1940–2009) created the highly influential Tanztheater Wuppertal, a company devoted to the director's unique blend of dance and theater.

Roberto Benigni (b. 1952) is an Italian clown best known for his Oscar-winning film *Life is Beautiful*.

Tony Bennett (b. 1926) is one of America's best-loved crooners, a singer of traditional pop standards, show tunes, and jazz.

Jack Benny (1894–1974) was a huge influence on American radio and television comedy, thanks to the enormously popular *Jack Benny Program*, a weekly radio show that ran for over 20 years.

The **Big Apple Circus**, founded by Paul Binder, is a one-ring circus based in New York. Since its opening in 1977, it has become a part of the cultural landscape of the city, winning numerous awards for its tireless contribution to culture and education.

Paul Binder (born New York, 1942) and his partner, Michael Christensen, made their living as street performers in Europe before participating in circus and television in France. When they returned to America in 1977, they founded the Big Apple Circus, of which Binder remained ringmaster and artistic director until 2008. The New York Landmarks Conservancy society declared Binder a "New York City Living Landmark" in 2001.

Herb Blau (1926–2013), a director and theoretician of performance, was the Byron W. and Alice L. Lockwood Professor in the Humanities at the University of Washington. As a co-founder of The Actor's Workshop in San Francisco and co-director of the Repertory Theater of Lincoln Center in New York City, Blau introduced American audiences to avant-garde drama in some of the country's first productions of Samuel Beckett, Jean Genet, and Harold Pinter.

Emanuel Blumenfeld became the director of the Circus E. Blumenfeld in 1834. His work bringing attention to horse training was influential developing modern circus. Circus Blumenfeld was one of the largest circuses of its time.

Victor Borge (1909–2000), the so-called "Clown Prince of Denmark," was a brilliant musician whose comic escapades while performing classical music made him a huge star in the USA and Europe.

Bozo the Clown is a popular clown character, featured on television in the United States in the 1960s. The character was originally created by Alan Livingston and portrayed by Pinto Colvig.

Peter Brook (b. 1925) is an innovative English theater and film director. His influential theater work includes productions of *The Mahabharata* and *Tierno Bokar*.

Debbie Brown (b. 1950) is the principal choreographer for Cirque du Soleil and an Emmy Award winner for her choreography of the 74th Academy Awards ceremony.

Lenny Bruce (1925–66) is one of the great American stand-up comics. His frank and deliberately provocative style paved the way for a whole new generation of comedians. He was convicted of obscenity just before his drug-related death in 1966. The conviction was overturned posthumously.

Phil Burgers, aka Dr. Brown (b. 1977) trained with Philippe Gaulier. Since 2009 he has toured his remarkable solo clown shows, for adults and children, across the world, winning numerous awards.

Hovey Burgess taught circus technique at New York University, and several other prestigious institutions, beginning in 1966, and has performed, directed, and created circus performance around the world including with Circo Dell'Arte, Circus Flora. He choreographed and appeared in the 1980 film *Popeye*.

Pierre Byland is a clown teacher and director. He taught at the Ecole Jacques Lecoq in Paris, and co-founded the Compagnie Byland-Gaulier with Philippe Gaulier, as well as the Centre National des Arts du Cirque, where he established FAC (Formation for Actors of Circus and the Art of Clown).

C

Sid Caesar (1922–2014) is best known for the 1950s live television series *Your Show of Shows* and the follow-up *Caesar's Hour*, which influenced a next generation of American comics including Mel Brooks, Woody Allen, and Neil Simon.

The Cairoli Brothers are a clown duo made up of Jean-Marie and Carletto Cairoli.

The **Canestrelli Circus** was a fixture in Europe for over 50 years during the twentieth century, although their family roots can be traced back to the early 1700s.

Cantinflas, the stage name of Mario Fortino Alfonso Moreno Reyes (1911–93), was a Mexican comedian and author. His clown character, a poor *campesino* or peasant, came to be associated with the national identity of Mexico, and was examined by media critics, philosophers, and linguists, who saw him variably as a danger to Mexican society, a bourgeois puppet, a kind philanthropist, a transgressor of gender roles, a pious Catholic, a verbal innovator, and a picaresque underdog. He won a Golden Globe Award for his role in the 1956 film *Around the World in 80 Days*.

The **Cardinalis** are a clown duo who have performed around Europe, including engagements with Cirque Pinder and Cirque Medrano in France.

George Carlin (1937–2008) was a staple of stand-up comedy in the twentieth century, often regarded as one of the great stand-up comedians in history. His comedy focused on social commentary, satirizing American culture and politics. He made numerous television appearances, including hosting the first episode of *Saturday Night Live*.

Art Carney (1918–2003) was an American comic and film actor best known for his role in the sitcom *The Honeymooners* where he played opposite Jackie Gleason. Carney won an Academy Award for the film *Harry and Tonto*.

Francesco Caroli (1922–2004) worked with his brothers in the Caroli Brothers, a bareback-riding troupe. They enjoyed success throughout Europe with all the top circuses, such as Benneweis in Denmark, Krone in Germany, and Knie in Switzerland. Francesco starred in *The White-Face Clown Is Dead – We Don't Need Him Anymore* in 1983 and worked as a clown from 1990 to 2001.

Roy Castle (1932–94) was an English vaudevillian who became a popular television presenter.

The **Cavallini Family** are trapeze flyers from Las Vegas.

The Chipperfield Circus is an English circus that is nearly 350 years old. Its heyday came after World War Two, when it was very popular as a touring circus in Europe. After a period of decline, it returned to the limelight in 2010, minus any animal acts, in an effort to rebrand itself as a more modern organization.

Michael Christensen (born Walla Walla, WA, 1947) toured Europe with his partner, Paul Binder, with whom he later co-founded the Big Apple Circus. In 1986, he formed the Big Apple Circus Clown Care Unit, the first organization in the USA devoted to medical clowning.

Ryszard Cieslak (1937–90) was an actor and a central figure in the Polish Laboratory Theater. In 1962, Cieslak joined the Laboratory Theater, which Jerzy Grotowski founded in 1959 in Poland as a vehicle for experimental drama. After its dissolution in 1977, Cieslak worked with Grotowski on numerous dramatic projects.

Cirque du Soleil is a Canadian circus that was founded by Guy Laliberté and Gilles Ste-Croix in Baie-Saint-Paul in 1984. Their theatrical acrobatics and character-driven approach to circus, including the absence of animals, became a trademark of contemporary circus.

Clowns Without Borders is a humanitarian organization founded in Barcelona, Spain. They send clowns to offer free performances for children affected by war in regions including the former Yugoslavia, Palestine, and the Eastern DR Congo.

Carlo Colombaioni (1933–2008) worked for over 30 years with his brother, Alberto Vitali, under the name of I Colombaioni. He featured in Fellini's *I Clowns*.

Chester Conklin (1886–1971) was a silent film comedian and clown. He appeared in Charlie Chaplin's first Keystone film *Making a Living*, and is said to have influenced Chaplin's development of the famous Tramp character.

Billy Connolly (born Scotland, 1942), originally a folk singer, became a stand-up comedian and actor famous for his working-class origins and his no-holds-barred comic tirades.

Gerry Cottle (born England, 1945) left home at 15 years old to join the Robert Brothers Circus. He developed a famous juggling act, and he toured England as the star of the Gerry Cottle Circus during the 1970s.

D

Michael Davis (born San Francisco, 1953) is a renowned comic juggler who has appeared several times on *Saturday Night Live*.

Sammy Davis Jr (1925–90) was an American dancer, singer, musician, and actor. He had an extensive film career, and was noted for his impersonations.

Etienne Decroux (1898–1991) was born in Paris. He studied at Jacques Copeau's Ecole du Vieux-Colombier, and later developed a style of isolated movements that developed the structure of what became modern mime. He was a major influence on performers Jean-Louis Barrault and Marcel Marceau.

Dell'Arte is a performance school located in northern California. It offers training in ensemble-based Physical Theater, focusing on acting, voice, movement, devised theater, and related physical skills, with specific attention to the areas of mask, commedia dell'arte, tragedy, and clown.

Franco Dragone (b. 1952) was a central figure in the early years of Cirque du Soleil. Dragone has directed several internationally renowned productions for the company, including *Nouvelle Expérience*, *Saltimbanco*, *Mystère*, *Alegría*, and *O*.

Margaret Dumont (1882–1965) was an American comic actress. She is largely remembered as the comic foil to Groucho Marx in several Marx Brothers films. Groucho referred to her as "practically the fifth Marx brother."

E

Edinburgh Festival Fringe is the world's largest arts festival. Established in 1947 surrounding the Edinburgh International Festival, the festival is held annually in August. It is a showcase for performing arts, and is an unjuried, open festival.

Leonid Engibarov (1935–72) was a highly influential Soviet Russian circus clown, whose routines included a component of intellectual reflection in addition to his comedic brilliance.

F

Kenneth Feld (born Washington D.C., 1948) is the CEO of Feld Entertainment, which owns Ringling Bros and Barnum & Bailey Circus, and many other significant performance events.

Federico Fellini (1920–93) was one of the greatest film directors of the twentieth century. His films include *La Scala* and *I Clowns*.

Flying Karamazov Brothers (FKB) are a juggling and comedy troupe that began in 1973. They started as street artists in Santa Cruz, California, and have since performed worldwide.

The Fossett's Circus is Ireland's National Circus. Run by the Fossett family, it has been playing for more than a century.

The Fourth Way is a book written by P.D. Ouspensky about the Fourth Way system of self-development as introduced by Greek-Georgian philosopher G.I. Gurdjieff. The text is a compilation of Ouspensky's lectures between 1921 and 1946.

Frankfurter Autoren Theater (FAT) is a variety theater in Frankfurt, Germany.

The **Fratellini Family** was a famous European circus family. Their engagement at the Circus Medrano in Paris in the 1920s was so successful that it sparked growing interest in circus around France and other regions in Europe.

Friends Roadshow was a communal theater group founded by Jango Edwards and Nola Rae that worked in Britain, America, North Africa, and Europe. They performed a variety of lighthearted shows utilizing a mixture of mime, magic, clowning, puppetry, music, song, and dance.

G

Philippe Gaulier (born Paris, 1943) studied and taught with Jacques Lecoq until he branched out to begin his own school, the Ecole Philippe Gaulier. The teacher and muse behind individuals and groups as diverse as Complicite and Sacha Baron Cohen, Gaulier is renowned as one of the world's most influential and inspiring theater pedagogues.

Mark Gindick is a graduate of the Ringling Bros Clown College, and was the second person to play Barry Lubin's famous "Grandma" character at the Big Apple Circus in *Big Top Doo Wop* and *Dreams Of A City*.

Jackie Gleason (1916–87) was an American comedian and musician. Known for his brash visual and verbal comedy style, he was also known for his character Ralph Kramden in *The Honeymooners*.

"The Golden Age of Comedy" (1957) is a compilation of silent comedy films from the Hal Roach and Mack Sennett studios.

Jeff Gordon (born Pennsylvania, 1954) performed in Ringling Bros and Barnum & Bailey Circus, and the Big Apple Circus, where he performed as "Gordoon" for five seasons, and later starred in *Clown Around Town*.

The Great Dictator (1940), a film by Charlie Chaplin, satirized Adolf Hitler and made a plea for tolerance and peace.

Otto Griebling (1896–1972) was a German circus clown. He performed with the Cole Brothers and Ringling Bros and Barnum & Bailey Circuses. He was one of only four clowns given the title Master Clown by Irvin Feld.

Grock (1880–1959), born Charles Adrien Wettach, was a Swiss clown, composer, and musician. Called "the king of clowns" and "the greatest of Europe's clowns," Grock was once the most highly paid entertainer in the world.

Jerzy Grotowski (1933–99) was a Polish theater director and leading figure in avant-garde theater in the twentieth century. He was a seminal innovator in experimental theater, founding and directing the Polish Laboratory Theater from 1959 to 1977, and establishing conceptual models of a theater laboratory, and "poor theater" concepts.

H

The House of Bernarda Alba is the last play written by Spanish playwright Federico García Lorca.

Gardi Hutter (b. 1953) is a hugely popular and multi-award-winning Swiss female clown.

I

I Clowns (also known as *The Clowns*) is a 1970 film by Federico Fellini, made for TV but both broadcast on TV and released as a feature film. It focuses on the human fascination with clowns and circuses, as a part documentary, part fantasy film.

Inter-Action is a group that fronts for new artists, playwrights, writers, poets, designers, composers, and song writers. The group puts these often-serious creations on a multi-arts bus that visits locations in an entertaining fashion where they can interact with marginalized people on housing estates and elsewhere.

J

Lou Jacobs (1903–92) was the clown star of the Ringling Bros and Barnum & Bailey Circus for over 60 years. Jacobs is credited with inventing the clown car. Soon after Irvin Feld founded the Clown College in 1968, Jacobs became one of its most influential teachers. One of the first clowns to be inducted into the Clown Hall of Fame.

Andrey Jigalov (b. 1966) is one of Russia's best-known and most idiosyncratic clowns.

Keith Johnstone (b. 1933) is a pioneer of the modern improvisational movement. His seminal text *Impro: Improvisation and the Theatre*, based on his own experiences as a practitioner at the Royal Court in London in the 1950s and

'60s, has become one of the most influential books in modern theater. John-stone founded Theatresports in Calgary, Canada, in 1977.

Desmond Jones was the founder and director of the longest-running School of Mime and Physical Theatre in Britain. He closed his school in August 2004. He is now working as an independent teacher, choreographer, and director.

K

Mikhail Nikolayevich Rumyantsev (1901–83), stage name **Karandash** (which means *pencil*), was an immensely popular Soviet clown, a People's Artist of the USSR, and the teacher of the famous Russian clowns Oleg Popov and Yuri Nikulin. The Moscow Circus School is named after him.

To this day, **Emmett Kelly** (1898–1979) remains one of America's best-known circus clowns. Kelly's inimitable clown figure Willie epitomized the struggles and the tragedies of the Depression era in the USA. Famous sketches included trying to sweep up a spotlight and opening a peanut with a sledgehammer, but Willie is best remembered for the extraordinary empathy he created with his audiences over many decades. From 1942 to 1956, Kelly performed with the Ringling Bros and Barnum & Bailey Circus, where he was a major attraction. He also landed a number of Broadway and film roles, including the role of "Willie" in Cecil B. DeMille's *The Greatest Show on Earth* (1952).

Claude Kipnis (1938–81) was a French mime and founder of the Israeli Mime Theater and the Claude Kipnis Mime Theater.

Bobby Klein (born New York City, 1942) is an American stand-up comedian. He was a member of the Chicago-based sketch comedy troupe Second City.

Circus Knie is the largest circus in Switzerland, based in Rapperswil. It was founded in 1803 by the Knie family and has continued in its current form since 1919. It is famous for its animals, including its featured horse acts, and now operates a zoo and a museum in Rapperswil.

Ernie Kovacs (1919–62) was an American comedian, actor, and writer. His uninhibited, frequently improvised, and visually experimental comic style influenced several television comedy programs.

Circus Krone is one of the largest circuses in Europe. Founded in 1905 by Carl Krone, and based in Munich, it is one of the few circuses to be housed in its own building.

L

Guy Laliberté (born Canada, 1959) is the current CEO of Cirque du Soleil. He began his career as a busker, stiltwalker and fire-eater. He founded Cirque du Soleil in 1984.

The Last Circus *(Balada Triste de Trompeta)* (2010), a Spanish film from director Alex de la Iglesia, chronicles the violent aftermath of the Spanish Civil War, focusing on the travails of a circus troupe.

Laurel and Hardy refers to Stan Laurel (1890–1965) and Oliver Hardy (1892–1957), one of cinema's most enduring comic double acts. The naïve Laurel and the pompous Hardy starred in film classics both during and after the silent era.

Jacques Lecoq (1921–99), founder of L'Ecole Internationale de Théâtre Jacques Lecoq in 1956, inspired many generations of theater, stage, and circus artists with the depth and range of his remarkable teachings.

Robert Lepage (b. 1957) is a Canadian playwright and director. He was the artistic director of the National Arts Centre's Théâtre Français, and in 1994 founded Ex Machina, a multidisciplinary production company. He directed *Ka* and *Totem* for Cirque du Soleil.

Jerry Lewis (b. 1926) is an American comedian, actor, and film director. He is known primarily for his slapstick comedy on film and television, and as one half of the comedy team, Martin and Lewis.

The Little Prince, first published in 1943, is the signature work of the French writer and aviator Antoine de Saint-Exupéry (1900–44). It is both the most-read and most-translated book in the French language, and received a vote in France as the best book of the twentieth century.

Joan Littlewood (1914–2002) was an English theater director, known for her role in developing the left-wing Theatre Workshop. She has been called "The Mother of Modern Theater."

London Mime Theatre was a theater troupe founded by Nola Rae and Matthew Ridout that later developed into the London International Mime Festival, now the longest-running mime festival in the world.

Siegmund Lubin (1851–1923) was a German-American motion picture pioneer. As director of the Lubin Film Company, he produced more than 1,000 films prior to 1917.

M

Marcel Marceau (1923–2007) was a French actor and mime most famous for his stage persona as "Bip." Among his various awards and honors, he was made Grand Officier de la Legion d'Honneur and was awarded the National Order of Merit in France. Marceau's school, established in 1959, continues to exert an influence on mimes.

Dean Martin (1917–95) was an American singer, actor, and comedian. He was one of the most popular entertainers of the mid-twentieth century, and was called the "King of Cool" for his confidence and effortless charisma.

The **Marx Brothers** (Groucho [1890–1977], Chico [1887–1961], Harpo [1888–1964], and, initially, Zeppo [1901–79]) took Hollywood by storm with their irrepressibly zany comedies, including *Duck Soup*, *Animal Crackers*, *A Night at the Opera*, and *A Day at the Races*. Combining madcap antics, verbal witticisms, slapstick, and musical prowess, their brand of mayhem is still beloved of clown enthusiasts and movie buffs worldwide.

Giulietta Masina (1921–94), sometimes known as "the female Charlie Chaplin," was an Italian film and stage actress who starred in *La Strada* and *Nights of Cabiria*, both winners of the Academy Award for Best Foreign Language Film.

Carlo Mazzone-Clementi (1920–2000) was an Italian performer, commedia dell'arte specialist, and the founder of the Dell'Arte school in northern California.

Simon McBurney (b. 1957) is an English actor, writer, and director. He is the founder and artistic director of Théâtre de Complicité in England, now called Complicité, which performs throughout the world.

The Monte-Carlo International Circus Festival is an annual festival celebrating the circus, created in 1974 in Monte Carlo, Monaco. It includes the awarding of the Clown d'Or (Golden Clown) award as well as awards for other circus skills. A permanent venue, the Chapiteau (circus tent) de Fontvieille, was built especially for this festival.

Sue Morrison, based in Canada, is an internationally respected teacher of the Richard Pochinko clown pedagogy. Her book, *Clown Through Mask*, articulates in great detail her training methods and philosophy.

John Mowat (b. 1947) is an English theater director and co-founder of Odd-Bodies Theatre Company in London. As a performer and director, Mowat has presented his highly visual style of comedy to audiences in over 40 countries.

Mummers and Dadas was a performance company, founded in 1985 and based in Bristol, England.

N

The Navigator is a 1924 film directed by and starring Buster Keaton. The film is regarded as one of Keaton's masterpieces.

The **New Vaudeville** was a term coined by *New York Times* theater critic Mel Gussow.

Bob Newhart (b. 1929) is an American stand-up comedian and actor. Noted for his deadpan and slightly stammering delivery, Newhart came to prominence in the 1960s when his album of comedic monologues *The Button-Down Mind of Bob Newhart* was a worldwide bestseller and reached number one on the Billboard pop album chart. Newhart later went into acting in both film and television.

David Nicksay entered the entertainment industry in the mid-1970s and has overseen the production of several feature films and television programs.

Yuri Nikulin (1921–97) was a popular Soviet and Russian clown who starred in several films. He was awarded the title of People's Artist of the USSR in 1973. He received a number of honors, including the prestigious Order of Lenin, which he was awarded twice.

The origins of **Circus Nock** date back as far as the seventeenth century. In 1860, Joseph Nock founded the circus that continues to this day, based in Zurich, Switzerland.

Pio Nock (1921–98) was a Swiss clown and high-wire artist, and a member of the famous Nock circus family. Known for his slapstick and musical clowning, he toured with leading circuses in Europe and the USA, including the Ringling Bros and Barnum & Bailey Circus.

Buck Nolan (real name Charles Logan Buxton, 1936–2004) stood 7'4" tall and was known as the tallest clown in the world. He toured with the Clyde Beatty–Cole Bros. Circus.

The **Nouveau Clown Institute** was created by Jango Edwards in Barcelona in 2009. The Institute teaches and promotes the art of clowning.

O

Sally Owen is a contemporary dancer who performed with Nola Rae in *And The Ship Sailed On*, representing a Mediterranean sensibility in the wordless comic drama.

P

Patrick Page (b. 1962) is an American actor and playwright. He played Scar in *The Lion King*, Brutus in *Julius Caesar*, and is recognized as a leading classical stage actor.

Monika Pagneux (born Germany, 1927) is a leading European movement teacher in contemporary theater. She has worked with Jacques Lecoq, Moshé Feldenkrais, Peter Brook, Complicite, and Philippe Gaulier. Her style of teaching encourages actors to explore flow between their inner psyche and outer expression.

Michael Parkinson (b. 1935) is an English journalist and author. His television talk show *Parkinson* enjoyed a long and acclaimed run in England, as well as other television programs in the UK and abroad.

Penn and Teller (b. 1955 and 1948 respectively) are American illusionists and entertainers. They have performed as a duo since the 1970s. Their act famously combines elements of magic with comedy, and has been featured on numerous stage and television shows.

Boleslav Polivka (b. 1949) is a Czech film and theater actor, mime, playwright, director, and screenwriter. His work is inspired by clowning, commedia dell'arte, and early comedy films.

Monty Python was an English surreal comedy group that created *Monty Python's Flying Circus*, a British sketch comedy show that premiered on the BBC in 1969. The show's innovative stream-of-consciousness approach extended the boundaries of style and content in contemporary comedy programs.

R

Kenny Raskin is a leading clown and physical comedian in the United States and Europe.

Ringling Bros and Barnum & Bailey Circus is an American circus company, started in 1919 when the circus created by James Anthony Bailey and P.T. Barnum was merged with the Ringling Brothers Circus.

Ringling Bros Barnum & Bailey Clown College was an American clown college rooted in the American type of clown performance, with an accent toward broad and slapstick-type humor.

Rhum (real name Henri Sprocani, 1904–53) was one of the great French clowns of his era, partner to Pipo and friend of Jacques Tati.

Josep Andreu i Lasserre (1896–1983), known as **Charlie Rivel**, was an internationally known Spanish circus clown whose definitive routine featured a guitar and a chair. In post-war Barcelona he was the star of Circo Price, where his routine of the ululating clown is still remembered. Rivel appeared in Federico Fellini's film *I Clowns*.

Circus Roncalli, founded in 1976 by Bernhard Paul and André Heller, is a popular touring German circus.

S

The **San Francisco Mime Troupe** is a satirical political theater that offers free performances in parks in the San Francisco Bay Area and around California. The Troupe does not, however, perform silent mime, but each year creates an original musical comedy that combines aspects of commedia dell'arte, comedy, and farce with topical political themes.

Erica Schmidt (b. 1975) is an American theater director whose credits include Manhattan Theatre Club, Paper Mill Playhouse, Playwrights Horizons, and many others. Schmidt co-wrote and directed the solo show *Humor Abuse* with Lorenzo Pisoni.

Phil Silvers (1911–85) was an American entertainer and comedian, known as "The King of Chutzpah." He starred as Sergeant Bilko on *The Phil Silvers Show*, a 1950s sitcom.

Johnny Simons is a theater writer and director who utilizes mime, pantomime, music, dance, puppetry, and spoken word in his work. He is artistic director and resident playwright of Hip Pocket Theatre in Fort Worth, Texas.

Red Skelton (1913–97) was an American comedian who featured in television performances in the mid-twentieth century. He was the host of *The Red Skelton Show*, and appeared in vaudeville, films, and casinos. His 70-year career as an entertainer has influenced comic performers for generations.

Cirque du Soleil *see C.*

Some Like It Hot is a 1959 American comedy film directed by Billy Wilder. It stars Marilyn Monroe, Tony Curtis, and Jack Lemmon, telling the story of two musicians who witness a mobster massacre and disguise themselves as women in a band to escape.

Konstantin Stanislavsky (1863–1938) was a Russian actor, theater director, and teacher. He founded the Moscow Art Theatre, and became known as the father of Western acting pedagogy, writing several books including *An Actor Prepares* and *My Life in Art*.

Steel Pier Water Circus was a circus hosted by Steel Pier in Atlantic City, New Jersey. Steel Pier was a popular entertainment venue in New Jersey until the 1980s.

Daniel Stein (b. 1952) is an American modern performer of physical theater who studied under Etienne Decroux, specializing in corporeal mime.

Story Theatre was created in the 1960s by Paul Sills, whose mother was Viola Spolin. Story Theatre uses the absolute basic ingredients of the theater – actors and a bare stage – as the foundation for stage interpretations of existing folk stories such as Aesop's Fables or tales from the Brother's Grimm.

T

Andrei Tarkovsky (1932–86) was a Russian filmmaker, writer, and director. His work is known for strong spiritual and metaphysical themes, unconventional structure, and distinct cinematography. He is regarded as one of the greatest filmmakers in history.

Jacques Tati (1907–82) was a French filmmaker who worked as a comic actor, writer, and director. In a poll conducted by *Entertainment Weekly* of the Greatest Movie Directors, Tati was voted the forty-sixth greatest of all time.

Theatre of the Oppressed is an umbrella term for a range of highly interactive theatrical forms developed by Brazilian theater artist Augusto Boal.

These theatrical forms include Forum Theatre, Image Theatre, Invisible Theatre, and several others, and are designed to propel social and political change.

The Three Stooges were an American comedy act during the mid-twentieth century. They made many short subject films that continue to play regularly in syndication with their trademark slapstick comedy. Their group was comprised of Moe Howard, Curly Howard, and Larry Fine.

Top Banana is a musical with music and lyrics by Johnny Mercer and a book by Hy Kraft. It premiered on Broadway in 1954, and starred comedian Phil Silvers.

John Towsen (b. 1948) is an American clown, actor, and teacher who has worked in circus, theater, and television. He is the author of *Clowns: A Panoramic History* and co-founded with Fred Yockers the clown-arts organization If Every Fool, Inc. He also created and writes the blog "All Fall Down: The Craft and Art of Physical Comedy."

Carlos Trafic is an actor and director who developed his style working with research and avant-garde groups in the '60s and '70s, including Grupo Lobo in Buenos Aires, Dharma Theatre in Sao Paolo, and the Living Theatre in New York.

W

Sam Waterston (b. 1940) is an American actor and director. He is noted for his Academy Award-nominated performance as Sydney Schanberg in *The Killing Fields*, and his Golden Globe-winning performance as Jack McCoy on the television series *Law & Order*.

Robin Williams (1951–2014) was an American actor, voice actor, and stand-up comedian. He became known first as Mork on the television series *Mork & Mindy*. Williams later established a highly successful career in both stand-up comedy and film acting, winning an Academy Award for his performance in *Good Will Hunting*.

Jonathan Winters (1925–2013) was an American comedian who recorded several classic comedy albums for the Verve Records label. Winters also appeared on numerous television shows and won the Mark Twain Prize for American Humor.

Z

Zippos Circus is a UK-based circus whose shows regularly tour England and Scotland.

Index